THE CREATIVITY
OF SOCIAL DREAMING

THE CREATIVITY OF SOCIAL DREAMING

Editor
W. Gordon Lawrence

KARNAC

First published in 2010 by
Karnac Books Ltd
118 Finchley Road
London NW3 5HT

Copyright © 2010 by W. Gordon Lawrence

The right of W. Gordon Lawrence to be identified as the author of this work has been asserted in accordance with §§ 77 and 78 of the Copyright Design and Patents Act 1988.

All rights reserved. No part of this publication may be reproduced, stored in a retrieval system, or transmitted, in any form or by any means, electronic, mechanical, photocopying, recording, or otherwise, without the prior written permission of the publisher.

British Library Cataloguing in Publication Data

A C.I.P. for this book is available from the British Library

ISBN-13: 978-1-85575-682-3

Typeset by Vikatan Publishing Solutions (P) Ltd., Chennai, India

www.karnacbooks.com

With profound gratitude to Bipin Patel who wholeheartedly has supported the Social Dreaming venture from its beginning.

Vision

Perplexed, I view
the spinning static,
flat spheroid world:
rivulets, tornadoes, seething crowds.
And I look on.

The sun burns all us sons.
The moon soughs, sea-weeding daughters.
Men stiffen into hoary trees.
Hills shiver and melt
as aging women do.

And I age wishing to share
perplexity, writing it down in
woefully inadequate words because …
it's what I'm part of, what I see
(if disconnected, unacknowledged).

Poetry is the finest form of seeing.
I am the child who blurts
'Look! The Emperor has nothing on.'
This raw truth insulting taste and
reason is vehemently denied;

the endless procession continues.
The poet-child sees
the infinite truncated by our reality,
speaks it, only to be dismissed.
Rail, rail against blindness!

—Francis Oeser

CONTENTS

ACKNOWLEDGEMENTS   xi

THE EDITORS AND CONTRIBUTORS   xiii

INTRODUCTION   xxiii

CHAPTER ONE
Working note on Social Dreaming and creativity   1
Gordon Lawrence

CHAPTER TWO
Social Dreaming to creativity   9
Francis Oeser

CHAPTER THREE
Image to gesture: Social Dreaming
   with student theatre directors   25
Laurie Slade

CHAPTER FOUR
A master plan experience with Social Dreaming   41
Domenico Agresta and Eleonora Planera

CHAPTER FIVE
Low-shot on reality: Dreaming in a primary school   53
Laura Selvaggi

CHAPTER SIX
The slavery in the mind: Inhibition and exhibition   65
Julian Manley

CHAPTER SEVEN
Migrant dreams: Integrating political refugees
    and immigrants in the local Italian community   83
Donatella Ortona and Eleonora Planera

CHAPTER EIGHT
Selection of cadet pilots   95
Tiziana Liccardo

CHAPTER NINE
The training of family mediators   105
Francesco Tortono

CHAPTER TEN
Social Dreaming with lawyers   119
Mattia Tortono

CHAPTER ELEVEN
Totalitarian toddlers:
    Consulting in the mental health service   131
Franca Fubini

CHAPTER TWELVE
Dreaming to emergence in a general hospital   147
Lilia Baglioni

CHAPTER THIRTEEN
Social Dreaming with black rappers in New York 169
Wolf Werdigier

CHAPTER FOURTEEN
Learning to host a Social Dreaming Matrix 177
Angela Eden

CHAPTER FIFTEEN
Creative role synthesis 187
Halina Brunning

CHAPTER SIXTEEN
The priesthood of dreamers 199
Thomas A. Michael

CHAPTER SEVENTEEN
The creative frame of mind 213
Gordon Lawrence and Susan D. Long

BIBLIOGRAPHY 233

INDEX 243

ACKNOWLEDGEMENTS

To Lilia Baglioni and Franca Fubini I am grateful for their 'hosting' of the Social Dreaming training programme in Italy. From the last programme the idea for this book was born. I had been curious to know what the Italian participants had done with Social Dreaming. As I listened to the accounts, I felt that I was being given gifts. Their chapters are in this book. To them I owe a debt, as I do to all of the other writers.

Wolf Verdigier donated the arresting front cover of the book, for which I give thanks.

Shivani Patel and Ashish Patel both kept the manuscript on track by their efficient computer work, compensating for my incompetence, and have my heartfelt gratitude for this. To the staff of the London Library and John Wilkes I am grateful for their help with references.

Any mistakes or omissions in the text, however, are mine, for which I apologize.

THE EDITORS AND CONTRIBUTORS

Domenico Agresta is a psychologist, musician, and composer. He is a Fellow in the Department of Biomedical Sciences, University of G. D'Annunzio Chieti-Pescara, Chair of Clinical Psychology (Holder Prof. M. Fulcheri). He specialized in Psycho-oncology at the Universita Cattolica del Sacro Cuore of Rome. He is specializing in Psychotherapy at the Institute of Analytic Antropological Existential Psychotherapy (IPAAE), Pescara, Italy. He is Deputy Director of the Centre for Studies of Clinical Psychology and Psychosomatics of Pescara, Italy. He is a member of the Italian Psychosomatic Medicine Society (SIMP). He is a member of Social Dreaming Ltd, UK as Licensed Host of Social Dreaming Matrix (SDM). He has written articles on training through the Social Dreaming and Balint Group and Occupational Clinical Psychology. He organized several music festivals and he has produced demo tapes and musical events. He lives and works in Pescara.

Lilia Baglioni is a director of Social Dreaming Ltd, UK and co-founder of Social Dreaming Italy, the Italian Association for the Study and Application of Social Dreaming. A former researcher of the Italian National Research Council, she is a member of the International Psychoanalytic Association (IPA), the Italian Psychoanalytic Society (SPI) and the International Association of Group Therapists (IAGP). She is in private practice as an individual and group therapist and organizational consultant. Her main areas of study are: affective regulation; unconscious processes; intuition and collective creativity; and psychosocial pathologies. In the last 10 years she has introduced the Social Dreaming Matrix method in her action-research work with organizations and in her practice with experiential and training groups. She has held experiential workshops and has lectured on SD at international professional conferences and at Italian Universities. With Franca Fubini and Gordon Lawrence she has organized for six consecutive years an International Experiential Workshop on Social Dreaming and Creativity in Rome. As director of Social Dreaming Ltd, she has been training colleagues in hosting SDM s and supervising their projects in social and institutional contexts in Italy.

Halina Brunning is a Clinical Psychologist, Organizational Consultant, and Executive Coach. She has worked in the British and Polish National Health Service (NHS) as a psychologist, therapist, manager, and consultant. She has published extensively on clinical and organizational issues, co-editing five books and writing 27 articles on these subjects. Her book *Executive Coaching Systems-Psychodynamic Perspective* published by Karnac Books in 2006 was translated into Italian in 2009. She has recently co-edited *Psychoanalytic Studies of Organizations* (Karnac Books, 2009) and is in the process of co-editing *Psychoanalytic Perspectives on a Turbulent World* also by Karnac Books (2010).

Halina currently works as a freelance coach and consultant and runs her own international coaching practice in Europe. She is an Associate Fellow of the British Psychological Society, member of the International Society for the Psychoanalytic Study of Organizations (ISPSO), Organization for the Promotion of Understanding of Society (OPUS), Association of Coaching, and founder member of the Coaching Psychology Forum.

Angela Eden started her career in Theatre Education, moved into community development and finally worked as a training practitioner in several organizations. She is trained as an Organization Consultant, and is accredited as Mediator by the School of

Psychotherapy and Counselling. She researches and writes about leadership, mediation, and coaching. Her personal, more internal, world is formed by dreams, poetry, and painting. All of these came together in Social Dreaming, and she has participated in matrices for many years. More recently she is working to develop the concept of 'training' or learning about the principles of holding SD matrices.

Donatella Ortona Ferrario, Italian by birth and family upbringing, lived and was educated in the United States. She worked as a journalist for over thirty years, mainly with American Press and TV in Rome, as well as being promoter of the arts and mediator between different cultures as press officer. Her experience as volunteer/coordinator with an association for HIV+ children and their families induced her to complete a course in Gestalt Counselling. She was attracted to Social Dreaming when collaborating with Gordon Lawrence during his introduction of Social Dreaming at the University of Rome in 2001. Her journalistic background highlighted the socio-political context of dreams, while the Gestalt training and volunteer work enhanced her disposition to multi-versality and empathy, which are necessary in the kind of relatedness of SD. She participated in SD Ongoing Matrices and has conducted SDMs in institutions such as hospitals, volunteer organizations, and the University of Rome, with which she is a regular collaborator. She has co-hosted matrices for a twelve-month Social Dreaming Project for the integration of immigrants and political refugees with the Italian community. She is a member of Social Dreaming, Ltd, UK.

Franca Fubini is Director of Social Dreaming Institute Ltd, UK, and co-founder of Social Dreaming,Italy, the Italian Association for the Study and Application of Social Dreaming. For many years she has been studying, researching, and developing the methodology of Social Dreaming in the context of corporations, public institutions, universities, art events, and so forth. With Lilia Baglioni and Gordon Lawrence, she has hosted Social Dreaming events in Italy, including the first module for training hosts of Social Dreaming matrices.

She works as a group and individual psychotherapist, and as an organizational consultant, also for the universities of Rome, Perugia, and London. She is a consultant for the Group Relations Conferences in Italy. She has contributed to the creation of 'Blossoming in Europe' a programme which has, for 10 years, connected European countries through the medium of cultural and art events.

Gordon Lawrence, After a career in the army with a short service commission, and commerce, he taught sociology at Bede College, Durham. He joined the Tavistock of Human Relations and was there as a social scientist for 11 years. While there he was joint-director of the Institutes Group Relations Programme and research fellow in the Quality of Working Life, in addition to completing consultancy assignments. He discovered Social Dreaming in 1982 and resigned to join Shell International. He devotes his time to writing and consultancy. He has been a visiting professor at Cranfield University and the New Bulgarian University; is a Distinguished Member of The International Society for the Psychoanalytic Study of Organization; and is managing director of Social Dreaming Ltd.

Tiziana Liccardo is a psychologist and psychotherapist being representative psychologist of the Welcome Point for disabled university students of the University of Naples—Federico II. Liccardo is also a consultant of the Aeronautic Academy of Pozzuoli; member of the Social Dreaming Institute, London (UK), directed by Gordon Lawrence; member of the A.Ri.S.Me.F. (an Italian Association which deals in Development and Research on Family Mediation); charter member and President of the Association R.I.CREA (which deals in Research and Studies on Innovation and Creativity); supporter of the project 'Spazio famiglia' (Space for Families), organized by Naples town council, Chiaia-Posillipo department, in the pipeline, which uses the International Classification of Functioning Disability and Health (ICF) to identify barriers and facilitators to promote social inclusion of families with special needs; and technical adviser of Naples Court. She carries out a research activity on the use of ICF by technical advisers, in legal situations. She is author and co-author of many scientific publications, among which some about the use of ICF by technical advisers, in legal situations.

Susan Long, PhD, is Professor of Creative and Sustainable Organisations at Royal Melbourne Institute of Technology University, Australia. She is editor of *Socio-Analysis*, past President of the International Society for the Psychoanalytical Study of Organizations and President of Group Relations Australia. Her most recent book is *The Perverse Organisation and its Deadly Sins*, published by Karnac Books.

Julian Manley is Director of Ecowaves, a company that offers consultancy and training to organizations. He studied at St John's College,

Cambridge, where he was awarded the Master's Prize for creative writing. He went on to study at Middlesex University and the University of the West of England where his current research, at the Centre for Psycho-Social Studies, focuses on organizational communication and Social Dreaming. He has been involved in research, training, and consultancy for organizations in Spain and Britain since 2000. In 2004 he was awarded an MSc with Distinction in Group Relations and Society by the University of the West of England, Bristol and his dissertation won The Business West Prize for Outstanding Achievement and Contribution to the Business Community. In 2006/07 he spent eight months at Schumacher College, Devon, forging links between organizational communication and principles of holistic ecology and sustainability.

His overall aim is to contribute to the well-being and health of people in groups, teams, organizations, and communities so as to engender success and a sense of holistic achievement on many different levels, including a combination of aspects that are often deemed to be paradoxical in nature, such as the economical, ethical, psychological, and spiritual dimensions of organizational life.

Tom Michael has an A.B. degree from Wabash College where he was elected to the Phi Beta Kappa society. Following his undergraduate career he was awarded a Fulbright Scholarship to study at Marburg University in Germany. He earned an MDiv degree at the Union Theological Seminary (NYC), and a PhD degree from Drexel University. Ordained as a minister in the Presbyterian Church US, he served as pastor in two churches in New York, and then moved to Philadelphia where he worked in the personnel referral and career counselling unit of the Presbyterian Church. He taught organizational behaviour and development and business policy at Rowan University until his retirement in 1999. He is currently adjunct instructor at Rowan University, lecturer in the Psychiatry and Religion programme at the Union Theological Seminary in New York, and is a consultant with the Dialogue Center for Counseling and Consulting. He is Parish Associate at Calvary Presbyterian Church in Wyncote, PA, where he has hosted a Social Dreaming Matrix for the past seven years.

A member of the International Society for the Psychoanalytic Study of Organization, he has written articles and contributed chapters on Social Dreaming in organizations and communities (www.socialdreaming.com/index.php). He has also written articles on the mimetic theory of Rene Girard, and is a member of the Colloquium on Violence and Religion.

Francis Oeser studied architecture, journalism, and town planning at Melbourne University, and later Shakespeare Studies at the Shakespeare Institute, Stratford-upon-Avon (Birmingham University). A musician and poet, he was born in St. Andrews (Scotland), grew up and was educated in Australia, and now lives in London and Aegina (Greece). He has published 10 books of poetry since 1983. In 1997, he was awarded two first prizes for a libretto called *Islands* (music by Constantios Lignos), which he performed in Greece in 1996, and for an opera libretto called *Persephone* (sets by Mark Strizic). His professional work as an architect/planner and his experience at a Leicester-Tavistock Conference and International Foundation for Social Innovation (IFSI) conferences in Evry (France) were significant in his journey towards Social Dreaming. He has experienced 'being a stranger in a strange land'; he wants to share something of the enrichment of such 'displacement' that, for instance, a waking person dealing with dream material can experience.

Eleonora Planera is a psychologist, presently training as a systemic/relational psychotherapist in Family Psychotherapy (Accademia di Psicoterapia della Famiglia). Her main areas of study and action are: childhood disorders; primary prevention of adolescent disorders; and transcultural psychology.

Her thesis on Social Dreaming, which centered on a pilot experience in a United Nations (UN) Shelter Home in the Southern Italian town of Sezze for women seeking political refugee status, led to further application of Social Dreaming as a local government project for the integration of foreigners into the Italian community. Consequently she has promoted and hosted SD Matrices with children and adolescents, as well as adults, in several public institutions in Sezze: in a Junior High School and in a High School; in a shelter home for children; in a shelter home for African women seeking refugee status; for the local Social Service Department with social workers and immigrants; and in the Training Program for the Formation of Cultural Mediators. As a member of the Social Dreaming Ltd, UK, she has also collaborated with the University of Rome, Department of

Psychology, by hosting SD Matrices for students on special projects regarding immigration, drug addiction, and women groups

Laura Selvaggi is a psychoanalytic psychotherapist; group psychoanalyst; member of the Italian Institute of Group Psychoanalysis (IIPG); member of the European Federation for Psychoanalytic Psychotherapy (EFPP); and co-founder of Gruppo, an association for research and practice through small analytic groups. She is currently the editor of *Koinos: Group and Analytic Function*, the official review of the Insurance Industry Practice Group (IIPG). She has been involved in Social Dreaming since 2001 and in the last two years has been exploring the possibility of extending this technique to children and adolescents.

Laurie Slade is a United Kingdom Council for Physiotherapy (UKCP) registered analytical psychotherapist, in private practice in West London. He is a member of the Guild of Psychotherapists, the Confederation for Analytical Psychology, and the International Neuropsychoanalysis Association. He has a long-standing interest in working with dreams, and has led workshops in different contexts. He has been actively involved in Social Dreaming since 2001, hosting sessions in a variety of settings, in the UK and internationally. His paper 'Social Dreaming for a Queer Culture' appeared in *Self & Society* (Vol. 33, No. 3, 2005). He was involved in the creation of the first programme for professional development of Social Dreaming hosts (2007). He previously worked as a lawyer, specializing for nearly 20 years in consumer dispute resolution. Before that, he worked as a stage manager in professional theatre, and he continues to be actively involved in that field. His play *Joe & I* was performed at the King's Head Theatre in London (2005).

Francesco Tortono is a psychologist and psychotherapist; associate member of SIPP (Italian Society of Psychoanalytical Psychotherapy); contract professor of theory and technique for psychological technical advice in legal situations at the Postgraduate School in Clinical Psychology, University of Naples—Federico II; consultant of the Aeronautic Academy of Pozzuoli; member of the Social Dreaming Institute, London (UK), directed by Gordon Lawrence; charter member of A.RI.S.ME.F. (an Association which deals in Research and Studies on Family Mediation); supporter of the project

'Spazio Famiglia' (Space for Families), organized by Naples town council, Chiaia-Posillipo department, in the pipeline, which uses ICF to identify barriers and facilitators to promote social inclusion of families with special needs; technical adviser of Naples Court; and charter member of the Association R.I.CREA (which deals in Research and Studies on Innovation and Creativity). He carries out a research activity on the use of the International Classification of Functioning Disability and Health (ICF) by technical advisers, in legal situations. He is author and co-author of many scientific publications.

Mattia Tortono graduated in Psychology of Relational and Developmental Processes. He cooperates with the University of Naples—Federico II and with marketing research institutes to the realization of psycho-social research projects. He is a member of the Social Dreaming Institute, London (UK), directed by Gordon Lawrence. He took part in training courses organized by the Tavistock Institute in cooperation with Il Nodo, aimed to the acquisition of specific skills in detection and management of institutional dynamics. He took part in a socio-organizational intervention in Togo, with a humanitarian mission, and is a supporter of the project 'Spazio Famiglia' (Space for Families), organized by Naples town council, Chiaia-Posillipo department, in the pipeline, which uses ICF to identify barriers and facilitators to promote social inclusion of families with special needs. He carries out research activity on the use of ICF by technical advisers, in legal situations. He is co-author of publications on Social Dreaming and on the use of ICF by technical advisers, in legal situations, and is a charter member of the Association R.I.CREA (which deals in Research and Studies on Innovation and Creativity).

Wolf Werdigier was born in 1946, in Pegnitz, Germany. He studied architecture in Vienna and London as well as painting and design with Jaap Bakema, Xenia Hausner, Jakobo Borges, and Irina Nakhova. His works include urban designs, installations, and city interventions; he teaches methods of urban design at the University of Vienna; is visiting professor at the Pratt institute of New York for city design and at the University of Stuttgart; and works in the area of interactive art and paintings with exhibitions in Vienna, Barcelona, France, New York, Jerusalem, Philadelphia, and Venice.

Exhibitions and Events list

1. Installations and Art Exhibitions

1985
Les Fleurs du Mal
Paintings Exhibition, Depot, Vienna

1989
Sfarad
Paintings Exhibition
and Performance Kulisse, Vienna
cooperation: Leni Rothstein

1989
Sfarad
Paintings Exhibition
and Performance
Kulisse, Vienna
cooperation: Leni Rothstein

1991–2000
City Scenarios
www.urbanistik.at
Paris 1991
Vienna 1994
Atlanta 1995
Marseille 2000

2000
Denk-mal
www.denk-mal.at
Installation Volksoper

2002
Templates
www.paintings.at/frames_temp
Paintings Exhibtion Schloss
Hardegg, Austria

2003
Eurydice Project
www.eurydiceproject.com
Exhibition San Stare, Venice

2. Art Exhibitions and Social Dreaming Matrix Workshops

2003
Hidden Images
www.paintings.at/frames_ispa
Exhibition Jerusalem,
al-Wasiti Center
Exhibition Tel Aviv, Amalia
Arbel Art Gallery
Exhibition Ramallah,
League of Palestinian
Artists—al-Hallaj Art Hall

2005
Verborgene Bilder
www.paintings.at/frames_wien.html
Exhibition Vienna,
Aspang Warehouses

Exhibition New York,
Castillo Theatre
www.paintings.at/frames_usa.html

Immagini Nascoste
Exhibition Venice,
Palazzo Albrizzi

2006
Exhibition Philadelphia, Loews

Exhibition Cleveland,
Ohio University Art Gallery

Exhibition Vienna,
Atelier Gallery

2007
Colour and Identity
Exhibition Washington,
Austrian Cultural Forum

Berlin 33—Vienna 38
Presentation New York, Leo
Baeck Institute

Hidden Images
Book presentation Vienna,
ESRA psychosocial centre
Discussion and Book
presentation February 15th

Sex, Perversion and
Psychoanalysis
Exhibition Vienna,
Sigmund Freud University

"you shall (not) make yourself
a carved image"
Exhibition Vienna, Church of St.
Klaus von Flüe

Contact: www.paintings.at

INTRODUCTION

In Chapter one a summary is made of the Social Dreaming Matrix (SDM), conceptualized as a temporary system with its intakes, transformation processes, and outputs. This sets the scene for the remaining chapters of the book. It is a 'Working Note' stating the understanding of the SDM at this point in time. As such, it is not definitive and, likely, will be revised in the light of any new thinking that may emerge from the Social Dreaming project. Clearly the SDM is a collaborative effort of participants to understand their dreams, and always has surprising insights.

Francis Oeser (Chapter two) details the creative processes that have emerged for him from Social Dreaming. Francis is an architect, poet, and novelist, and is uniquely placed to show the clear connections between creativity and Social Dreaming. His paper is full of interesting insights and *apercus* that substantiate the use of dreaming in creativity. He has long taken part in Social Dreaming conferences and previously wrote a chapter on Shakespeare and the language of Social Dreaming (Lawrence, 1998: 75–90).

Laurie Slade (Chapter three) worked with student theatre directors at the Rose Bruford drama school, showing how the SDM transformed the students' understanding of the theatre. Specifically, the project was designed to enhance the students' creativity, which it surely did. Using Anton Ehrenzweig's work on creative thinking, Laurie devised with his colleague, Colin Ellwood, an efficacious programme that is now a permanent feature of the school's curriculum.

Following the life cycle, the next two chapters are reports of SDMs held with Italian children. Domenico Agresta and Eleonora Planera (Chapter four), and Laura Selvaggi (Chapter five), provide lively accounts of their work. The imagination of children is treated with respect and an enthralling account of the children's dreams is given. This can only have a beneficial effect on their peer relationships and their school work. Ron Balamuth pioneered SD with New York children (Lawrence, 2003: 122–141).

Working with general members of the public who had visited the exhibition on slavery at the British Empire and Commonwealth museum in Bristol, Julian Manley, with his colleague, Jacqueline Sirota, mounted an SDM as part of this exhibition experience (Chapter six). We are inhibited about discussing slavery. Dreams provide insights that can be voiced in the SDM. Many of these would have eluded them in conversation, but show a relating of the meanings of slavery at the times of its happening to what it means in contemporary times.

Immigrants pose problems for the host society, in this case Italy; Donatella Ortona (Chapter seven) has worked on this issue for a number of years, adapting the SDM technique for them. Fortunately, the director of the home for immigrants and the town council of Sezze Romano support her and Eleonara Planera in this work, despite the bureaucratic delays of Italy. There are some very moving dreams from the adult participants and their children as they come to a new country and are faced with making a living and other issues of survival.

The next three chapters show how the SDM can help cadet pilots, family mediators, and lawyers in Naples. In Chapter eight, Tiziana Liccardo introduces the SDM with cadet pilots who are undergoing training to be aviators at the Aeronautical Academy. Through the dreams they are able to voice their anxieties and gain an insight into their future roles. I was surprised, indeed astounded, when I visited Naples as a guest of the Director of the Academy to find how the SDM was treated very seriously by the officers on the staff.

In Chapter nine Francesco Tortona uses the SDM with family mediators. Although his colleagues on the staff of his university initially viewed the SDM with suspicion and hostility, students who had taken part were a powerful voice in having it accepted by the faculty. Matteo Tortona (Chapter ten) uses dreaming with lawyers. They are trained to use legal precedent and all their training is convergent in its orientation. Through the SDM Matteo showed them a more open way of thinking, allowing for divergent thought.

Both Franca Fubini and Lilia Baglioni worked with the SDM in hospitals. Franca, in Chapter eleven, addresses the organizational problem of a mental health facility. The staff, due to their anxiety and fear of working with acute mentally disturbed patients, and their wish for certainty in a bewildering organizational environment, became totalitarian in working with their patients. This intervention shows how the SDM can be used as a tool of action-research to surface the essential issues that are impeding the professional work of the staff. What is striking about Social Dreaming is that it collapses the functions of research gathering and understanding its implications—with people collaborating to find what the dreams might mean, compared to the two-step sequence of action research in which there is the collection of data followed by the working hypotheses on the implications of the data. Franca completed her assignment in a much shorter time than conventional research.

The same can be said of Lilia Baglioni in Chapter twelve who worked with a developing emergency service in a hospital. From the work of the SDM a basic organization began to emerge that was fit for its purpose, despite the complexities of recruitment.

The mood of the book changes with Wolf Verdigier's (Chapter thirteen) account of working with black rappers in New York and young immigrants in Vienna. He reports the dreams with gusto and offers interesting insights to schooling for Afro-American youngsters. Despite their unprivileged backgrounds they readily recounted their dreams rhythmically. His investigation of the folk heroes of Viennese immigrants is equally insightful. His pictures are available at www.paintings.at

Of recent years the training of hosts for the SDM has become a priority in Italy and the UK. Angela Eden (Chapter fourteen), who is responsible for training for Social Dreaming Ltd, sets out and discusses the issues. She outlines the principles and the method of

Social Dreaming. The training always includes practical work with the participants learning by doing.

Halina Bruning (Chapter fifteen) is experienced in coaching and uses Social Dreaming in her practice. As ever, she provides a stimulating account of her work.

The mood of the book changes once again with Thomas Michael's (Chapter sixteen) consideration of dreamers being a priesthood. Tom has hosted SDMs with the Presbyterian church of America for many years, very successfully. The Bible is a rich source of dreams and by doing Social Dreaming some members are continuing that tradition, and offering themselves solace and help from their dreaming work. Tom has previously published accounts of his work (Lawrence, 1998: 59–68; Lawrence, 2003: 142–156; Lawrence, 2007: 120–130).

In the final chapter, Susan Long and I offer our thoughts on creativity. Stanley Gold (1999) once wrote that creativity has become the great white whale to the Captain Ahab of psychoanalysis which has always defeated us. Nevertheless, we treat in Chapter seventeen the creative frame of mind, disentangling the conditions for fostering its development.

The central working hypothesis of that paper is that creativity always occurs outside of goal-orientated activities. All of the SDMs reported in this book have occurred outside of the goal-orientated activities of the institution. The SDM is a reflective space outside of the normal activities of the organization. This reflective space has a purpose which is the examination of dreams to find out what they may be saying about the organization as a system. It is marked off from other activities by its purpose, which is the examination of the dreaming of the participants.

Finally, the accounts of the SDM have taken place with diverse groupings of people: from children in school, through work with young theatre directors, immigrants, young pilots, family mediators, lawyers, visitors to an exhibition on slavery, hospitals, black rappers, to a church congregation. Hopefully, the reader will be persuaded that the SDM is a method for enhancing creativity and will try it with other diverse groupings.

CHAPTER ONE

Working note on Social Dreaming and creativity

Gordon Lawrence

This chapter is in the form of a working note, that is, a sketch of the reality of dreaming and the Social Dreaming Matrices as they have been experienced. Mostly it is a series of working hypotheses, that is, sketches of the truth, but knowing that absolute truth will never happen for it lies in the unconscious and is unknowable. Others, with their experiences of Social Dreaming, may arrive at different working hypotheses. A better sketch of the truth will be realized when one working hypothesis is made redundant by another which better captures the reality of the subject. In this fashion a better version of the reality of Social Dreaming will be attained that is more congruent with experience.

> In a broad sense, artistic creativity involves making new arrangements, or connections, not randomly but picturing or expressing in some way the emotional state of the artist. In other words artistic creativity, exactly like dreaming, involves making new connections, or making connections broadly guided by the dominant emotions. The work of art, much like the dream, contextualizes the emotion or emotional concern of its creator. (Ernest Hartmann 2000: 73)

Dreams occur when we are asleep, allowing the neural nets of the brain's cortex to relax. This *congé*, holiday, is from the rational logic of consciousness, like the 3Rs which all operate to rigid rules that make for absolute certainty: 2 and 2 do make 4. When we are asleep our brains become available for the unconscious which is a far freer state of the mind.

Ernest Hartmann has described the differences between the awake mind of consciousness and the unconscious sleeping mind. Essentially, the unconscious mind is more capable of making connections than the state of wakeful consciousness.

This echoes Anton Ehrenzweig's finding that:

> Unconscious vision ... [has] proved to be capable of gathering more information than a conscious scrutiny lasting a hundred times longer ... the undifferentiated structure of unconscious vision ... displays scanning powers that are superior to conscious vision. (Ehrenzweig, cited in Gray, 2002: 63)

In dreaming, these connections between experiences of the day, and life, become auto-associative, linking in diverse, unexpected, and surprising ways to weave a, sometimes bizarre, narrative. That surreal narrative will often contain the bright idea that would elude us while awake; evidence of which being that scientists, writers, and painters have been known to make use of these dream accounts in their work.

Social Dreaming viewed as a system

These diverse narratives are brought by participants to the Social Dreaming Matrix (SDM) as inputs to the temporary system of the Matrix.

Matrix was chosen rather than group to receive the Social Dreaming because it heightens the opportunity in waking life to recreate the Matrix of the undifferentiated unconscious while asleep. The word 'Matrix' is being used in its basic sense—a place out of which something grows—and refers to the emotions and feelings, both conscious and unconscious, that are present below the surface in any social gathering. This idea was subsequently construed as a 'mental

Faraday cage'—an invention of Faraday's to protect his experiments from electro-static interference (Lawrence, 2007: 39).

The chairs in the Matrix are arranged in clusters of four (snowflakes) that fill the room in a large circle. This is to provide anonymity and to be a different configuration than the large group with its chairs in a spiral. This is a physical statement of the different container structured for Social Dreaming.

The dreams that are intakes to the Matrix are social ones. From its inception Social Dreaming has focused on the knowledge and thinking of the dream, and not the dreamers with their psyches. By taking this vertex on dreaming a whole new vista on the dreaming process was made apparent. Social Dreaming takes place simultaneously with many; not in a one-to-one situation.

The differences between Social Dreaming and Individual, Therapeutic Dreaming, Hanni Biran and I worked out a few years ago:

> Whereas Individual, Therapeutic Dreaming has the Dreamer as the focus of attention, follows an egocentric path by concentrating on issues of self knowledge, by dramatizing the personal biography and occurs *within* the clinical situation, Social Dreaming follows a different orientation. It focuses on the dream by holding a socio-centric view-point. It is knowledge of the environment that is important, as individuals face the tragedy, and comedy, of being. This is *outside* the clinical situation. (Lawrence and Biran, 2002: 224)

Social Dreams of participants come into the Matrix which has the purpose of transforming the thinking of the dreams by means of free association so as to make links and connections between and among the dreams, and in this process be available for new thinking and thoughts.

To be sure, personal dreams will also be present but it has always been found that participants manage themselves to produce, and transact, only Social Dreams. People intuitively know the difference. After the statement of purpose by one of the hosts—the name given to the takers of the Matrix—the question is posed, 'What is the first dream?'

One dream is offered, perhaps another, and then another. Then, free associations begin to follow. One hunch is that the first dream of the Matrix is anticipating the others that go after, and contains the vestiges of the dreaming for the whole Matrix. Participants intuit that there will be no personal interpretations of a personal nature so engage with the Matrix with limited anxiety. Because it is spontaneous, they also intuit that they will not be asked for a dream except as a general injunction. Also they become aware that there is no hierarchy in the dreaming, that it is the dream that is important not the status or position of the dreamer. This provides the element of democracy in the Matrix.

The host's role is to enable the participants to follow the purpose and to only intervene when he or she has a working hypothesis that attempts to links the dreams. This they do by accessing their own unconscious, by moving into a dreamy state to respond to the dreams being presented in the Matrix. The beauty of the working hypothesis is that it is a method to arrive at the truth of the dreams voiced in the Matrix. As a sketch, it can be faulted if the evidence does not fit the hypothesis. Another hypothesis can be substituted. These are approximations of what the truth might be and a probing way of establishing meaning for the Matrix. The working hypothesis is based on the assumption that truth will never be known absolutely, but is always in a process of emergence.

A dream is a metaphor and Matrix exists to explore it and find what it symbolizes. The Matrix works at the meaning of the dreams and the free associations which are enhanced when the participants begin to lose their ideas of the ego and the self. In the Matrix the participants come to regard the dream as existing in its own right—disengaged from any personal obligations or ties. Participants are less preoccupied with the question, 'What does the dream mean for me?' and more with the idea of the dream bearing meanings for social life. This socio-centric thrust reveals the knowledge and the thinking of the dream thoughts of the narrative.

In the last two centuries when Western individuals have been narcissistically preoccupied with self and their ego, leading to a culture characterized by what has been identified, following Bion, as the basic assumption of Me-ness (Lawrence, Bain, and Gould, 1996) that leads to the selfishness, even hubris, of our times, the idea of losing one's ego, even temporarily, is regarded with suspicion, even horror. The idea of losing control, of losing one's ability to manage oneself, is fraught with fantasies of danger.

The Matrix invites this sublimation of ego for its purpose by mimicking, or recreating, the conditions of the undifferentiated unconscious. Then the dream can be engaged with in its own terms.

The output of the transformation of the Matrix is re-worked by thinking of the dreams as they are related to the social, political, and human issues of contemporary times. This is a result of the free association done by the participants, and the occasional amplification when the dream is related to a film, a novel, or contemporary problems.

The output, as here described, is contained substantially in the minds of participants, to be recollected in tranquillity when they are alone. This is described as 'Thinking as becoming' to give the sense of the participants struggling towards a realization of what they had never had the opportunity to think of before, as they expressed in their being.

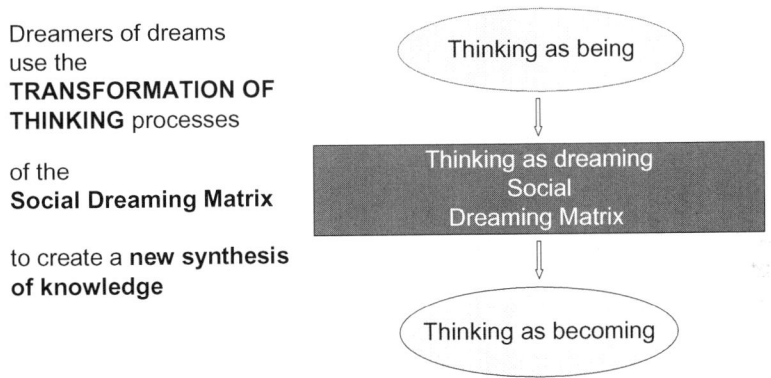

Often after the SDM a period is set aside to examine more fully the meaning of the dreams. This is called a Dream Reflection Dialogue. The participants implicitly are given the opportunity to regain their ego. The Matrix only lasts for an hour, or an hour and a half. In a sense the loss of ego is to be regained during the Dialogue when the thinking becomes more rational. Specifically, the participants are invited to identify the dreams and themes of the Matrix, to find any patterns that connect the dreams, and to make working hypotheses on the messages of the dream Matrix.

There is a difference between people congregating to share their dreams, as an experience, and when role-holders from an organizational system meet to do so. In the former the participants come from different contexts, whereas, in the latter, they will share the culture of their organization. This common background means that the dreams tend to be about their lives in the organization, but individual congregating will reflect through their dreams their disparateness. Alistair Bain has called the former SDM 'Organizational Dreaming' arguing that the organization is the container of dreams (cited in Lawrence, 2007: 148–161). Nevertheless, Social Dreaming is the generic term.

Because the SDM is dealing with the unconscious it is also engaging with the infinite, being used in a poetic rather than scientific sense. Essentially, when the ego is lost in regarding the dream, it exists in its own right as part of the infinite, unknown domain. It means looking at the dream as if it never existed before and as part of non-finite knowledge. In this way new meanings for the dreams are discovered.

The SDM is a place, or setting, outside of the goal-orientated configurations experienced in daily life. It is a special space for the mind to be reflective, to enlarge itself through considering dreams as a social phenomena.

In short, it is a unique, precious space for people to find the potential for being creative.

Dreaming opens the door to the infinite possibilities of the dream meanings through the exercise of free association (Lawrence, 2007). Wilfred Bion held the view that dreaming is an ongoing mental activity at the basis of our unconscious, and, therefore, of our thinking (Grotstein, 2007: 59ff).

Human beings dream all the time, though they may not always be aware of it. They certainly free associate to the objects in their environment situated in the events and happenings of a day. Free association—the uncontrolled thoughts which pass through the mind—as objects are encountered, like their system of work, are spontaneous and are not monitored. Free association is the human way of entertaining the unconscious⇔infinite. Free association leads to dreaming, whether by day or night.

These activities are essential for our thinking/dreaming as being, which is transformed by our ability to think as dreaming in the SDM. Once the social dreams have been examined, through the process of free association, and, if need be, amplification, the thought processes of the dream are transformed into new personal knowledge. With systems of organization this has been found to be thinking as becoming, that is, tapping into the emergent, hidden, system that exists, like a shadow, in every system, for example, family, community, or work.

Human beings have been dreaming for millennia. The unconscious is manifested through the cultural artefacts of our civilization. Every work of architecture, work of art, literature, film and the cultivated environment takes its shape and content because of the unconscious dreaming abilities of their creators. As we are exposed to these objects we resonate with our unconscious expressed by free association so we are surrounded by unconscious thinking and thought.

But we deny this unrivalled source of creativity because of the human demands of our egos which omnipotently claim exclusive right to creativity. Without dream, fantasy, and imagination, the creative act and artefact would not have existence.

Further thoughts

As has been implied, Social Dreaming is an intimation of absolute reality which is the unconscious and the infinite that cannot be known. Bion (1970: 88) proposed that absolute reality be termed 'O' which could be intuited by means of emotional experience. That emotional experience will be triggered by an emotionally charged event in daily life, to be transformed in the dream into a version of knowledge. And it is this knowledge that is the stuff of the SDM, that is, the sphinx perspective. The experience of the SDM also makes participants realize it is possible to have faith in the unconscious as it opens the gate to the infinite.

The dream is a metaphor of reality as it is experienced. What it is a metaphor of, the SDM exists to explore and, possibly, find. When, in the process of evolution, early forms of humankind experienced an unprecedented expansion of the prefrontal areas and of the visual area of the cortex, human beings could imagine themselves doing something even if they were not acting in actuality. This evolutionary jump allowed the emergence of culture, leading to religion (Frankl, 1979: 33). Human kind was released from the daily grind of simply surviving to look at their environment—where the sun rose and fell, the moon waxed and waned, and the seasons came and went—to ask the question as to why it all existed. Humankind looked for a *because clause*, to employ the phrase frequently used by

Pierre Turquet, a former Tavistock colleague, to postulate reason. Religion was used to bind the emergent societies together. Dreaming was postulated as being a gift of the gods. How else could it be explained?

Bion, one of the original psychoanalytic thinkers of the twentieth century, was aware that human beings exist with an awareness of death and recognized that his profession was a 'mystic science' because it deals with human 'emotions that are infinite and consequently complex and non-linear in nature' (Grotstein, 2007: 328). Bion was the first to use the ideas of complexity theory that acknowledges the non-linear attributes of phenomena and events. Mystic refers to 'numinous science based on the abandonment of memory, desire, understanding and a respect for relativity, complexity and uncertainty' (Ibid.: 24). In using the term 'numinous' Bion was pointing to the complexity of human relations and dreams whose wonder and astonishment robs us of words when awesome and uncanny experience is encountered to advocate a spiritual epistemology. Now, God is dead but dreaming remains as a vestige, a symbolic simile of the now defunct angels of the transcendent infinite.

These infinite qualities of dreaming are intuited subliminally by participants in the SDM through collaboration, their respect for other's dreams, and their faith in the quest for truth, which is grounded in the dream thoughts of the Matrix.

Objective truth is identified through consensus formation.

> The search for truth is a collective enterprise, in which we can learn from each other. As truth finding strategy, this is objectionable on the grounds that it is vague and slow; as a political prescription it can be criticized for endorsing woolly minded 'community politics'. But it has the merits which so far have been insufficiently praised: it is humane, undogmatic, solidly rooted in tradition, optimistic and, in effect, good for the individual who practises it and the society which benefits from it. (Fernandez-Armesto, 1997: 222)

In short, Social Dreaming celebrates the discovery of the unconscious, the inner voice of humanity present in the dream thoughts—surprising epiphanies—and attempts to find their truth, no matter to where it will lead.

CHAPTER TWO

Social Dreaming to creativity

Francis Oeser

Social Dreaming encourages 'associating' to dreams rather than the easier option of interpretation, steering away from conscious thought towards feeling and intuition. The work of Social Dreaming is less comfortable from an everyday viewpoint because it involves the imprudence of risk and trust. Similar risks and trust are confronted when painting, sculpting, or writing. Dreaming puts us in touch with the unconscious to which associating reaches. The artist and the social dream participant engage in similar ways. This process is examined here.

The anarchy in the creative act—bringing forward new ideas through the courage to go beyond the existing and institutionalized domains of knowledge—seems much the same as that in dreams. The risks of engagement are threefold:

1. Daring to allow the unbidden.
2. Owning/accepting it.
3. Risking telling it (sharing).

Creative work depends primarily on the feeling that everything is connected, is both right and wrong, obscene and ordinary, unnatural and natural, involving me, you, and them, a unity of the connected and separate. Gestation of the new is effectively supported by excluding interpretation and judgement until such time as it has a life of its own.

Children live in their world with the first and second risks, trusting in unity. The third belongs with the boundary between self and others: the family, the outside world. As Donald Winnicott (1970) says, maturity involves thought, knowledge, and choice; like the uncoerced man who enlists, then goes to fight.

Creativity is as risky as war. Although we readily declare war, Western societies shy away from attitudes which prefigure creativity. The shadow-consciousness of childhood, lost in adolescence, craves a place in adult lives. Without it our future is dire. This aspect of childhood is not lost—rather, it is repressed. Only artists and our dreams try to reconnect us with it.

I have a few tricks for getting back in touch. For instance, I resist writing pre-structured poems (such as sonnets or those with pre-set schemes). First drafts are scribbled down as they come out. Later I seek 'natural' structures embedded in each piece—stanza length, rhyming scheme, sense; the latter requiring reordering of usually disordered fragments. Tough honing is necessary to organize them all, to link (chaotic) thought with (orderly) expression.

Wallace Stevens (1997) said a poem contains two poems: one, the poet's intentions; the other, the characteristics imposed by language. Writing is a fierce struggle between the two systems: imagination and the recording of it. The odd thing is that in giving up the intentions for the sake of the other, nothing eventually is lost. This involves more than a belief in intuition. Rather, it trusts the warring process to encompass both. For when the poem becomes itself it holds both. Becoming itself entails a unity of the two protagonists, our immediate intention and an ancient system called language, both, the poem's parents. Trusting such an outcome involves risk, we are risking failure; surely a matter of life-and-death.

The Matrix of Social Dreaming has been likened to a Faraday cage—a metal screen invented by the scientist Faraday to keep his experiments free from extraneous interferences. The SDM screens out group dynamics to focus on the dream and dreaming. For the protective Social Dreaming Matrix (SDM) limits risk and nurtures trust. We share our dreams with others in the belief that insights will arise; we risk ridicule, break out of the thrall that dreams are personal property, to make the risky connection of *they* with *me*, in an outside world consisting of personal and public.

Years ago, an architect working with clients, I held the experience of the SDM during discussions about my clients' dreams (we never used this term) while establishing the brief for their buildings. (On the grounds that it is better to dream before scaling down, starting 'high' in this way is more reliable than first considering practicalities such as money, regulations, and other tangible objects which limit imaginative thought.) It worked. I remember having to contain the anxiety of many clients about the outcome. I think they said to themselves, 'How can such talk produce a building? Why doesn't he give us a sketch, a model, a cost estimate?' (The equivalent of a doctor's pill.) There was little belief that in the sharing of making a brief, a building (made from their aspirations and my skill) would eventuate. This sort of parenting is uncomfortable. Their doubt represents the risk. An architect carries a conviction that there will be a building. Its quality depends on the richness of such encounters. His Faraday cage protects doubt from being infected too early by extraneous matters, and represents a conviction that the building will be real and dreamlike; *The Bridge of Dread* crossed[1], it usually was. Finding ways for 'new thinking' results in the best outcome, whether of buildings or other work.

Associating leads to the unconscious, its riches and promise. I used another technique as a way in while engaged in the mundane task of drawing with a tee- and set-squares. When almost working to rote, one's mind is freed to wander. Many design solutions popped out during this 'waste of time'. Mechanistic activity forms a Faraday

---

[1] Edwin Muir, The Bridge of Dread
But when you reach the bridge of dread
Your flesh will huddle into its nest
For refuge and your naked head
Creep in the casement of your breast,

And your great bulk grow thin and small
And cower within its cage of bone,
While dazed you watch your footsteps crawl
Toadlike across the leagues of stone.
(Knight, R. [1980]. *Edwin Muir—An Introduction to his Work.* London: Longman, p. 150.)

cage perhaps because one's judgement is busy elsewhere. So, dreamlike, thoughts wander—we are susceptible to messages from the unconscious. Rich buildings are the result of either local engagement (builders who intimately know the environs, local materials and techniques and share the culture of the clients), or the traditional process of 'wasting time'—preparing drawings and allowing new thinking with appropriate results. Somehow, in the 'not concentrating', solutions arise. Surely not-concentrating is tied to concentrating. Everything is connected—'All in One and One in All' as Zen Buddhists say. Working with computers short circuits the process of new thinking as most new buildings blandly proclaim. Time may be money. It is also quality. Dreams and associations could be truncated in the SDM, saving time. Efficient? But pointless. Designing buildings is similar to designing poems. Intentions are enriched by allowing more intangible aspects. In this instance, Wallace Stevens' duality is made up of the intentions of the architect plus the systems in a design. This twinning occurs in the SDM. A personal dimension is joined to a social one in the telling of a dream also by the associations to that dream. The extremes are those bits which do not overlap. However the purely private and the public remain parts of the whole, making for unity—a vital characteristic of the unconscious.

The range of attributes making up unity is articulated by Peter, a boy-gardener, in my novel *Changes*[2]. Here is part of his prize-winning speech:

> ... in the Greek Myth of a goddess: Persephone who contained two extremes: death and life; of childishness and queenliness; of what is seen in the light and felt in darkness. Her life involved respect and love and duty as dictated by a law above the law as pronounced by Gaia, Mother Earth, the mother of all, who adjudicated on whether Persephone should inhabit either dark Hades or the bright living earth, by ruling she inhabit both. So every one accepted Persephone would spend time as Queen with her husband Hades for the time the earth was dormant

---

[2] A number of texts are considered throughout *Changes*: Bronte, Swift, Shakespeare, Brecht, and so on, plus the Bunyip Stories told to children in *Changes* 2–5, separately published as *After You've Brushed your Teeth* (Oeser, 2005). *Changes* 1–5 is due for publication in 2010.

(autumn and winter), spending the rest as kore, girl, with her mother Demeter, goddess of growth, during spring and summer. She can be called a Bridge between the extremes of light and dark. For instance, growing up involves extremes like Persephone's, between male and female, which tell children only boys may play football, drink beer, swagger and rule while only girls may do cookery or dancing or be creative. But I found the law above this law stating girls too may rule and play football, and boys too may be creative. Some of my friends think landscaping is girlish whereas I found my involvement makes me a fuller person. Like Persephone we contain contradictory characteristics, of male and female. We must face and deal with these extremes in ourselves and in the outside world. Otherwise everything fragments … . (Oeser, 2010)

To Peter, Persephone's Bridge represents the whole of sexuality. Pure male and pure female are the extreme ends of the bridge (in whichever way 'pure' is defined). Everywhere along the bridge is a mixture of male and female. The bridge centre represents half-male/half-female. Unlike current attitudes, we are not either male or female, any more than pure evil or pure good exist. The bridge connects extremes. We are located between, each in a unique place, and belonging to a sense of unity which brings us equilibrium and sanity.

Furthermore, *Changes* demonstrates how associating to stories (read and heard) clarifies confusion and reinforces experience. Stories, like dreams, are mirrors which, illuminating shadows in our reality, reveal the unseen. Working with stories or dreams is essential. We miss their wisdom and thrill by treating them only as entertainment. They help us see differently in their more neutral milieu much the same as in the SDM. The double view, a root of insightful experience, is a rewarding way to work. This is one form of transformation which acts by jolting us out of usual attitudes. I had supposed that change comes about in psychoanalysis in the juxtaposition of the patient's view with the interpretation of the analyst; that in the tiny 'friction' between statement and interpretation lies the impetus to change (one's mind, actions, position, and so forth). Experienced in the SDM, other truth and other power lie in the interstices between dream and associations. Transformation in a poem proposes alternative realities. Similarly, maybe in the arena between meanings, lies the energy to reach into the unconscious. Edith Södergan's poem *The Stars* for instance:

> When night comes
> I stand on the stairway and listen,
> the stars are swarming in the garden
> and I am standing in the dark.
> Listen, a star fell with a tinkle!
> Do not go out on the grass bare foot;
> my garden is full of splinters. (McDuff, 1984)

When stars are splinters of glass or tears or eyes or dreams, when most associations are true then all is one; in such a mental flux we are capable of new thinking either in a poem about stars and/or splinters, or in the SDM.

Drama is filled with energizing 'gaps' between words and situation. Think of Shakespeare's *The Winter's Tale* for example. The king, Polixenes (disguised) is talking to Florizel, his son (incognito to the rest). The audience is aware of threatening family and state politics (the external world) intruding, and is still smarting from the cruel misunderstanding in the first part of the play. Fury, banishment, death and 'EXIT pursued by a bear' are not far behind. The audience suddenly sees that the joyous love between Florizel and Perdita, a shepherdess, is doomed now in their agrarian paradise:

> POLIXENES—How now, fair shepherd,
> Your heart is full of something that does take
> Your mind from feasting. Sooth, when I was young,
> And handed love, as you do; I was wont
> To load my she with knacks; I would have ransack'd
> The pedlar's silken treasury, and have poured it
> To her acceptance. You have let him go
>
> And nothing smarted with him If your last
> Interpretation should abuse, and call this
> Your lack of love, or bounty, you were started
> For a reply, at least if you make care
> Of happy holding her.
> F L O R I Z E L—Old Sir, I know

> She prizes not such trifles as these are.
> The gifts she looks from me, are packed and locked
> Up in my heart, which I have given already,
> But not delivered. (Wells and Taylor, 1991; *The Winter's Tale* 4.4. 343ff)

This exchange comes in the midst of rustic revelry, the sly salesmanship of Autolycus the tinker singing 'Come buy, come buy,' the unsuspected presence of the wrathful king and the lover's confidences mixed with joy and doubt, the extremes of love. Beauty and innocence are threatened by the unmasking of king and prince. In the public cacophony we are startled by the inner calm of Florizel's reply that his gifts are packed and locked up in his heart for her. Its unwitting sincerity will bring about his and Perdita's downfall. We weep for them, stung by the unbridgeable gap between outer rules and inner feelings, lost for a moment in the familiar nowhere between the two extremes of outer role and inner conviction. We weep too for the prince's focus on what matters most, and in bravely out-facing a world implacably hostile to true love. We understand his princely stance, oscillating between our own hopes and fears, wishing this divided world could be made whole. With Shakespearian canniness the rest of the play resolves this. Hope, dreams, and love triumph. The audience gains a renewed vision of unity. The journeys between opposites negotiated in the play and in the SDM are similar. But a distinction is important: the material in the SDM is the participants' own dreams and associations. They experience 'the real' as an ingredient in their making a more complete world. A real achievement, surely with a more solid hope?

We strive in the SDM for feelings of satisfaction with pain and pleasure: intangible rewards of immeasurable value not the common currency of cash, position, or even admiration, yet a lasting enjoyment of ensemble. I am reminded of teaching the flute. An instrument with which one must shape every note with all of one's self: lips, fingers, eyes, hands, feet, torso, lungs, diaphragm, head. The goal is *not* to be the best but a journey in understanding and using self, all of one's self, plus accommodating the complexities of musical tradition. Each of my pupils, with unique characteristics, had to find ways of producing the best sound. The goal was replicating the dreamy sweetness of flute tone carried in our inner ear and achieved by experimenting in playing and responding and thinking. It's a personal struggle mastering music: body, feeling, fluency with the stave-language; always listening, honing the skill of cooperation, always feeling, not led by words.

I programmed an overlap of lessons so two pupils and I shared music making (infinitely more difficult than playing alone). The flute is a lonesome instrument without the comforts of harmony (double stopping on strings, chords on piano or xylophone). I suspect more was learned in these short trio spells than in longer solo lessons. Playing together another skill develops, of being lost in the musical texture. Losing one's self, yet still being there. Feeling simultaneously separate and part of the whole is thrilling.

I felt teaching should reinforce not carp. In reinforcing achievement errors wither. It was touching how often pupils replied, 'But I made a mistake in bar three.' The education system, inescapable, to which I said, 'I know. We both do. You'll fix it next time'—greeted with a sheepish nod. Insight gleaned from doing is by far the best teacher, particularly when teacher and pupil, equal but not the same, confront the Muse.

This sort of Faraday cage neutrality is precious. For doing involves all, often without defences. The security of sharing performance brings its own confidence and perceptions. I don't think anything I said was as effective as playing a few notes or playing together. Because interpretation is shared it becomes integral with playing, not an alien judgement.

In the SDM all dreams are valid as each part is in chamber music. The struggle, the sharing of making a piece of music whole, heartfelt, and evocative, also emerges in the SDM. There is a tension between private and public. Mood-sharing and struggle belong in music and the Matrix. It is hard to describe the flowering. But it is tangible if, more often then not, missing today. The fragmentation of families, societies, and nations is a needless failure of human imagination.

Now, something for you, the reader, to do: associate to the picture below. Let your gaze dwell, thoughts wander, see the shapes, try to say what they are—a pyramid of flowers? Falling water? Key holes? Arms or faces? Landscape? Yes, rather like a Rorschach ink blot. Tell its story!

Read no more until you've fixed its 'meaning' in your mind!

The poet saw doves, birds of paradise, masks, and great faces in a glimpse of imaginary life below the surface of a pond. A vision touching on how the fragmented is whole when embraced by the earth, on how this unity is alien to everyday life. Yet, how vital it is:

> Someone commands the silence
> clad in feathers with beaked head-dress.

> Great faces leer and beyond, doves coo.
> 'It's not my time, is it.'
> All heads grimly shake.
>
> Tangled tears course my cheeks.
> The doves coo softly, the faces stare.
> The bird-head starts to nod.
> 'This is not paradise,' it bills.
> 'I want a life, not paradise,' I say.
> 'Bravely said,' the beak snaps
> shut, 'Your sort are welcome here.'
> The doves, now birds of paradise,
> flutter iridescent wings in welcome,
> the great faces almost scowl as
> Earth's breasts engulf me.
> 'There is nothing else but life.'
> someone whispers as
> I float joyfully away. (Oeser, 2008: 73)

Hopefully the reader now has two visions of the picture—their own and the poet's, just as he had associated previously to Florizel's inner feelings, and Södergran's stars. This is enriching work leading to new thinking which may be defined as creative. A connection to the unconscious brings life to our work. Suggestions of unity forge fresh connections between feeling and thought. This spurs us to share the world in a different way. Maybe this is our last frontier, a beginning of new eras. I believe it's our last chance to achieve a wholesome future.

I find it difficult to explain Social Dreaming. I often think it's like trying to describe a sunset to a blind person. Even discussing dreams I seem to be speaking another language. (A friend announced recently that dreams are the garbage which the mind rejects, leaving it uncluttered, freed for thought.)

Why dreams are ignored, why so many ignore fruitful working methods, ignore each other, and the world, is perplexing. Turning a blind eye to what lies in the shadows is a continual rejection of a rich bit of our childhood. Yet we can't irrevocably grow up. Furthermore (remembering Freud's comments on sexual repression), I have been wondering if the current obsession with men's sexuality (from gayness to paedophilia) represents a struggle with a natural bent to be male and female which legal, moral, and religious restrictions can't possibly contain; it's our inability to accept deep truths. One of the threads of polyphony in *Changes* explores this. The novel begins with a damaged boy who embraces homosexual love yet heroically grows into maturity, marriage, and grandfatherhood. Peter, the boy-gardener, has a similar experience. His mention of Persephone's Bridge is partly a cipher. This raises the question: Are they complete men? If so, are we?

Academia too, is part of the eye-blind brigade by insisting on ana-lysing rather than associating. Scholars' reactions to my book *Reflections* have concentrated on the source of the pictures (like the one above) and biographical messages in the text. Certainly *not* the point as Virginia Woolf [3] complained in 1932 (Woolf, 1944: 39ff). The book reader is invited (as above) to hide the words and 'see' the pictures and afterwards compare their view with the text. Hopefully a richer reading result. Have we forgotten how to relate to stories and to daily events with a duality of vision?

Whatever the answers, it seems to me that creativity is neutered; both for the work of artists and for the less visible acts of others that enliven the everyday. (Such as working with stories.) The loneliness of being a poet is deadening. I hanker after the collective energy in the Social Dreaming Matrix, the skills honed there, and the hope gained that a richer world can be thought about, shared, and then made.

Some characteristics of Social Dreaming and of creativity may be understood by now looking at two World War I poems of Wilfred Owen:

---

[3] Woolf, V. (1994). *The Second Common Reader*. Harmondsworth: Penguin, pp. 39ff, "Robinson Crusoe": 'Nobody who has any slight acquaintance with English literature needs to be told how many hours can be spent and how many lives have been spent in tracing the development of the novel and in examining the chins of novelists ... However ... our first task, and it is often formidable enough, is to master his perspective. Until we know how the novelist orders his [sic] world, the ornaments of that world, which the critics press upon us, the adventures of the writer, to which biographers draw attention, are superfluous possessions of which we can make no use. All alone we must climb onto the novelist's shoulders and gaze through his eyes until we, too, understand in what order he ranges ...'

> I saw his round mouth's crimson deepen as it fell,
> Like a Sun, in his last deep hour;
> Watched the magnificent recession of farewell,
>
> Clouding, half gleam, half glower,
> And a last splendour burn the heavens of his cheek.
> And in his eyes
> The cold stars lighting, very old and bleak,
> In different skies. (Lewis, 1969: 110)

In this fragment we see the structures of rhyme and meter, although holding the words, overwhelmed by the poet's feelings which bring life and meaning. The tussle between form and content extends the subject of war not so much by intellectual engagement as in our emotional involvement. For, feelings, like dreams, are largely communal.

Tension predominates. Although its subject is death, the piece reads like a love poem. Love colluding with disgust and despair at the loss of life. The dying soldier in his last hour, with fresh cheeks and the life, warmth and majesty of the sun, is transformed into an angel in different skies. Feelings are so strong that the banal ugliness of war is eclipsed.

The heroic ordinariness of humankind—the great qualities of youth, beauty, and nobility—dazzles us. The poem's structure is overshadowed by feelings of loss. The transfiguration of the corpse highlights the futility of war. Its scale change from person to universe (the transformations of mouth to sun, of cheek to heaven) carries with it the impression that the death of a soldier is equally the end of the world; an enormity of destruction.

The gush of pain is so powerful that the obvious trench scenes of mud, blood, guts, rats, the obscenity of the dead, and the screams of guns, are obliterated. Sightless, we are transported into war wrestling with our own emotions. The poem is magnificent.

The 'different skies' shocks us by suggesting that angels belong in different skies, not on battlefields or in the ordinary world over which the poet longs for the protection of skies with benevolent stars (as care-filled eyes), the antithesis of war. Here, feelings act as a screen excluding the seen and objective commentary. This is in contrast to the second poem:

> I knew a simple soldier boy
> Who grinned at life in empty joy,
> Slept soundly through the lonesome dark,
> And whistled early with the lark.
>
> In winter trenches, cowed and glum,
> With crumps and lice and lack of rum,
> He put a bullet through his brain.
>
> ****
> No one spoke of him again.
> You smug-faced crowds with kindling eye
> Who cheer when soldier lads march by,
> Sneak home and pray you'll never know
> The hell where youth and laughter go. (Sassoon, 1968: 28)

The folksy meter and rhyme are poor choices more suited to a ribald ditty than to war. The poem does not chime to our sympathies. It reflects on waste, loss, and obscenity. It works at the level where words and concepts dominate. The poet seems unconnected to his feelings which get little expression. Apart from grim irony, feelings are not spoken of, adding to a sense of carelessness. The reader has little space in which to react. Nothing stirs their rage or tears. The poem is reminiscent of television programmes featuring misted images of bloody horror castrated by intermittent adverts for beauty products and breakfast food, the pain having been tailored out.

'Rum' properly rhymes with 'glum', but trivializes life in winter trenches. Natty rhymes sit uncomfortably with the unspeakable horror of trench warfare. The imposition of structure inhibits the flow of feeling, further disabling readers' involvement, as is work with dreams without the protective SDM. The poem is akin to propaganda—a words-led form, abstract and unyielding, which banishes feelings and dialogue. It is, by Wallace Steven's (1997) criteria, half a poem. A good poem mixes the specific and the unspecific; its unity being their accommodation and the reader's involvement.

These fine poems show how difficult dreams and poems are, and how essential is finding neutrality (like the SDM) in which we can embrace both the measured and the immeasurable. Beyond the creative arena I find the world infiltrated by power (and impotence), greed (and poverty of expectation), and constricting systems of control which deny the freedoms experienced by social dreamers and poets fishing in the anarchy of our unconscious. It is easy to despair of such a lifeless and stupid world. But the shadow side of despair is hope; with this I go on, knowing that human society can change.

Finally, after completing the first draft, I had a dream:

> *I am showing a huge building to someone. Drawing back a very large steel sliding wall panel consisting of decrepit corrugated iron sheets, a much older, more characterful medieval building is revealed. Wanting to show its quality rather than bulk, I point out the massive gnarled wooden structure supporting everything. It is immensely strong, extensive and intricate belying the stolid simplicity of the whole. The decrepit facade, reminiscent of temporary corrugated iron fences around abandoned urban sites after demolition and before rebuilding, is a rusting rather fragile skin compared to the rugged complexity of the natural timber building behind.*

I associate the contemporary sliding wall with current language and attitudes. The building behind, an original, is the parent of modern life and thought. The corrugated iron screen represents a mask of language and attitudes with which we describe our dreams that obscures an ancient and intricate system of support (of being) for which we have images but no language. The old, hidden behind a failing contemporary facade, has surprising permanence, a powerful character of real usefulness supporting a slippery veneer of current attitudes.

At first glance this dream seems couched in 'either-or' terms (either new or old, outside or inside, fragile or solid, vague or clear). But the newer corrugated iron wall is supported off the old. The two systems are interdependent. So we must abandon the deficient 'either-or' concept in order to explain the dream.

The new is a rusting (uncared for) parasite, the old, a hoary yet effective if invisible support structure. Innovation inevitably grows out of (is supported by) older ideas, images, and structures. The whole building is a unity, a combination of old and new in much the same way as new thought co-exists with the old thoughts after we experience transformation. *Both* have resonance and power because each belongs by contributing to a unity. Similarly the grown-up protects the child, their adulthood shielding the (juvenile) older structure yet supported by it. *Both* contribute to our sense of being.

The dream represents ancient structures embodying private and public—personal and social, now and then. Hidden, they lurk, supporting each of us as individuals and as members of matrices. We share bits of the ancient unconscious as we do a contemporary shell of behaviour and values. As always, working and dreaming contribute to our sense of being, and represent the essential resources into which we must dip in order to creatively re-think and build another sort of world.

CHAPTER THREE

Image to gesture: Social Dreaming with student theatre directors

Laurie Slade

> It is the privilege of the artist to combine the ambiguity of dreaming with the tensions of being fully awake.
>
> (Anton Ehrenzweig, 1967. *The Hidden Order of Art*.)

The project

Image to Gesture was an experimental project at Rose Bruford College, conducted in 2005–08. The project was developed jointly by Colin Ellwood and I. Colin heads the Directing Programme at Rose Bruford. The College gave us space to work in, and—when resources were available—occasional funding. We proceeded regardless when they were not.

Our progress depended on the voluntary participation of four successive year groups of students. Sessions were often held outside of college hours, and the students were otherwise engaged in a very demanding course. Despite this, they were enthusiastic and always ready to participate, a great incentive for us to keep going.

The project evolved during the four years of its existence, each step being informed by our experience of what had gone before.

As it progressed, it became clearer what Colin and I were trying to do, and how we might do it better.

Our general aim was clear from the start. We wanted to identify possible applications of Social Dreaming for theatrical work. This aim was underpinned by two assumptions:

- that Social Dreaming has a potential contribution to make, in theatrical production; and
- more specifically, that it can develop the creativity of aspiring theatre directors.

These assumptions, in their turn, presupposed that we knew what we meant by creativity.

Creative consciousness

A conversation about creativity was where the project began. Colin and I were working together in another context when I 'pitched' to him a model of creativity I work with. It derives mainly from Anton Ehrenzweig's (1967) study in the psychology of artistic imagination *The Hidden Order of Art*.

Ehrenzweig suggested that creativity involves complementary modes of thought:

- *differentiated thinking*, that is, 'our normal logical habits of thinking', and;
- *undifferentiated thinking*, that is, 'a diffuse, scattered kind of attention'.

The creative thinker, Ehrenzweig said, 'is capable of alternating between differentiated and undifferentiated modes of thinking, harnessing them together to give him service for solving very definite tasks' (Ehrenzweig, 1967: xii–xiii).

In a sense, there is nothing new in this. More than two centuries ago, the painter Francisco Goya famously observed:

> Imagination, deserted by reason, begets impossible monsters. United with reason, she is the mother of all arts, and the source of their wonders. (López-Rey, 1953, Vol I:. 80–81)

As a psychological theory, Ehrenzweig's approach derives from Freud's distinction between *primary* and *secondary process* (Freud, 1900: 600). However, Ehrenzweig felt that Freud's concept of primary process was too limited. He argued that Freud did not sufficiently recognize the deep level structuring which undifferentiated thinking can provide—the 'hidden order of art' (Ehrenzweig, 1967: 260ff).

The converse criticism can be made of Ehrenzweig. Janet Sayers suggests that he did not distinguish sufficiently between psychotic disintegration and undifferentiated thinking. They are radically different manifestations of primary process (Sayers, 2007: 123). To be fair, Ehrenzweig recognized that a particular ego strength is required to harness primary and secondary process creatively (Ehrenzweig, 1967: 205, 291–2).

Ehrenzweig's approach was rooted in psychoanalytic theory, but partial in its perspective. He was condescending—if not dismissive—of Jung's views on creativity (Ehrenzweig, 1967: 181). Rosemary Gordon, a contemporary of Ehrenzweig, noted the 'curiously close affinities' which his ideas had with those of analytical psychology (Gordon, 1978:.137). Ehrenzweig's failure to recognize such affinities is puzzling.

Whatever the reservations, the model which Ehrenzweig advocated has been validated by empirical research. Colin Martindale observes that there is a surprising consensus: 'psychoanalytic, behavioural, cognitive and neurological perspectives all confirm that complementary thought processes are involved in creative functioning' (Martindale, 1995: 249). The different levels of cortical arousal involved in the exercise of these complementary processes can be measured by an Electroencephalogram (EEG) (Martindale and Hasenfus, 1978).

I call this capacity for complementary functioning *creative consciousness*. Creativity itself is not the prerogative of artists—but anyone wanting to make a living through the arts has to develop this particular mental muscle, and has to develop an awareness of what using it involves. Ehrenzweig (1967: 12) called it 'the privilege of the artist', to work in this way. I call it a necessity.

Martindale has shown that the critical element is primary process or undifferentiated thinking. Less creative subjects can score equally on focused, secondary process thinking, but lack the capacity to let go and allow new ideas to 'bubble up' (Claxton 2006: 268).

Research suggests that this capacity to let go and experience inspirational thinking can be cultivated (Howard Jones and Murray, 2003; Claxton, 2006: 268). Ehrenzweig took a similar view. He was a lecturer in Art Education, concerned with developing creativity in art students. This is what caught my attention when I first read Ehrenzweig—and what caught Colin's attention when I explained Ehrenzweig's views to him.

Enter Social Dreaming

This was where Social Dreaming came in. In the course of our free-flowing conversations, I had told Colin about my involvement in Social Dreaming. As Freud maintained, dreams are the prime manifestation of undifferentiated thinking:

> At bottom, dreams are nothing other than a particular form of thinking, made possible by the conditions of sleep. (Freud, 1900: 505 n.2)

Social Dreaming offers the possibility of a dialogue with our dreams—conducted through the medium of undifferentiated thought. Freud insisted that the *interpretation* of dreams was the 'royal road' to understanding unconscious process (Freud, 1900: 607). Social Dreaming avoids interpretation, on the grounds that it objectifies the dream. The emphasis is on experience.

Gordon Lawrence staked out the ambition of Social Dreaming in the prologue to his first book on the subject:

> We need a methodology that is congruent with unconscious processes, does not betray them, and does not seek refuge in conscious, unwittingly defensive, boundary-bound, reductionist ratiocination. (Lawrence, 1998: 2)

With this goal in mind Lawrence identified the essence of Social Dreaming through the primary task. This has been defined in different ways at different times, suggesting that there is no magical formula (compare Lawrence, 1998: 18 and 30; Neri, 2003: 17; and Lawrence 2005: 13). For me, the primary task can be reduced to a simple proposition: we meet in the Matrix to share dreams and our associations to them, making connections where possible. We dive into a pool of undifferentiated thinking, emerging when the Matrix ends. We can then see where we have got to, from a differentiated perspective. It is an exercise in complementary functioning.

Colin had no previous experience of Social Dreaming—but he told me that the director Robert Lepage asked his cast to share dreams when rehearsing *A Midsummer Night's Dream* for the National Theatre (Irvin, 2003). Here was the germ of an idea: through Social Dreaming, we could explore the connection between dreams and theatre.

Such a connection has long been recognized. It can be traced back to the sanctuaries of Asclepius in classical Greece. Seamus Heaney describes how he:

> ... realized at Epidaurus
> That the whole place was a sanatorium
> With theatre and gymnasium and baths,
> A site of incubation, where 'incubation'
> Was technical and ritual, meaning sleep
> When epiphany occurred and you met the god ...
>
> (Heaney, 2001: 8)

So Colin asked me to introduce Social Dreaming to his students.

Our initial aim was to develop the creative consciousness of these students—to enrich their work in unexpected and potentially fruitful ways. But Colin wanted to address a further issue. He felt his students came to the Directing Programme on a wave of enthusiasm for the life-choice that they had made. During their studies, as they engaged with the demands of the course, this primal enthusiasm got lost. Acquiring competence prevailed, sometimes at the expense of authenticity. A successful director needs both. Colin hoped that dream-work of the kind we were contemplating would remind his students why they were there in the first place, reinforcing their personal motivation as artists. Empirical research confirms the soundness of his intuition:

> It would seem that anything that increases intrinsic motivation will improve creativity. (Howard-Jones and Murray, 2003: 165)

Workshop 1 (YG 2004): 7 March 2005

Our first experiment was in 2005. We devised a workshop using Social Dreaming to engage with emotional themes in a stage text.

The workshop was part of a module taught by Colin to 1st Year Directing and Design students (2004 year group: 'YG 2004'). The text we worked on was *The Ticket-of-Leave Man*, by Tom Taylor. This was selected at random, one of a series of texts representing period genres which Colin was exploring with his students.

- **Preparation**. We met the students a week beforehand. We asked them to do exercises designed to identify passages in the text which had particular emotional resonance for them. I gave a brief introduction to the idea of Social Dreaming and how it works. We asked the students to prepare for the next session by reading the text, and attending to their dreams. They were advised not to try to make connections at that stage.

The programme for the workshop was as follows:

- **Social Dreaming Matrix**. Thirty-seven dreams were shared in the space of an hour. These students needed no encouragement to work in this way!
- **Reflections.** The students were asked to think about the experience of the Matrix. Participants were encouraged to make connections with the passages in the text which they had previously identified. A sense of helplessness in some of the dreams, for example, could be linked to the predicament of the central character in the play. Dreams of death and gravestones could be linked to the last scene of the play, which took place in a graveyard. And so on.
- **Improvisations**. The students broke up into groups. We asked them to improvise scenarios which amplified or developed the connections being made. The groups took turns to perform their scenarios. We explored how it felt for the performers, and how it affected the rest of us to watch each mini-performance. The group performances were repeated in a single sequence as a finale.
- **Closure.**

Feedback suggested that most of the students enjoyed the workshop. At least some of them felt immediately empowered, saying that they had a clearer idea of how they might develop their engagement with the text in a meaningful way. A few months later, a number of students reported to Colin that they were more aware of their dreams, in connection with other projects that they were also involved with.

Re-formulating the project

Colin and I felt that the first experiment had been sufficiently successful for us to develop a more comprehensive project.

We were concerned that we had overloaded the students in *Workshop 1* by introducing them to Social Dreaming at the same time as we had asked them to apply it to a text. We decided that we needed to take it in stages. We would start by giving the students an experience of Social Dreaming for its own sake.

We realized we had a new aim for the project. This came about through a parallel process. *Workshop 1* had been Colin's first experience of Social Dreaming. He was struck by the intimacy of the process—the 'honouring of interiority', as he put it. I have noted elsewhere how deeply this intimacy may affect participants in a Matrix (Slade, 2005). Colin insisted that it was 'gold-dust' for theatre directors. He said—somewhat ruefully—that a director might spend days or weeks in rehearsal, trying to generate in some other way a comparable atmosphere of safety and mutual respect.

Meanwhile, I was involved elsewhere in the production of a play I had written. I was reminded that theatre is a collaborative art. A novelist or painter may work in isolation, give or take a little help from their friends. A playwright offers a new script as the medium for a dynamic exchange with the director, the designers, and the actors—and they are all involved in a similar interplay among themselves.

From our different perspectives, Colin and I had reached the same conclusion. Social Dreaming can do more than facilitate creative consciousness for participants as individuals; it can facilitate *creative collaboration*—the essence of theatrical production.

A comparison makes clear the significance of this. Robert Bosnak and Janet Sonenburg did dream-work with the Royal Shakespeare Company in Stratford, in 2003. Actors in the company were encouraged to treat their dreams as if dreamt on behalf of the character they were playing—as if the character were dreaming 'by proxy' (Bosnak, 2007: 88).

Bosnak describes working on a scene from *Romeo and Juliet*. Actors playing Juliet and the Nurse ran the scene. Then Bosnak worked with the actor playing the Nurse, engaging her imaginatively and physically with one of her dreams. They ran the scene again. Bosnak worked in the same way with the actor playing Juliet. They ran the scene a third time:

> The result is breath-taking ... None of us has ever seen this scene played with so many layers of reality present simultaneously. The performance feels entirely instinctive. (Bosnak, 2007: 104)

From Bosnak's description, dream-work of this kind can be highly effective—and deeply affecting. The difference for Colin and I is that we do not focus specifically on the link between the dreamer and the dream. In a Matrix, everyone pools their resources. Anyone's dream may be treated as if dreamt on behalf of anyone else—whether as proxy for characters they are playing, or for the production as a whole.

We felt this aspect of Social Dreaming would be useful for first year students, and that they should experience it in their first term, when they need to begin developing their capacity for creative collaboration. A new intake was due—YG 2005. Ideally, we thought, we would provide them with sessions at intervals, during their progression through the college, and see where we got to by the end. Specific applications could be explored as we went along, once the students had had an introductory experience.

Workshop 2 (YG 2005): 19 November 2005

- **Preparation**. We met the students a week beforehand. I outlined my idea of creative consciousness, and how Social Dreaming works. We talked about the programme for the workshop, laying down ground rules regarding confidentiality and the need for participants to respect each other's contributions. They were asked to attend to their dreams as the week progressed.

The programme for the workshop was as follows:

- **Social Dreaming Matrix.**
- **Reflections** on the experience of the Matrix.

- **Break.**
- **Improvisations.** Students formed into groups, with instructions to improvise a response to the experience of the Matrix. No instruction was given as to the content of these improvisations. Colin and I withdrew. The groups had limited time to work, and then we returned.
- **Playback.** Each group performed its improvisation for the others. After discussion, the groups came together to develop a further piece, for which Colin and I were the audience.
- **Closure.**

It is impossible to do justice to the quality of the material which was generated. We were struck that the students responded as much to their experience of dream *process* as to the actual content of the dreams. One of their improvisations conveys a strong sense of this:

> We were led into a darkened room. At the other end of the room there were plate glass windows, against which blinds had been lowered. Sunshine outside was backlighting the blinds. We were instructed to stand on a mattress. It felt wobbly, destabilizing. We looked around. Furniture was scattered around the room—upended chairs, debris. On a table, a script lay open—inert. Our guide had vanished. There was no sign of the performers. We wondered what was happening. Eventually, we stepped off the mattress, to inspect our surroundings. At that point, we became aware of shadows on the blinds—dancing shadows—and we heard banging. We rushed over to raise the blinds. Outside, the performers were flashing torches, banging, gesticulating, and mouthing words we couldn't hear. I said, 'These are dreams, trying to get in.'

The students were energized. They scarcely believed how fresh they felt at the end of the day's work, coming as it did at the end of a heavy week in college. We explained that we were still developing the project, and would be offering further sessions. They welcomed the prospect.

A few months later, Colin told me that YG 2005 had done a module on improvisation elsewhere on their course. They had noticed the difference. Their spokesperson said that their dream-work with us had prepared them in some way for the improvisations they did in *Workshop 2*. This 'state of readiness' had not been there when they tried to improvise without first doing the dream-work. They wanted another workshop. This was the best possible validation of the project. From then on, it acquired a momentum of its own.

Developments

Further workshops were held as follows:

Workshop 3 (YG 2005): 20 May 2006. As requested.

Workshop 4 (YG 2005): 20–21 October 2006. Two-day intensive.

Workshop 5 (YG 2006): 11 November 2006. Introductory, for the next year group.

Workshop 6 (YG 2006): 20 January 2007. Using the process to inform work on scenes from Pinter's *Old Times*.

Workshop 7 (Rose Bruford Annual Symposium): 16 April 2007. Participation was not restricted to students on the Directors Programme.

Workshop 8 (YG 2006 and YG 2007): 27 October 2007. Follow-up for YG 2006 and introductory for YG 2007.

Workshop 9 (YG 2005, YG 2006, and YG 2007): 24 June 2008. A final session for all participants.

Additionally, members of YG 2005 were given the option of having a Social Dreaming Matrix in the course of rehearsals for their 3rd year showcase productions. Two (out of six) students opted for this, with matrices held as follows:

Production 1: 18 February 2008. Participants: Director, actors and stage manager for Ibsen's *The Master Builder* (Act 2).

Production 2: 25 February 2008. Participants: Director, actors and stage manager for Buchner's *Woyzeck*.

The student-director of *Woyzeck* said that the Social Dreaming during rehearsal seemed to put our ideas into a structure. I felt he had experienced Ehrenzweig's 'hidden order of art'. The use of Social

Dreaming in these showcase productions is to receive a separate evaluation within Rose Bruford.

Image to gesture

When we began, Colin and I knew that in adapting Ehrenzweig's approach for theatre students we had a major challenge on our hands. Images generated in a Matrix may be inspired, but they lack substance. The primary language of theatre is visceral—images need to be embodied in gesture. We could see that we would have to help students bridge the gap. Dream-work in the Matrix would need to be complemented by something which gave physical form to the creativity of the Matrix. Our thinking as to how we might achieve this developed considerably over the course of the project.

We knew from *Workshop 2* that our basic format was working well. When the students asked for a repeat performance, it confirmed this. However, Colin sensed that more was needed in order to counter a tendency he sensed to intellectualization. I saw his point. We decided some structured body-work was required. As Heaney pointed out, a gymnasium was part of the complex at Epidaurus.

So, in *Workshop 3*, between the Matrix/reflection session and the improvisations, we introduced a session called 'Embodying the Energy of the Matrix'. At that point, we were not aware of Bosnak's way of working with dreams—or that he would call his book on the subject *Embodiment* (Bosnak, 2007).

Our embodiment session was led by Colin to complement my hosting of the Matrix. We started with warm-up exercises, getting centred in our bodies, exploring the space in the room, and interacting with each other. Then we played a free-association game. This was a particularly fruitful innovation by Colin. Free association, in itself, is fundamental to psychoanalytic technique, as a way of gaining access to unconscious process (Laplanche and Pontalis, 1973: 169). But Colin's intuitive sense of what was needed is also validated—once again—by empirical research. Sarnoff Mednick (1962) argued that creativity is bound up with a capacity for associative thinking, and developed tests to predict creative potential on this basis.

In the game we played, anyone in the group could call out *'Let's be ...'* We had to respond with appropriate actions, until someone else called the next instruction. The sequence ran:

> Let's be: Hamsters on a wheel—Palm-trees—Chopping wood—Carving sculpture—Placing our carvings in an exhibition—Critics and viewers—Arsonists with matches—Flames—An explosion—Survivors—Firefighters pulling survivors out—Water from the fire-fighters' hoses—People living in sewers—Crocodiles in sewers—On a beach—It's raining—The sun's come out.

We lay down, exhilarated and exhausted. Relaxation exercises followed. Colin asked us to think back over the day, to dreams in the Matrix, the associations, the reflective discussion, the physical workout. We had to identify an image which now engaged us, and respond to this image physically, as we lay on the floor—not aiming for a literal representation, but rather articulating a feeling response. When we had a sense of this, we worked in pairs, each sculpting the other in the form that their image took. The sculpting had to be done without verbal instructions—through gesture and manipulation. When we were ready, we went around the room, viewing each sculpture in turn and relating it to the experience of the day. Only then were the students let loose to embark on their improvisations.

The difference was noticeable. In *Workshop 2*, the improvisation I describe above suggested that the dreams were outside, trying to get in. This time:

> Colin and I were led blind-fold into a room. A piano started to play. A voice whispered 'Don't you want to see ...' We realized it was up to us to remove our blindfolds and open our eyes. When we did so, we saw each member of the group was engaged in some activity. They moved around, now speaking to each other, now ignoring each other, now interacting physically with each other. Some activities were mundane, such as checking a mobile phone, or trying to negotiate appointments in a diary. Others were more surreal. The pianist had stopped playing. He was stuck in a cage, asking for help. A stranger—a member of the college staff—walked in from outside, looking

for something. He was incorporated in the action, bewildered but game-for-a-laugh, until he cut loose and made his escape. One by one, the participants followed. Colin and I were left in the empty room. I felt the dreams had been there, with us. We had seen a presentation of process in a dream Matrix.

Colin and I knew that we had further to go. Something in the transition from sculpt to improvisation was still not working. We experimented in different ways. By the time we got to *Workshop 6*, feedback suggested we were hitting the mark. One student commented:

> The whole process, in fact, is almost perfect in its timing and placing of activities.

But, in other ways, *Workshop 6* suggested that we still had not resolved a critical issue. A dream was shared in the Matrix:

> *I've had two dreams I remember since the last Matrix. One was this bizarre insect-beetle thing. It was transparent. It gets worse. It was being attacked by ants ... It was attacked by ants. One got inside. It was climbing up inside. As it got closer to the head, I woke myself up.*

No-one offered any association to this disturbing dream. As if to pre-empt the space, another dream was quickly introduced. When the Matrix ended, in our reflective discussion I suggested that the insect dream had been difficult to respond to. There was general agreement. Still no associations were forthcoming. We moved on, to the embodiment session. When we got to the mutual sculpting, a number of us focused on the insect dream. Only when the dream had been embodied in this way was it possible for us to begin talking about it.

Colin and I did not immediately grasp the implication of this. But after *Workshop 7* we realized that too much chat was dissipating energy in the embodiment session. We took this on board when planning the next workshop.

Workshop 8 (YG 2006 and 2007): 27 October 2007

- **Preparation**. This was as before.

The revised programme was as follows:

- **Social Dreaming Matrix.**
- **Reflections.** Students were asked to think about the experience of the Matrix. Participants were asked to move from chairs to the floor. Pens and paper were available. While the conversation continued, participants were invited to jot down themes and images from the Matrix which felt significant. Everyone was asked to make at least one physical mark on paper at this stage, to make sure that the process of embodiment got underway.
- **Break.**
- **Physical workout.** This included the free-association exercise.
- **Sculpting images in pairs.** As for *Workshop 3* above. Each pair was viewed as a unit, so the relationship between the living sculptures created a spontaneous tableau. Responses were not verbalized, but could be noted on paper. This was to ensure that responses were physical before they were put into words.
- **Improvisations**. An instruction was given that each improvisation must incorporate a reference to material or images generated previously during the day.
- **Playback**. Improvisations were performed and discussed.
- **Closure**.

Colin and I now felt that we had a workable model. It would remain under review, and open to further development.

Evaluating the project

The project has been an exploration, not a formal research project. We did not know where it would take us, so we could not build in from the outset criteria for measuring progress.

As the project came to a close, it was clear that we had only scratched the surface. For example, our exploration of the 'social' dimension of Social Dreaming was mainly focused on the internal processes of a creative group. We did not begin to explore seriously the ways in which Social Dreaming might highlight connections between the work of that group—the play, the production—and its potential audience. 'Why do this play now?' 'How shall we do it?' 'For whom?' Can Social Dreaming help a production team address such questions? There is scope for further exploration here, in the context of specific productions, whether text-based or devised from scratch.

Nevertheless, within the limits of the project, we achieved some success. Evidence of this comes from responses we received from participants. Some extracts follow. They show that the aims we identified for the project were all met, at least to some extent.

We aimed to:

i. **Develop the creative consciousness of participants.**
   - Through the workshops so far I have accessed thoughts, emotions, and feelings that I did not know were there, discovering world and self.
   - I came thinking I would empty myself. I leave feeling I have a whole backpack of things I can make use of.
   - A way of working where images and ideas are quick to crystallize and become forms visible to performers and audience.
   - A brilliant way of talking and opening up ideas, often quite private ones.

ii. **Develop the capacity of participants for creative collaboration.**
   - Bring(s) a company together as people.
   - Learnt that are able to incorporate ideas of others into stream of overall story.
   - I think it would be particularly effective when a company has become bored, stodgy, and in a rut to liven things up and reawaken the imagination.
   - It seems to me that any healthy collaborative process is, and should be, understood as an act of Social Dreaming … Precious secrets bubble in the Matrix and float into the space. Everyone can share sensitivity towards a space brimming with endless thoughts and images.

iii. **Motivate participants in their work.**
   - I truly believe that Social Dreaming can open up areas in one's creative consciousness allowing my work to be more exciting, creative, resonant, and truthful.
   - From a poem written during a break in *Workshop 7*:

   And in this minute I am me,
   the sum of past, present and rapid changes
   in between, changes by the second that in fact I'm so little of
   what I used to be. I've read books, traveled seas, seen oddities,
   lived life up close, pulled it tight against my skin,
   but I must confess, never has it been like this, never like this.

- A dream from *Workshop 8*:

    It's like Manchester Library Theatre. In a circle. Underneath, there's another theatre, also a circle. I was walking to college—had to walk through college. Guys were running through, with duffel bags. They dumped them. I saw—I listened—I heard ticking. I thought—'Those are bombs. I've got to get the crowded Library Theatre clear.' I tried to ring 999. It was a new phone. The lady didn't respond. The whole place exploded. But the beautiful Library Theatre had fallen into the theatre below. There were flickering red flames. The balcony was held up by a Greek woman's head. Singed red seats. There was a cinema next door. I sat to watch a film, but I couldn't take my eyes off her face. I suddenly realized it was six hours since I'd been in college. I woke up crying. It was beautiful.

Reflections

It is tempting to analyse this dream for the dreamer—to see in it the expression of a seismic shift of consciousness for her, in relation to her work and workplace, if not in other ways.

It is tempting to link the imagery of explosion and fire in this dream with similar imagery in the free-association exercise in *Workshop 3*—suggesting that the dreamer's fears may be shared by other young artists in the making.

It is tempting to link these explosive images with the insect dream in *Workshop 6*—seeing the devouring insect and the devouring flames as examples of archetypal oral imagery. Ehrenzweig (1967: chapter 14) associated images of this kind with the surrender of ego consciousness required for undifferentiated thinking.

Such speculations belong to a different discourse. This has been a Social Dreaming project, so I end with my association to the Library Theatre dream. Heaney said it for me:

When epiphany occurred and you met the god ... (Heaney, 2001: 8)

Or, in our case, when we met the goddess: 'a Greek woman's head', supporting the superstructure.

To work with these students, in this way, has been to experience at times—like the dreamer—an awesome beauty.

CHAPTER FOUR

A master plan experience with Social Dreaming

Domenico Agresta and Eleonora Planera

Social Dreaming at School is a project which took place at the *Pacifici e De Magistris High School* in Sezze, an Italian small town near Rome. Students and teachers of the school, which provides different courses of studies—humanities, science, social sciences, and accounting—were invited. Our aim was to provide adolescents with aid to their psychophysical growth through a primary prevention agency that fosters peer cooperation. According to us, Social Dreaming supplies useful instruments to students and teachers to analyse both school and city context.

Our working hypothesis was that the Social Dreaming Matrix (SDM) could create a safe space to experiment with new ways to communicate and relate, since in the SDM roles and abilities of each participant are put aside; the *dreamer role* is the only one allowed. This kind of space is fundamental in order to share participants' experiences which are very similar. They also help to discover new points of view and creative solutions for what deals with social reality, in our specific case, the school and the class.

This paper is about a pilot experience conducted in November 2007 during three non-consecutive weeks. The SDM lasted 45 minutes; participants were from two classes, enrolled in the final year of the

Social Science High School. A standard modality of Social Dreaming was applied to a specific context as a school: a) short theoretical introduction to Social Dreaming and a Matrix's evolution; b) a Matrix, Dream Reflection Group (DRG); and c) the morning after a new Matrix, a DRG, and another Matrix.

After 15 days we had a new session that was scheduled in the same way and was to end with another meeting to summarize what had been done to understand and highlight what had arisen with students in the last Matrix. Participants suggested activities based on cooperation and sharing, such as listening to music and watching movies together, on specific themes that had emerged during the Matrix.

Network of dreams

The following dreams and free associations which came out form five matrices which are described and connected according to the authors' ideas, as Fubini (2002) already said. The first SDM collected 52 dreams. In the first dream, an attack of thousands of terrifying snakes was described which pulled a long associative chain about what permeates the whole SDM—**death**: one's own death or a beloved one's; a slow and painful death because of an incurable disease; or a violent and unannounced death because of a car accident.

Car was another basic theme: a remote-controlled car that brings someone home; out-of-control cars with brakes out of order and driven without license, linked to death topic, and hearses.

> *I had a car accident because I couldn't reach pedals.*
> *I hold the wheel but I didn't drive because it went its own way.*

Free associations on the meaning of cars brought the representation of life. Taking the driver seat is like taking control of one's own life; besides, cars enable displacements and the car could be seen as a medium to reach another person.

Then the theme of **escaping** appeared, where lions (the white Lion is the symbol of Sezze) chased citizens.

> *Lions escaped from Sezze and chased us. Suddenly we are in another town climbing to reach balconies, but they're not balconies, they are thin poles, too narrow to sit on. A boy went to the bathroom and never came back. I was looking for him and I found him dead on the floor.*

Associations linked this sense of instability and intense oscillatory movement to constant changing moods and to frequent alternate feelings still hidden and unfathomable. Then a chain of dreams flowed about dead beloved ones. Two dreams referred to secret identities of parents; dreamers conceived of their parents as members of the Central Intelligence Agency and the Mafia. A very peculiar sequence of dreams began with heroic fights against hordes of aliens, and then the effort to cover up trails after having run someone down, until it soaked in dreams of **powerlessness**:

> *I was in the middle of a punch up with strangers but I feel powerless.*
> *I pummelled but I didn't harm them. My fists were painless.*
> *I beat with soft fists, flabby at the impact; it drove me mad!*
> *In the effort of running away, escaping, I was stuck in the starting point.*

When a boy said: 'I am aware while I'm dreaming,' and another one added: 'According to me we can put our dreams under control; we can decide what we want to dream,' it seemed like an attempt to dominate the increasing feelings of anguish, just as the dream that followed. It concerned the will to manage and tidy up thoughts and feelings: *The door locked my aunt out of the house while she was tidying logs up. She could get in by climbing the stacking logs. The day after burglars got in her house the same way.*

It seems like the dream is speaking about the uselessness of the effort of tiding one's own thoughts up in order to hold burning feelings (like logs) under control. Fear, like that evoked by burglars violating home cosiness, is too strong and frightening to be kept under control.

A new association brought the *Panopticòn*, the prison, shaped in a circle, in order to have just one guardian watching all prisoners at the same time. We considered it as a school's belief that keeping everything under control as the only way to bring well-being inside a system felt almost hard and persecuting. Is it possible to keep everything under control to defeat fear? Are we always able to control everything? The *Panopticòn* project reminds us that when we bring some kind of fantasies and thoughts back to the context where they were imagined, they seem like nothing but utopia. According to the students, the institution of school needs rules and respect of roles but these two factors add to a lack of dialogue and exchange of ideas between students and role holders, producing a constricting and persecuting context.

Nevertheless the *Panopticòn's* association is very useful for us to underline two important requests: a) communication improvement; and b) development of the ability to understand the importance of respecting rules and roles. Hosts found very interesting reckoning with this peculiar fantasy which arose from the Matrix as an image– that belongs to the context of school—of what concerns **the rules**, more or less accepted by students and related to how they live in everyday life.

This could be considered as an example of one of the Matrix's abilities: letting oneself think about an experience while living it. The first Matrix closed with new dreams about death. The first dream of the second Matrix, hosted during the afternoon of that same day, took place in a theatre.

> *I'm attending my acting class; am in a theatre with a stairway. I wish they would assign me the starring role; they give it to a 30 year-old girl instead. I can see her; she stands across the stairway, and she's wearing a brown dress and a cloak. She doesn't engender envy but dread inside of me.*

Associations concerned a dark theatre where panic-stricken actors could confuse their lines with somebody else's. Then, as the Matrix explored the possibility of a sunken world, a number of dreams followed regarding going down sets of stairs, or climbing up, diving and scuba diving. The unconscious, like the sea biologist, popped up in one of these dreams. In the last part of this Matrix dreams about natural catastrophes made an appearance: dreamers could reach a shelter and observe the terrifying sight of giant waves swallowing cities, and overflowed rivers covering huge plots of land.

> *Sezze was overcrowded by water. We sat on my roof very close to other survivors. People moved on by tiny boats.*
> *We were on the beach watching a huge wave rising up!*

The next morning we had our third Matrix; the first dream described a young boy transforming himself into a demon: *he was pale but very intriguing and dangerous—for his friends too*. Ghoulish figures, like Dracula, the Not-death, appeared, representing oscillations between day and night, death and life, transgression and secret, along with strength and difference.

The following dreams caught a glimpse of this **ambiguity**: girls with male sex organs and vice-versa. Masks replace body's transformation; they are useful to **hide one's own identity**, like the protagonist of *Eyes Wide Shut* (1999). This Kubrick movie shows a person who, wearing a mask and mingling in the crowd, lives a sexual transgression. The movie suggests two different ways of transgression and cheating: action or dream; both ways are about a desire for pleasing that have consequences in real life.

Then this dream: *Swimming pool's protective cap protrudes and the whirlpool sucks in everything. Suddenly the pool becomes the sea.*

Followed by dreams about **lack of control**:

> *I was driving on a high hill way and suddenly I got off the road. I didn't fall but I flew instead and landed on a field. The ground was soft and I was alive.*
> *I get in the car. When it moves I discover that it has no brakes. I can't stop it.*

Feeling of being lifted: *My whole class was sitting on a bench, like a chair lift. Looking down, while we were lifted, I saw that our small town became a jungle.*

By contrasting these dreams another one was shared about immobility: the darkness provokes paralysis. *I couldn't turn the light on so everything was dark. I couldn't see and I couldn't move, which bothered me.*

A new chain of associations and thoughts emerge, an example of verbalization about how important it is to hold everything under control and how high an anguish level can be reached when a person cannot have control any longer:

Not respecting my schedules and my programmes scares me; I get lost when I'm late.

When I go to bed I'm frightened by dreams. I reject them. I'm afraid they can come true. This is the reason why I try to repress everything.

The Matrix was closed by a long dream and association sequence that concerned bugs, spiders, and ants sticking, all observed for researches, transforming like in Kafka's *Metamorphosis*.

Two weeks later we had the fourth Matrix. Its first dream, and its main topics, seemed a perfect synthesis of previous matrices: *I am in a water park with two colleagues. We reach a lake. I can see the teacher, Mary, lay down tanning. Then Antonio, another teacher, and his children drop me off the car. The road is on a sea cliff. I can see a sea lion diving. There are two black people sweeping the road. They are in the middle of the street and don't want to move over although the car could smash them up. Antonio and I were surprised by their attitude.*

The nucleus of the following dreams was **competitiveness** that compromises relationships and prevents trusting another person or finding friends. Dreams concerning final exams were linked to high risks of falling over while passing through impervious mountain roads; a straight road that connects the top of the hill to the level plane would be better, as another dream suggested.

> *I am in my new home. Out of my window I can see vast and boundless ocean, a mass of calm water. I ask my mother why there is the ocean instead of the landscape I know.*

Sexuality was a new topic: first sexual love experiences, first love and cheating that is generally allowed only in dream life.

The day after had the last Matrix. It started up with bad final exams, then jealousy that causes **acts of violence**, especially in girl's dreams.

A lot of girls had dreamed about hitting children and then feeling that those children belonged to them. Or had dreams of pregnancies, but said that they didn't have sex—they just suddenly found themselves with a huge belly:

> *Suddenly I had a big belly—I was pregnant—while I was walking on a gravel road. And I put my hands between my legs to catch the baby stepping out of me.*

Furthermore emerged the image of the swimming pool where the dreamer felt **vulnerable**, everybody was naked and exposed to everyone else's gaze.

Another sequence of dreams revolved around communication and an inability to speak, culminating in a dream about gigantic teeth that keep growing until they explode or another one where the mouth is entrapped by an abruptly materialized brace.

The last Matrix ended with dreams of turbulent weddings: wedding attendants thumped by explosive charges; a wedding messed up by the church's garden; a birthday party for someone turning eighteen turned into a wedding party. The bride was worried because she had to schedule the week in order to spend time with her groom in their new house and dedicate the rest to her parents.

Adolescence according to adolescents

Social Dreaming supplies students with a democratic and equal space which helps them to confront each other about issues central to adolescence and everyday life: clubs; use and abuse of alcohol; family; school; sexual love; first couple experiences; final exams; leaving school to go to university; and problems concerned with integration and growth. What emerged from the dreams shows experiencing **transgressions** as an important and essential way to affirm one's own identity and one's own way of being in the world. The importance of **physical contact** and discovering another person by **sexual experiences** become a real **workshop about building and testing one's own identity** because of their communicative and relational value.

However we won't linger on analysing these topics since we believe it would be better to focus on our specific context. Through this experience we observed and tried to analyse expectations, fantasies, fears and interpersonal dynamics belonging to a **class**, as a scale representation of society. It was possible to observe modalities and relational and communicative models developed by the class, through the language of dreams and thoughts that let us find codes, markers, signs and symbols specific to a different class that attended the matrices. As said before, dreams suggested a very interesting reading connected to the **sharing dimension**, relationship sharing, memories sharing, even of specific objects that belong to a class or to a small part of it. During this specific experience we avoided underlining and working on strong group dynamics:

a. We used dreams and thoughts from Dream Reflection Groups in order to facilitate communication among class members.
b. We also observed the ways in which the system reorganizes itself. Group dynamics weren't encouraged or interpreted, but we used

them as facilitator factors to better understand the dreams of the Matrix. However we couldn't avoid thinking about student–teacher relationships, relationships among teachers, among class members and between students considering themselves to be very close friends. Exploring group dimension, according to us, is helpful to define and organize the complexity that is typical of relationships, roles, and tasks of the class.

For this reason Social Dreaming seemed the perfect methodology to discover and observe, from a new point of view, fantasies, feelings, and dynamics that students live everyday in their classroom and school. By focusing on dreams, Social Dreaming sets aside individual problems and focuses on collective topics belonging to all participants; this is what makes it unique and useful in taking out the peculiar characteristics of the system. People consider dreams their most spontaneous and honest private dimension but, at the same time, they can share them according to anthropological value. In a collective dimension considered similar, democratic, non-judgemental, non–discriminating and without any aim of providing advice, SD facilitated an equal exchange of feelings and sensations.

The task of the Matrix was to face what a group of students of the same age is experiencing, or will experience, in becoming adults. A dream, when it's shared, heard, and lived through other people's thoughts and associations could become a bridge, an instrument that creates links, relationships and helps individual growth.

The Matrix holds at the same time an intimate dimension and a social space where adolescents can have training in communication, to dialogue, and in relationship. In this sense the hypothesis of Social Dreaming as a gym is not unusual; the training, concerning getting in contact with the 'Thought of *Other*', underlines the importance of the intersubjective and the context in which we live and deal, in and through which we build ourselves, our personality, and our corporeality.

Due to its dynamic and complex nature, the Matrix can facilitate discovering the connection between school and families through students' dreams. Dreams are an important instrument to observe the context in which a person works and lives. In this way, language and thoughts related to dreams and inserted in the Matrix, are unique elements that can help indicate infinite meanings regarding social reality. The dreams find images useful to shape reality from a new and complex perspective, one which is socio-centric rather than ego-centric.

The Matrix portrays adolescence as an ocean of feelings, a moment to experience fears, new things, disappointments, and genuine competition. Dreams tell us about manifold phenomena, social instances, and every kind of experience.

The Matrix's experience, like plunging in the ocean

Depicting the Matrix as an **ocean into which to plunge**, gives an ideal representation of relationships and feelings established during this experience. Deep in this ocean participants could get in contact with someone else's private ideas, thoughts, and feelings. Social Dreaming's work needs everybody's cooperation to reach a dreamlike dimension; this is its peculiarity.

It could facilitate thoughts about oneself, although personal stories are not requested and it triggers new images of the context in which participants live, as a balanced and democratic instrument. Participants must dive in, must fly in the void, in order to get into the Matrix in which, as dreams said, they are carried away and go off-road, plummeting into an emptiness but surviving because they landed on soft ground.

The space created by the Matrix is like the one described in one of the first dreams, like thin high poles that provide swinging and precarious shelter; the oscillation between what is rational—the logical thought—and what is purely associative, spawned by a creative act, between consolidate knowledge and incomplete intuition, and between what is considered as private property and what belongs to everybody. The deep involvement of participants causes a continued oscillation between a desire to, and a fear of, living that involvement.

Looking at the development of the matrices, it's clearly visible that the dreams of the second Matrix were focused on Social Dreaming itself; they wondered the possible meaning of sharing dreams with other people, what is the nature of the thought of the dream and how it develops. During the Matrix participants got in touch with their **fear** of what they were living: a dream was about the risk that a person takes participating in scuba diving. When scuba diving it is very important to constantly monitor the time, as if the air inside the oxygen tank runs out a person could die in the deep water. Nevertheless the Matrix is a protecting shelter too: it provides a safe point of view to observe natural catastrophes, as in the dream about floods where the people ultimately survived in a shelter holding altogether.

Gaburri and Ambrosiana (2003) define the experience of the feeling of plunging into a shared universe as the *oceanic feeling*. Darkness (blindness) and loss of a personal role (anonymity), as happened in the dream set in a theatre, generate extreme unease and yet simultaneously help people to get in contact with each other. If persons manage to tolerate the uncomfortable feelings aroused they can extend their personal boundaries.

Giving birth without fertilization is possible in this way. Matrix/womb gives hospitality to thoughts/babies through the minds of participants, like in those dreams in which dreamers gave birth to babies despite the fact that they were not pregnant. According to Ambrosiano (2003) we can assert that the experience of Social Dreaming enables participants to connect with those auto-generative thoughts that don't belong directly to them. Being pregnant of these unfamiliar thoughts transforms the idea of individual growth and the experience of sharing; it strengthens the trust in learning from experience. The dream-like state, that gradually appears, relates the unconscious to mind's generative dimension.

The benefits of an instrument grounded on the cooperation of a collective of people

According to several studies about the school context, participant observation with students, when allowed by teachers, helps to better evaluate the life of the class: this shapes the way that the role holders consider the system. The fact that participants (students, headmaster) invited teachers to the Matrix didn't interfere with our host role: we preserved an open road to manage and organize the work frame. Even though everyone appreciated this experience and students valued teachers' attitude towards Matrix, in the second part of the pilot project students didn't renew the invitation to teachers. We can assume that some ideas needed a stronger delimitation, and maybe students wanted to share their intimacy with their classmates, people of the same age.

This echoes back to *Panopticòn's* association and also to the will of learning how to get news and a creative dimension through tiny first steps: the peer sharing. Taking into consideration the importance that dreams represented to students and their observations about several topics (sex, drugs, relationships, school, teachers) we accepted to modify the work frame. When we illustrated the reasons of our decision to teachers, they accepted it in a positive way.

Conclusions

Our working hypothesis was confirmed by several dreams concerning specific elements about participants whose attitude, as student and as person too, was very participating. The observations of the students, collected during the DRG, supported our hypothesis. In the middle of a very delicate period that is constituted by important development through important and sudden psycho–physical changes it is essential to let young people express their thoughts about living their life here and now in order to help them in their growth.

We reckon Bion's (1962: 95ff)) concept about 'learning from experience' is apt to the context of our specific experience. Learning groups are necessary in order to analyse and establish clear rules suitable for the class. Furthermore, these groups provide a deeper knowledge about complexity that belongs to classroom's relationships, tasks, and roles. Social Dreaming could be a concrete instrument to discover new definitions of several interpersonal dynamics, fantasies, and feelings which students live everyday with their classmates.

Conclusions are dedicated to further observations about methodologies applied to schools. Even though the group provides a space for looking at topics and interpersonal dynamics in their various dimensions, applied psychology and school psychologists do not use experiential activities and especially group activities as much as psychometrics instrument or courses about specific topics. Social Dreaming, as we all know, uses a unique 'frame', the Matrix that is different from a classic group setting. The Matrix can be considered both as the way the host thinks, that builds and organizes a specific working context useful to sharing thoughts and observations, and as a real and complex space; very archaic in a metaphorical sense, a kind of cauldron full of stories, feelings, fears and relationships, not completely known but part of the system yet, in which they express themselves. This is the reason why using dreams and dream's thought in a class is an original and useful didactic and pedagogical instrument for students and teachers.

Dream is not a lie and it suggests a lot of things about the dreamers: their mind, and their way of living and feeling in the social and relational context in which they think and live. Following Bion's insight, Lawrence (2003) states that knowledge and awareness are generated by the thought based on the dream. School issues are often caused by students that don't respect rules, tasks, and roles, by mistaken communications and difficulties in managing rules too. Bullying episodes are assimilating, in general, to problematical school integration; sometimes the class is the place where the bully finds his/her own identity, regarding a missing or distort role that belongs to its family's system and so on. There is also a problem regarding power and lack of professional updating; it can create atmosphere that doesn't facilitate relationship between the teacher and the learner.

The class of a school is a complex system that needs educational activities and spaces to read its complexity in order to transform itself and make it usable and thinkable to each member without shaking its inner and deep balance. Social Dreaming, according to us, has the requirements to be implemented in the school context.

CHAPTER FIVE

Low-shot on reality: Dreaming in a primary school

Laura Selvaggi

This paper reports experiences of Social Dreaming with children six to ten years of age and underlines the special characteristics of both setting and aims. The cases examined show how Social Dreaming can be a pleasant and interesting activity for the young participants and how it represents, at the same time, a considerable contribution to foster creative thinking, communication, and tolerance.

My intention was to study how Social Dreaming can spread its beneficial educational and transformative potential in the early years. Furthermore, I had the hunch that the image of social reality emerging from the children could in some way be different from that of the adult. Particularly, I thought that through Social Dreaming we could explore the children's perception of those structural and cultural aspects of Western society that systematically violate children's rights. At the same time I expected that it might offer a concrete opening to cope with these indirect forms of violence and abuse. Starting from this hypothesis, I 'imagined' the special contribution Social Dreaming could offer to contemporary education.

The setting

Working with children entails in the first place the effort to arrange the setting (participants, primary task, and locale) so that the young participants can understand and use it.

I preferred an open-order arrangement, since I wanted the children to be free to choose their own place (sitting or lying down on the floor; leaning on a chair to draw; sitting with their back to the room; sitting close to one of the hosts or facing the wall). I thought that a very fixed layout, in a snowflake or spiral pattern, would interfere with the possibility of thinking and associating freely, since it would have brought back the participants within the stiff framework found in school.

I stated the primary task in simple words, using an involving tone:

> Now we're going to play together with our dreams: our task is to recall dreams, telling them by talking or drawing. We are going to tell and draw and play with dreams, as well as with everything dreams may make us think of. Some of these thoughts may be very fast, others may be slow: we have to catch them all! Who has the first dream?

Furthermore, I decided to allow the teachers to be present not only as a part of the required authorization, but also because their presence would create a more stable environment, fostering a full and free participation. Anyway the teachers, very cooperative in both cases, knew that the experience would be quite different from the ordinary scholastic activities.

The matrices included six to ten-year old children; they were kept for 1 hour, followed by a further 15 minute reflection about dreams and the experience within the Matrix. The first experiment took place in a summer recreational centre (two matrices in the course of a week), and the second in a Montessori primary school (three matrices in the space of two weeks). An informative report specially designed for children and caregivers was given out a few days before the meeting. In both cases, Social Dreaming had been included among the daily activities as a 'guided game'.

On a formal level, I first noticed that children preferred to express free associations and amplification in the form of tales, jokes, songs and, obviously, drawings. With tales and jokes they often came back to an ordinary and conventional way of thinking: for instance, jokes rarely aimed to make everybody laugh and mostly they were offered as something that everybody knew both in the dynamics and in their punch lines. It was a sort of flight from the creativity embedded in the thinking of the dreams. Swinging between creative and conventional ways of thinking probably allowed the children to adopt gradually the creative, so it encouraged participation. Even if I intended drawing as a means of telling dreams, children often used it to express moods and thoughts about dreaming and about Matrix.

A six-year-old girl drew a beautiful tiger and told a story she had invented: a male tiger was questing for a wife, but he could find her only with the help of a friend. Perhaps there was the underlying thought about the use of the Matrix, since it offers the possibility to work in a group at something which is usually an individual matter.

An eight-year-old boy drew a wonderful dinosaur; I asked (quite dumbly): 'Did you dream about a dinosaur?' He answered: 'No, but my dream made me think of a dinosaur!'

Drawing was essential in one case, when one of the younger children didn't manage to describe with words a dream in which two people, one without his head, faced each other with their arms out. As expected because of the age, dream telling was facilitated by turning to different means of expression (gestures, sounds, dramatizations) or to the backing of the adult host (short questions or the mere closeness).

The dreams

The material I collected in the five matrices is quite rich (81 dreams) and varied; it obviously includes many characters and situations from television programmes. It was striking that there were many bad dreams or actual nightmares, sometimes connected with something the children had seen on television (on the news or a fictional show).

The first Matrix at the summer recreational centre opens with an especially representative sequence: *I am sitting on a volcano and it's boiling hot and I go poops in the volcano.* Everybody laughs and they calm down only when another child began to tell his story: *I met three wolves in the woods. I was throwing stones at them ... I hit one in the belly and one on the paw. I kept throwing stones and hitting them, throwing stones and hitting them. In the end they ran away to the hills.*

After a brief group discussion on the fear of the dark and scary movies another dream comes along: *I was on the stairs, it was night and I was falling. When I got to the bottom it was full of witches.*

The content of these dreams is not surprising and is consistent with the literature about children's fears and about specific difficulties of the developmental stage. Nevertheless, it is noteworthy that some of the themes that appeared from the beginning would be confirmed in the next Matrix and in the ones at the Montessori school.

Even if I am aware of a certain degree of straining, I think it can be useful to list the dreams by subject, underlying some of their characteristics.

Clowning around

The above mentioned dream 1 seems to be—by content and teller's intent—one way of attracting attention by playing the clown. The following dreams are quite similar, both in structure and in the reaction they caused: *I got up really early and, since I didn't want to make a fuss, I started drawing. I drew a broom and then* Fantozzi *[an Italian comic]; the broom hit me on my behind and then* Fantozzi *pulled down his underpants.* (summer centre, Matrix 1)

> *I dreamt that Giacomo was a Power Ranger, the Red one, and he threw a spit-ball at his enemies and they became chickens.* (Montessori, Matrix 1)
>
> *I dreamt that Francesco became a Ninja, but he couldn't jump because he was too fat!* (Montessori, Matrix 2)
>
> *I dreamt that Claudio ate a live bee and so the bee stung him and he got all blown up!* (Montessori, Matrix 2)

Hyperbole

In this group I include the above stated dream of wolves and also: *There was a three-headed dragon and I cut off his tail, he came at me even without his tail and so I cut off his legs, then the body and he kept walking on his heads. And I said to him: 'Oh gross, what are you, an octopus with poisonous tentacles?'* (summer centre, Matrix 1)

> *I was in the mountains. I was flying with a parachute when a plane came. The plane broke down and the blade fell, bum, it flew right in*

front of me and cut off the strings of my parachute, zap, as I'm falling it cut off my head, right in half ... like this ... zap. (summer centre, Matrix 1)

I'm in a field near the road and there are all zombies who kill me. I scream and scream and scream so much but the people don't hear me. (Montessori, Matrix 1)

Falling

In addition to dream 3, this group includes: *I'm walking along a waterfall, then I slip and I fall near a tractor that runs me over.* (Montessori, Matrix 1)

I was on vacation at my favourite place. I was on a wall structure really long [he might be referring to a jetty], that went down into the water. There's a man, I go up to talk to him and I fall into the water [he mimes the movement of falling backwards] ... Yup, I fell back. (Montessori, Matrix 2)

There's Marco [a schoolmate]. He fell down the stairs and broke his neck. (Montessori, Matrix 2)

I dreamt that I was in a canoe all by myself and I heard the noise from a waterfall. The noise got louder and closer; in the end I fell. [He screams and moves as though he was falling.] (Montessori, Matrix 2)

Also one of the teachers shares in the theme of falling. *In her dream, two men chase after her; in order to escape them she entered a building under construction. She felt as though she were running 'slowly' and, when she reached the top, she was so scared to be caught that she threw herself down. She woke up with the sensation of falling.*

Clownish dreams (or sometimes associations) provoke laughter starting from a sadistic aspect, which moves from dream to all the participants. Laughter, biting remarks, and modest physical assaults draw attention to the children's need for relieving themselves of something extreme and violent, that one can't work out by himself/herself. Apart from their content, this kind of dream has an effect that displays the social nature of the embedded emotion. In fact it tends to show conflicts among children as well as those between young people and teachers, who on those occasions intervene by force to restore order.

The dreams in the second group directly represent the necessity to recover from one's temper; they are characterized by a crescendo of emotion tending to hyperbole that is expressed through a repetition of the main action and through modes of non-verbal communication (excited or very loud tone of voice; frenetic movements). These dreams seem to signify directly a need for containment when excitement or fear grows. This request is addressed also to the Matrix 'game'.

As regards dreams about falling, it is plain to me that they entail a failure of the containing function, that can't offer sufficient protection (falling down) or that can be oppressive (being crushed or drowning).

Death

In order to supplement the survey on the most frequent themes, I add a group of dreams about death. These are some examples:

> *I dreamt someone killed me.* The other children ask for some explanations: how, where, and when? But the young dreamer had nothing else to say: someone killed him and that's it. (summer centre, Matrix 2)
>
> *One time, after fighting with my sister, I dreamt that she was talking with me in Spanish and I pushed her and she hit her head on a chair and died.* (Montessori, Matrix 1)
>
> *My mother was dead, in the dream, and I went to see where she was. I saw the flowers but there was also my mum laying on the ground. A wolf ate my mum.* (Montessori, Matrix 1)
>
> *I dreamt we were on a school trip with the first grade. I went to go pee and when I came back I found all my friends dead. I don't remember anything else.* (Montessori, Matrix 2)

These dreams are always followed by manifestations of relief for they are not real events. That introduces a distinction between dream and reality that the young participants will carefully investigate.

Did you really dream it?

Both groups of children discussed the problem of 'false' dreams, that is to say the stories they can tell without an actual oneiric experience.

Is it allowed within a Matrix to invent a story that can look like a dream or is it a violation of the primary task? Furthermore, how can we ascertain whether a dream told is true or not?

During the second Matrix at the summer centre, a boy we'll call Giovanni presents as a dream a fantastic yarn which follows closely the movie *The Gladiator*. When the other children remark that it is an 'invented' dream, Giovanni answers that he reads a lot and sees many films, so his ability to invent tales is considerably developed. Soon after, another boy tells a dream of being killed. Giovanni insistently asks him to enrich the story with details and offers possible versions of it.

A third child passes off a story with a moral as a dream: a wolf comes to punish him for one of his pranks. The idea comes out that a younger child, four or five years of age, could have 'real' dreams, so one offers to go and call his younger brother. In that moment the following dream arrives: *There are some bogey men around me, one of them wants to hurt me. I don't know how, but all the bad ones were killed and an ugly old lady appears and there's a waterfall next to her. So I throw myself into the water to get free. I fall down and then I wake up and my face is in the sand. I want to go home, but I can't find the way. There are wild beasts and perhaps they are going to attack me. There's a part I can't remember and then I wake up at the sound of a hunter's shot. The hunter and the shot were in the dream—it wasn't a real sound.*

At the Montessori School, 'invented' dreams caused a lively debate from the first Matrix, giving rise to some interesting proposals. Marco says: *We were on a mission against the zombies. Paolo got killed and we buried him. On the grave we put an alien's body. We went on and a zombie ate Sara's head [a lot of noise; all of the children were enjoying themselves]. In the end we get to a castle. Me and Riccardo were the only ones left alive. There was a big heart that went ba-bam [pulses]. It was the chief zombie's heart. The chief came along, he had a beard and a hat ... anyway, in the end we killed the chief and we hit his heart with a stick that turned all black.*

Some girls accuse the dreamer of having invented the dream. Marco defends himself by saying that he is the only one that knows whether it's true or not. The children try to lay down the rules according to how they can ascertain whether this dream is true: it is false because the story meets the dreamer's wishes (his friend is safe, while those he dislikes are killed); it is too consistent; he told it with a faltering voice as he was inventing offhand; and he was able to provide too many details.

Unbelievably enough, their criteria are suitable to the task. This fact shows great powers of observation, despite the young age of the participants. Even more interesting is the fact that such a profound perspicacity is used to tell reality from imagination, to tell experiences from creations. More exactly, these children broaden their reflection to distinguish reality from 'true' dreams and from fantasies, trying to differentiate the emotional impact of these three levels.

Dreams, drawings, and reality

During the second Matrix at the Montessori school, Luigi says: *I often have dreams that come true. Once I dreamt a pack of cards and I found it the day after.*

Barbara: *So have I! I had put a sweater in my rucksack, then I forgot about that and I couldn't find it. One night I dreamt exactly that I was putting the sweater in my rucksack, so I could find it the day after.*

Andrea: *Once I had hidden a slip of paper and I could find it again only when I dreamt about it!*

Examples multiply, but nobody is really sure that dreams can simply foresee reality.

Suddenly, Marcello advances this hypothesis: *In my opinion while dreaming we keep on thinking of what happened when we are awake!*

In the following Matrix, we keep on talking about the relationship between what we dream and what is real.

Massimo: *Sometimes I dream I'm piddling! But I don't piddle actually.*

Simone: *I often dream about a girl who chases me and, while she's running, her hair falls all on her face.* The schoolmates immediately recognize the reference to the little girl of a horror movie, *The Ring*, called Samara.

I had a dream that Samara wanted to kill me with a dagger.

So I learned that almost all of the children in the Matrix usually see scary movies like the one mentioned, in which Samara, a satanic child, is buried alive in a well by her mother.

Stefania: *But it's only a movie!*
Giacomo: *But my fear is real!*
Paolo: *Once I dreamt that a teacher I had never seen before was chasing me. I run into a classroom and locked the door, but the teacher came in all the same.*

Riccardo shows a drawing of an enormous robot attacking a small town. Tanks and superheroes intervene, but they can hardly prevail against the monster, which only retreated after it had already created much destruction. The explosion of the robot is emphasized by movements and shouts, in a general loud noise which is explosive in its turn.

Clara: *I was at the playground with dad and mum. A squall rose and blew my balloon away.*
Giulio: *I was in the street and there were two men, one of them had a gun and the other had a knife. I was hidden behind a wall, but they encircle me all the same. Then I kicked them and got free!*

No associations from the children, but the adults (teachers and hosts) painfully recognize the echoes of a terrible story on the current news bulletins: in a small town near Rome, the teachers of a nursery school were charged with very serious abuse against the babies they took care of. The fear of the bogey man seemed to have come true, both for children and for parents. However dramatic and baffling, this is only one of the many examples of terrible news which is impossible to keep from children.

Conclusions

Such a direct influence of a real event on a child's dream is not surprising, but in this paper I would try to leave aside what is known from infantile psychology about traumata to adopt a vertex that is more consistent with Social Dreaming.

The main hypothesis in Social Dreaming is that dreams contain information about the reality that dreamers share; this information is not available in waking life. A single event, and its traumatic impact, is not the most interesting aspect of the material we collect. What is really important, I think, is the idea coming from the sequence of dreams and associations, which reveals the structural aspect of the violence the children are exposed to. The chasing killer is not always a character out of a work of fiction, sometimes the killer can be a teacher or a male stranger; since our world seems to work on a basis of abuse, parents themselves aren't sufficient to prevent a rosy and childish view of life from disappearing (the blown away balloon).

The image of society that emerges from dreams, mirroring the one offered by TV or videogames, is burdened with a violence that goes beyond any single traumatic episode to become an inherent cultural characteristic. Modalities of communication to which our children are exposed are often in themselves violent (swift, noisy, excessive) even when their actual content is not.

Therefore the problem we have is not only about the traumatic impact, but about giving the youngest the possibility of thinking in a way that is different from the prevailing culture. In this connection, I was inspired by a small handbook by the French psychoanalyst Serge Tisseron (2004) about the negative effects the mass media could have on children's development. Tisseron (2004: 15) openly states that any censure or attempt to cut children off from mass media bombardment is impractical and counterproductive within a 'society of image'. His well constructed argument is based instead on providing children with means that can help them to cope with the violent and sometimes worrying stimuli coming from the mass media. In other words, as we teach children how to read and write, so we should also foster an early development of abilities at understanding and creatively using the mass of stimuli coming from television, videogames, and the Internet.

From this point of view, all of the activities aimed to improve imagination would be very useful, if imagination is seen as:

> the power to make use of the imagery, that belongs to internal reality, in order to transform the environment. Imagination can be addressed towards the actual daily experience, artistic creation or scientific research. In any case it bridges our sensations, emotions and bodily states on one side, and relational world on the other. If you have a very developed imagery, but you don't apply it to the world, you run the risk of becoming alienated.

On the contrary, imagination is quite socializing. (Tisseron, 2004: 21)

I add to this what Fulvio Scaparro (2003) wrote about how important it can be for children to 'cultivate' dreams:

> ... so that in time they start to talk to us. Then dreams will allow us to discover that we are enormously richer, more conflicting and complicated than it appears from our social masks. (Scaparro, 2003: 12)

Perhaps what we find in this way is less presentable and consistent than we would like, but it also gives a more realistic image of ourselves and others. According to Scaparro, cultivating dreams helps to 'transform what is boiling within us in positive and constructive energies that we can use to cope with challenges in our life' (Ibid.).

So we can now understand how Social Dreaming could be a very powerful pedagogic instrument, producing great benefits both for the young participants and for society as a whole. If we imagine a more lasting application of Social Dreaming to the age of development, we can formulate our working hypothesis as follows:

- **Dreaming for dreaming's sake**: In Social Dreaming dreams are offered without the prejudice of any kind of interpretation. So telling dreams becomes a game, that is an activity useful for itself, apart from its product, and which allows them to experiment with and literally try on a multiverse of possibilities.
- **Building a social container**: Sharing dreams in a group of peers is a means to create a stable relationship, one that helps to develop one's talents, as well as meeting the basic needs for protection and containment.
- **Developing imagination**: Playing with dreams strengthens the ability to connect the internal and external world, useful both to modulate the impact from the outside and to use unconscious thinking in order to transform creatively the surrounding reality.

CHAPTER SIX

The slavery in the mind: Inhibition and exhibition

Julian Manley

Introduction

Social Dreaming is a means of understanding the inexplicable. Human existence is seemingly replete with events and happenings that defy the limits of our comprehension and the theme of this chapter is one of these impossible conundrums: the legally sanctioned slave trade between Britain and North America. For most of us today, the idea of shipping black people, chained together in ultra-inhuman conditions across the Atlantic to then be sold as property to other human beings (if, of course, they survived the appalling journey across the ocean in the first place), so that they could be subjected to a cruel existence of humiliation and degradation in the service of their masters, which included physical and psychological pain and torture, beggars belief. And yet it happened and still happens in many different guises and disguises today.

This chapter discusses the possibilities of a deeper and more meaningful understanding of these issues through the creative thinking that is engendered in Social Dreaming. The title 'The Slavery in the Mind' is a reference to the patterns of slavery which are patterned in our minds and which give us a propensity for enslavement.[1] It also makes reference to how our minds are enslaved by limited conscious patterns of thought that Social Dreaming attempts to free through the sharing of dreams and associations. The 'inhibition' of the title is a reference to the reluctance of each of us to delve deeply into the pain and psychological truth of an awful fact such as the slave trade. The 'exhibition' refers to both the museum exhibition and the possibility of 'exhibiting' what was once 'inhibited' in the sense discussed above.

I begin with a brief background to the Social Dreaming sessions. Then, the bulk of the chapter analyses some of the major images and thoughts that emerged from the Social Dreaming matrices themselves. My conclusion discusses what new understandings the Social Dreaming workshops brought out and why.

Background

On 23 April 2007, the British Empire & Commonwealth Museum opened an exhibition, 'Breaking the Chains', to commemorate the bicentenary of the passing of the Parliamentary Act to abolish the transatlantic slave trade. The purpose of the exhibition, in the words of a leaflet produced by the museum, was 'to remember the lives of millions of black people enslaved under British authority and to honour the actions of those, both black and white, who were responsible for finally bringing legally sanctioned slavery to an end'. The exhibition was divided into six main sections:

1. What is slavery?
   What made the transatlantic slave trade so different from all other forms of human bondage?

---

[1] This is akin to the idea of patterns in the mind such as 'the organization in the mind', David Armstrong's (2005: 29ff) seminal concept that suggests that we all apply our own subjective mind images to the organizations that we might work in so that our understanding of an organization is tainted by a psychological preconception that we carry around in our minds rather than an objective vision of a reality. Similarly, we may bring preconceived concepts of slavery that prevent us from seeing the issues as they really are. This is particularly true of the slave trade as a process that appears to be so awfully incomprehensible that it may be too painful to objectively confront.

2. Africa and Europe
   How the slave trade dramatically changed the lives of both Africans and Europeans.
3. The Caribbean
   The reality of life and death in the Americas.
4. The Age of Abolition
   What brought the slave trade to an end.
5. In slavery's footsteps
   Life in the Caribbean after abolition.
6. Legacies
   Past and present—heroes in the fight against slavery.

Together with my colleague, Jacqueline Sirota, we proposed a series of Social Dreaming workshops to be held at the museum and to coincide with the exhibition, which would draw on people's experiences of viewing the galleries. The aim of the Social Dreaming project to be held within the museum was to open out a space for the sharing of images from the exhibition and those that arise from our unconscious in the form of dreams, associations, and other images. These, together with their corresponding feelings and ideas, would create new thoughts and understandings. In this way we hoped to reach a new understanding of some of the complex issues behind the slave trade.

The programme was divided into three sections: (1) The viewing of the exhibition; (2) The Social Dreaming Matrix; and (3) Dialogue and discussion. There were four sessions in total. This chapter discusses the first two, held respectively on 16 June 2007 and 1 December 2007.

Images and thoughts arising from the Social Dreaming Matrices

Mother, father and child

Both matrices brought out images of relationships between parents and their children. The first Matrix (speaker here is male) began with a dream about a father/son, father/daughter relationship:

> *This is a short dream about my father and daughter whose loss I mourn. It's just about how I'm getting into a big car, like a*

> *limousine, and I'm worried because I've left my father and daughter behind.*[2] *(I)*

And the second Matrix (speaker is again a male) began with a mother/son relationship:

> *I'm in my mother's house; I'm staying there. And somebody called on my house. She was looking for me and she was working on the Abolition project. I wanted to know what she wanted but she didn't say. In another way, I was trying to avoid her. She was in a room, not saying much. I wanted to ask her, 'Why are you coming to my house?' (II)*

These dreams bring out the emotional reality of the slave trade, of feeling unsafe and that things are unnatural as fathers, mothers, sons, and daughters are separated. In the first dream the 'big car, like a limousine' includes the possibility of being a hearse taking the dreamer away to his death, like the slaves in the slave ships. In the second dream the comfort of the maternal home is disturbed by an uninvited female who is bringing disturbing and unsolicited information on the 'Abolition project', that brings out the uncomfortable nature of the enquiry of the Social Dreaming Matrix itself that will bring the participants out of their comfort zones, out of their 'enslaved minds', and into a painful confrontation of the real emotional truths behind slavery. The feeling that the slave trade affects us all, not just the victims and perpetrators of the time, is brought out in these initial dreams, where the intimate and loving relationships that are common to humankind help us to understand the pain and suffering of the breaking up of those relationships for the slaves as they were cut off from their families and forcibly deported. Through our own subjective experiences, expressed in the containing space of the Matrix, we are able to empathize with the plight of the slaves. This 'family relationships' theme was reiterated throughout the matrices as a reminder to the participants that the emotional truths of the slave trade are human truths and as relevant to us in a subjective, personal, and visceral way as they were for the slaves. In this way, we are able to understand some of the emotional

---

[2] A contribution from the first Matrix is denominated by a (I) and the second a (II).

meanings of slavery, so that our comprehension is no longer limited to the sphere of rational and logical argument. Slavery, in this sense, is about robbing us of the basic, natural and absolute human right to a loving, caring, and nurturing relationship between parent and child. The purpose of these dreams at the beginning of the matrices was to establish a common ground between our emotional understanding, our affect, and that of the slaves before Abolition. In this way, the first dreams of the matrices ensured personal participant commitment to the exploratory nature of the matrices in an immediate and applied fashion. Thus, in both matrices, there were many references to this shared relationship. Poignantly and tellingly, for example, the following contribution:

> *When I was little my mother suffered great grief at my father being away at sea for years on end ... She had this dream that a large black man would take her in her arms and rock her back to sleep.*[3] *(II)*

In this dream and its context, the connections between ourselves, our unconscious knowledge, and the emotional reality of the forcible separation of families resulting from the slave trade are made strikingly clear. This dream associates the grief of an absent husband and father with a black man as harbinger of sleep and dream in such a way as to suggest that the participants in the Matrix were embracing such a link in their shared unconscious. This was made clear by associations made soon after this dream contribution:

> *Reminds me of the exhibition where family members are being divided up and separated being sent in different directions. (II)*

Later:

> *I have this feeling of the exhibition as having been present in many lands, protected, indulged and carrying the dream of the past, going to a place we have never been but we have been there, something about what we pass on. (II)*

---

[3] In the quotations from the Social Dreaming matrices, a 'D' denotes a dream account and an 'A' an association or any other kind of contribution.

By this time it was clear to the shared thinking in the second Matrix that the exhibition was like a dream space that enabled participants to carry 'the dream of the past' and allowed them to go to a place that they had never physically been to but yet, at the same time, had in some sense 'been to'. That is to say, the Social Dreaming Matrix had allowed participants to come closer to a subjective understanding of the issues by tapping the sources of their creative imaginations that were harboured in their shared or 'social' unconscious.

This unnatural separation of families was quickly developed into thinking about responsibility and guilt. In the first Matrix, for example, one of the early dreams recounts:

> *This is a dream about a family at a zoo. Everybody is looking at a crocodile and we all knew that if you went too close to the water the croc would get you, and eat you. There was a little girl by the water and suddenly the crocodile took her. You could hear her screaming in the belly of the crocodile. Eventually they managed to get her out, but it wasn't easy and they put screens in front of the scene so that you couldn't see what was happening. It was very scary. Everybody was blaming the parents for not looking after their child properly. (I)*

The final line of the dream brings out the theme of parental responsibility as a means of helping us to understand our responsibility for the human disaster of the slave trade. By illuminating a common responsibility, the participants could understand what it was like to share responsibility for common human suffering and avoid the 'I wasn't there' statement of avoidance of that responsibility. This was made clear in later associations:

> *It's a question of heritage. Who's where? I have a friend who is from a rich southern family and he discovered that all the people with his last name were black people, so that he must have had black ancestors to do with the slave trade. Names of people, like a family, and not a family ... (A)*
>
> *This connects to the pottery in the exhibition that states: 'Am I not a brother?' The logo on the pottery. (A) (I)*

By enabling the participants to become truly responsible in the issues of the slave trade, the Matrix opened out the possibility of an emotional understanding and, therefore, empathy, which is otherwise difficult to achieve in the conscious and rational mind. A beautiful example of how this works arose in the second Matrix with the image of the chimney sweep.

The chimney sweep

There are many obstacles in the way of understanding the issues of the transatlantic slave trade. These include, as we have seen, on the one hand, the historical distance between then and now and, on the other, the fact that as white descendants of the people who sanctioned the slave trade we are less likely to enter into empathy with the realities of another race.[4] The second Matrix found a beautiful way of solving the latter problem in the figure of the chimney sweep.

The seed for the emergence of this image was a very short, simple dream sequence:

> *A dream connecting being condensed into a square ... ashes? Art? The water had gone and had been condensed. (D) (II)*

This was a very enigmatic contribution, the kind of dream image that is impossible to even begin to understand out of the context of the Matrix. Its meaning started to emerge later, in the course of the session. The first feeling that was picked up was the feeling of being 'condensed':

> *The sounds outside give me the feeling of being condensed into a small space; reminds me of the pictures of slaves stacked up. You can see the soles of their feet. You can hear the sound of the ship's engines in the exhibition, like the sounds from outside ... (A) (II)*

The image referred to in the association was of a photograph of black slaves being stacked up, shoulder-to-shoulder, one on top of the other with almost no room for breathing or moving. It was an image that arose in both the matrices. This image, in the second Matrix, immediately brought about a shared identification:

---

[4] To my knowledge, of all the participants in the two matrices, only two were of coloured or mixed descent.

> *I was struck about coming through the door here and the door being locked behind us; a sense of claustrophobia ... Like in the ships, being left here, but in this case we're in a gracious Jacobean room. (A) (II)*

This leads later to the introduction of the image of the chimney sweep:

> *Remembering a Jacobean fireplace in a big room and a black man who lived up a chimney. (A) (II)*

Note, once again, the extremely enigmatic nature of the contribution, as if there is something difficult waiting to be said which leads to further contributions:

> *Reminds me of Anna O's description of psychoanalysis: chimney sweeping. (A)*
>   *There were plenty of children going up chimneys in 1807 ... (A) (II)*

The importance of the use of unconscious imagery is made clear here by the reference to the famous case study that heralded the beginnings of psychoanalysis, thus indicating the accepted validity of such thinking to the shared emerging thought of the Matrix. This reference is linked to the key date of the exhibition, 1807, and the image of the chimney sweeper. In this way the difficult issues of the slave trade can be thought about within the unconscious thought processes of the Matrix. From this moment on the Matrix was able to talk about children, an emotional reality close to the participants, as if they were talking about the slaves before 1807:

> *Last night I had a dream, and an image comes to mind, an image of a little girl, past a toddler. She was showing off to a group of people who were paying her a lot of attention. I remember feeling how free she was and how soon that freedom would come to an end. As a young girl she was protected and indulged. (II)*

So the image of the child is identified with freedom before the 'slavery' of being an adult. This dream brought about further dreams from childhood, ones equivalent to a shared identification with a child's freedom lost:

The first dream I ever had, when I was about four or five years old, keeps coming back to me now. I was in a house that was burning and when I picked up a book it burst into flames. I was both terrified and trapped. (D)

My first dream memories were traumatic, about being taken away by or to the man in the moon. (Dream) (II)

These child dreams led back to the figure of the child chimney sweep and the struggle to identify this child with the black face of the slave:

The image of the man in the moon stealing you away ... the moon is intensely, dazzlingly white ... (Association)

As an adult I love the dark ... (A)

Connecting the various ideas of the chimney sweep, the innocent children, their innocent white faces turned black through the ashes, the ashes representing death and blackness, water taking away the blackness. I'm reminded of William Blake's poem of the chimney sweep ... (A)

Darkness and light ... the world seemed bright and happy, now hiding in the dark ... (A)

The dark is where seeds germinate before they go into the light ... (A)

When you paint pictures of faces, if you paint a black face you can only shape the face by highlighting, while for a white face it's with shadows ... (A) (II)

The image of the chimney sweep made it possible for the participants of the Matrix to understand that their 'whiteness' could be equally 'dark'. So the issues of the slave trade could belong to them as much as to the black slaves before 1807. In this way, the association of William Blake's poem of the chimney sweep to the images of the Matrix makes his poem 'The Chimney-Sweeper' from *Songs of Innocence* relevant and instructive to our understanding of the Social Dreaming Matrix itself (Blake, 1979: 51). The poem and the dream within it can then contribute to the thinking of the Matrix (even though the verses were not actually quoted), where black and white are interchangeable and equality is viewed in a spiritual sense:

'And so he was quiet, and that very night,
As Tom was asleeping, he had such a sight!

> That thousands of sweepers, Dick, Joe, Ned and Jack,
> Were all of them locked up in coffins of black.
>
> And by came an angel, who had a bright key,
> And he opened the coffins, and set them all free;
> Then down a green plain, leaping and laughing, they run
> And wash in a river, and shine in the sun.'

(Blake, 1979: 51–52)

This is followed up in the second poem by Blake from *Songs of Experience*, with the same title, where the parental responsibility for the slavery of the child chimney sweep is made clear:

> 'A little black thing among the snow,
> Crying "Weep! Weep!" in notes of woe!
> "Where are thy father and mother? Say!"
> "They are both gone to the church to pray."'

(Blake, 1979: 71)

Children

Further references to children in the second Matrix can then be seen in this light, as symbols of innocence enslaved by the parents in exact parallel to the black man whose innocence was enslaved by the slave traders. Towards the end of the Matrix, then, the question arose as to whether children should be allowed by the adults to see the exhibition in the museum, reminding us of the opening dream that asked, 'Why are you coming to stay in my house?'

> *They had little children and thought that they 'couldn't bring them into a thing like this' ... (A)*
>
> *The perception transferred to children, children running around ... (A)*
>
> *Taken away, logged together, in chains ... (A)*
>
> *I remember the whalebone corsets in the exhibition, how uncomfortable ... (A)*
>
> *I'm reminded of a poem by Dylan Thomas, 'I sang in my chains like the sea' ... (A)*
>
> *What most affected me was not upstairs, but a little screen showing a newsreel of people emigrating to the US and Australia. I was moved by how people held their children ... (A)*

> *In the 50 s and 60 s, children sent off to Australia ... (A)*
> *Reminds me of 12th century children's crusade in Palestine and Jerusalem, children became slaves ... (A) (II)*

This exchange shows how some of the issues concerning the slave trade in the exhibition were understood by the shared Matrix. The poem by Dylan Thomas is a marvellous example of how the imagery that arises in a Matrix can take on its own meaning and force. Thomas' lines are about the lost innocence of childhood but the imagery used in the original poem takes on an added force and power in the context of the Matrix where we have had references to the singing of the sailors who manned the slave ships (see he section 'Sailors and songs' below), the chains of the title of the exhibition and the sea as the passage from freedom to slavery:

> 'Oh as I was young and easy in the mercy of his means,
> Time held me green and dying
> Though I sang in my chains like the sea.'
>
> (Thomas, 1975: 944)

Similarly, images which were not part of the 'Breaking the Chains' exhibition, but part of the permanent exhibition, such as the emigration newsreel mentioned above, take on a new significance in the context of the Matrix. The care of the child, as represented in the holding of the hand, becomes the clinging on to hope on a journey across the Atlantic, the desire from the shared thoughts of the Matrix that there should be some hope in the face of desperation. This is a good example of how the thinking of the Matrix can transform thought from the simply rational to the deeply creative and how connections and links can be made where before there were none. Even after the Matrix, these thoughts remain creative and new thinking has emerged and continues to emerge. The effects of the Matrix on creative thinking can last beyond the Matrix itself. At the moment of writing, for example, my mind sees the painting 'The Last of England' by Ford Madox Brown—where an emigrating couple cling to their child's little hand as they make their journey to a new land—in a different light. It is as if the couple in the painting represent the inhumanity of being forced away from one's homeland, slaves to circumstance, as if the little child will never experience the freedom of childhood as understood in the Matrix. This thought helps me to understand the plight of the slaves on their transatlantic journey.

Ford Madox Brown, 'The Last of England', 1855

Just as the creative thinking engendered in a Matrix can continue out of and after the Matrix, as discussed above, so can one Matrix help us to understand another. In the quotation above, for example, the reference to 'whale bone corsets' seems rather obscure unless you had participated in the first Matrix where the following reference was made:

> *Being trapped in something, like a ship or a crocodile reminds me of Jonah being trapped in the whale ... (A)*
>
> *Being in a ship and the fear of being trapped in a ship, away from the known world, like a scary dream, not being able to see out, like the Titanic ... and the exhibition ... reminded of the image of the feet and the heads stacked in the slave ship. I found that image very moving ... (A) (I)*

This makes it clear that the whalebone corsets represent the feeling of being trapped in a cavernous ocean-going vessel, the kind of sensation that is identified with the image of the stacking of slaves mentioned in both matrices.

Sailors and songs

Another image that emerged in the course of the second Matrix was that of the sailor and his songs. In a similar way to the image of the enslaving of innocent children combined with the hope they represented, discussed above, the sailor's song was representative of the double possibility of joy and despair, just as the negro spiritual represented both hope and despair and contained hidden messages:

> *That's the funny thing about the human species, minor differences are highlighted. I have this song going around in my head, I don't know if anyone else can hear it. It goes something like 'Sailor ... Sailor ...' in a voice that isn't mine, like a song from the deep ... (A)*
> *Is it a waltz, a tango or a foxtrot ...? (A)*
> *As if it came from a mermaid, deeply inviting ... (A)*
> *Spirituals were made on hidden songs and hidden codes ... (A) (II)*

As the Matrix developed, this sailor's song became ever more sinister, a song that could be expressed in childlike innocence and could yet embrace the corruption of reality, such as the reality of the sailors' cargo, representative therefore of our blind turning away from the truth through a screen of song and drunkenness:

> *I wonder if the sailor's song referred to had something to do with soul music ... (A)*
>
> *Sailors had a brutal life. The song reminds me of 'What shall we do with the drunken sailor?' I remember singing this at school—how sailors had to cope with such a hard life, maybe by being drunk, and how innocent this was singing the song as a child at school, how the innocent mixes with the harsh realities ... (A)*
>
> *The song is quite a violent one too, one of the lines being 'shave his balls with a rusty razor'. (A) (II)*

Screens and fences

The refusal to face up to the realities of the slave trade was represented in the first Matrix by images of screens and fences. As discussed above in 'Mother, father and child', one of the opening dreams of the first Matrix concerned the lack of care shown by the parents whose child had to be rescued from the belly of a crocodile. In the same dream, the operation of rescuing the child from the crocodile happens behind some screens:

> *Eventually they managed to get her out, but it wasn't easy and they put screens in front of the scene so that you couldn't see what was happening. (D) (I)*

The screening of the horror represents society's tendency to not look into the horrors of the slave trade. This image was developed later in the same Matrix where the 'screen' is a fence that impedes movement of people but allows the movement of water, that is to say the movement of creative, possibly unconscious, thoughts through the medium of the Matrix:

> *I had a dream that I was looking at the globe—the earth—from high above. It looked completely blue. Then I found myself up to my knees, my thighs, in what looked like an endless ocean. It was like the sea in its vastness but completely calm like a lake. I was absolutely alone, no other features, either from nature or from man. Then I seemed to turn and find that there was a fence in front of me. It was one of those criss-crossing wire fences slightly taller than me and with barbed wire along the top. I was thinking how the barbed wire was there to stop people getting across when I noticed that the water had begun to flow and was now flowing through the wire of the fence. I remember thinking how useless the fence was because it couldn't stop the water crossing over to the other side. (D) (I)*

The significance of this dream for the creative thinking of the Matrix was quickly pointed out:

> *I have an association to the screen and the wire fence, to this exhibition, about how we try to screen out our thoughts to slavery and what it means to us, yet the water, like the feeling, gets through anyway. (A) (I)*

In the process of creative thinking in the Matrix, these dreams and association opened out the way for thinking 'without screens'.

Ships and boats

The first Matrix gave rise to a long list of ships and boats, clearly in an effort to understand the inhuman shipping of human beings across the Atlantic. These included the *Matthew* (John Cabot's 1497 pioneering ship), RMS *Titanic*, the *Poseidon* (from the film *The Poseidon Adventure*), a 'huge ship, like a disused ferry or liner' (quoted from the Matrix session; see Note 5), immigrant boats from Africa to Spain, Wagner's *The Flying Dutchman* and the *Exodus* (Jews trying to reach the Promised land in 1947). The nature of each ship or boat adds, so to speak, a piece of thought to the endeavour of the participants' attempt to understand the nature of the slave passage across the Atlantic. This is a good example of how the Matrix works in 'collage', by piecing together disparate elements into a new creative picture, so that the slave ship becomes a conglomeration of our understanding of all these different vessels put together. It includes the hope and pioneering spirit of the discovery of the New World in the image of the *Matthew*, which contrasts with the reality of the slave trade to the New World; the *Titanic* as a representation of the unsinkable being sunk, and so the impossible being made possible, reflecting the 'impossible' nature of human suffering nevertheless made possible through the slave trade; the *Poseidon*, the ship that trapped people under its hull as it floated upside down, representing the world turned upside down; the terror of a huge dream ship which depicts the terror of the slaves;[5] the mirror image of the contemporary emigration from Africa to Spain and the awful conditions of this journey, often leading to death and terrible suffering; *The Flying Dutchman*, the ghost ship that can never go home, like the slaves once transported to north America; and finally the *Exodus*, a ship of Jewish emigrants trying desperately to find the Promised Land, representing the desperation of a race.

Conclusion

What these matrices at the Empire & Commonwealth Museum showed was how essential it is to reach for the truths and realities of human issues through the shared unconscious. We all have a 'slavery in the mind' that chains us to our rational thoughts and ideas about human dilemmas. This 'slavery in the mind' reminds me of the 'map' in Alfred Korzybski's famous statement 'the map is not the territory' (Bateson, 2000: 455). That is to say, the 'map' we have in our conscious minds of the problem of the transatlantic slave trade can never be the same and can never be complete

---

[5] I'm on a huge ship, like a disused ferry or liner and I'm running up and down in the ship, trying to gain control. Sometimes we're out at sea, sometimes in port, but there always seems to be some imminent danger somewhere. (D)

until we encounter the reality of the 'territory'. This fundamental message can be understood in the following dream from the first Matrix:

> I had a dream last night. I'm in a room twice the size of this one. It's wood panelled. It seems to be a conference with people going in and out, different places, and tables. Some people seem to be at special tables and they are going to cross the Atlantic. They are dressed in costumes that seem to be made of maps. They are going to sail on the Matthew. (D) (I)

In this dream, the people whose clothes are made of maps are those of us who have preconceived 'maps' of the problem of the transatlantic slave trade. These people might be the participants in the Matrix. Through the Social Dreaming Matrix, these people will travel on a ship of hope (the *Matthew*), to the New World where they will encounter the 'territory' for real. This 'real territory' is the shared thinking of the Social Dreaming Matrix, where unconscious emotional realities can be truly and subjectively understood, so that we are transported from now to then.

In the case of the Social Dreaming matrices held at the museum, we also had the benefit of the reality of the images and artefacts on display, more 'territory', so to speak. The shared unconscious of the Matrix was able to play with the objectivity of these images and the subjectivity of the mind. I use the word 'play' on purpose because it seems to me that there is a sense of play in the Social Dreaming process. We are 'playing' with 'objectivity' through 'subjectivity' and this 'play' between our two worlds, akin to consciousness and unconsciousness, is the creative germ for new thought. It is a process that resonates with some of Winnicott's (1999: 50) ideas from his book *Playing and Reality*: 'Playing is an experience, always a creative experience, and it is an experience in the space-time continuum, a basic form of living. [...] The precariousness of play belongs to the fact that it is always on the theoretical line between the subjective and that which is objectively perceived.'

This process of 'play' also aptly describes the nature of the thinking within the Matrix. Thoughts are no longer simply linear in their everyday, rational sense, as expressed in words in a sentence. Instead, the thoughts are expressed and understood in a series of what I have called 'collages', a network of images that communicate to us simultaneously, on a multilevel. The mind imaginatively 'plays' with the images as they are shifted, created and recreated into pictures of vitality. This is the thinking process of the Matrix. In this process, humanity can 'break the chains' and come closer to nature. The sentences of everyday speech, the thinking and wording of our rational and conscious minds are sometimes like chains to our creativity. In the Social Dreaming Matrix, these chains of words are transformed into a network or web of images. In the case of the issues and problems of the transatlantic slave trade, where our linear and rational thinking seems to face an incomprehensible complexity, the collage of visual thinking that arises from the sharing of dreams, associations, and images in the Matrix gives the complexity of the unbelievable a new sense and meaning. It is a process that works like nature in all its complexity, a complexity that cannot be explained through chains of words only, but rather in interlocking and coexisting visual multiplicities. Just as nature is to be understood in networks, so is the Social Dreaming process a network. Our conscious thoughts are limited by our linear expression and this is what is freed by the unconscious in the process of Social Dreaming. It is a natural process, as is borne out by the ease with which the participants in the Matrix are able to contribute their dreams and images. It is 'natural' to think in images and networks because that is the process of nature itself:

'Nature connects its genera in a network, not in a chain; whereas men can only follow chains, as they cannot present several things at once in their speech.' (Albrecht Von Haller, cited in Arnheim, 1997: 234)

CHAPTER SEVEN

Migrant dreams: Integrating political refugees and immigrants in the local Italian community

Donatella Ortona and Eleonora Planera

When our Social Dreaming pilot experience at the UN Shelter Home for women and their children in the ancient hill-town of Sezze Romano was concluded in December of 2003, Dr. Marie Therese Mukamitsindo's initial diffidence had turned into enthusiasm. And, as Rwandan director of the Karibù Cooperative which hosts African women applying for political refugee status, she decided to apply Social Dreaming as a regular activity for her guests.

As in all political-bureaucratic, Italian matters, almost three years went by before the project finally took shape. Meanwhile the town of Sezze Romano was surnamed Sezze *Rumeno* as Rumanians now constitute a rumoured 30% (only 3% are officially registered!) of its total population of some 23,000 in a nationwide atmosphere of an alarming rise of xenophobia.

Thanks to Dr. Mukamitsindo's keenness and the unrelenting determination of one of us, a Sezzenese herself, the Project *Sognando & Sognando* (Dreaming & Dreaming) was finally approved by the Town Council in early 2006. Its goal: the application of Social Dreaming as an instrument supporting the integration of foreigners (immigrants and political refugees) within the Italian community.

Within this plan that stretched over 15 months, we co-hosted 11 Social Dreaming Matrices (SDM) for African political refugees, Rumanian immigrants, and Italian social workers, which we conducted in Italian, French and English, and with an alternative translation into Pidgin English and various African dialects. The sites, difficult to pin down each time, varied, but always included the presence of children (from babies to 10-year olds). Needless to say, unorthodox setting accommodations, spontaneous freedom of movement, and our own trust-inducing contributions of dreams and associations were essential to the process.

The 2003 pilot experience had taken place in the Karibù shelter-home, a big country house immersed in the green hills 15 km from town, where all the guests lived together, but from where they were scheduled to soon move out. At the time, their dreams and associations expressed their anxiety for yet another upcoming separation and transfer. Now, these women, used to communal space, were living scattered in separate apartments in two different hectic historical centres and their preoccupation was poor communication and local rather than trans-continental transport.

The first dream of the first Matrix, held at night-time in a dimly lit apartment filled with many pregnant black women and mothers, was charged with solitude, disorientation, fear, craving for guidance and search for identity:

> *I am alone; I am alone in the plains. I walk and walk but I don't know where I am going.*
>
> *I am afraid. I run. My legs are in pain, my feet wounded. I lost my way. I am alone.*
>
> *I look for my mother, but she is not there.*
>
> *I walk. I fall to the ground and wake up in a forest. I forget what day it is and I don't know who I am. I hear the voices of animals that make fun of me. I walk, I cry. I no longer know who I am.*
>
> *I recognize myself, but I don't know who I am.*

The emotional sharing of all participants was very strong, as they related not only to their present life experience, but also to the native landscapes of their past. The dreams that followed were tied to reference figures for protection and guidance: the **mother** and the **angel**. The associations concerned the word *'madre'* = mother (mother-earth, motherland, mother-tongue, mother superior, *madre-casa* = headquarters) and 'angel' (a protective guardian, an entity who magically appears and offers help and guidance).

The need for guidance and protection emerged in many dreams with **angels**:

> *A beautiful woman appeared saying, 'If someone hurts you, you must let me know.'*
>
> *A crowd of people behind barbed wire and a closed door behind which is open empty space. A young woman appears who is the only person who can move in both directions as she is transformed into a spirit and intermediator. (This woman was associated to: [i] an angel, or the director of Karibù, as an akin, bridging figure; and [ii] Social Dreaming linking the conscious and unconscious, transcending all boundaries into the infinite.)*

Many dreams had also clearly revealed a search for a **mother-figure**, the delusion and sense of abandonment and bewilderment for the absence of an authentic mother: *There is a woman beckoning me. The woman insists she is my mother. I realize that her face is not that of my mother and I wake up upset.*

At the end of this first Matrix we questioned ourselves: could the absence of the director of Karibù, an essential presence as a key initiator and participator during our pilot experience in 2003, have influenced this first Matrix? Our hypothesis: the guests of Karibù seek psychological support, beyond its institutional-bureaucratic task of providing political asylum and living quarters, but perhaps there is no clear-cut mother-figure for the guests to refer to.

Our hypothesis was confirmed when the director explained to us that a period of transition and redistribution of roles was taking place at Karibù. It had become necessary for her to limit her work to a more institutional, less maternal, and less personally engaging role. To our satisfaction, our Matrix had in fact revealed the symptoms of disorientation within the organization itself, as well as among the guests of Karibù.

The first dream of the third Matrix, confirming Lorenz's Butterfly Effect in SD, was very revealing of the social context of our work, indicating, on the one hand, the political refugees' **search of identity and acceptance**, and, on the other, the lack of clarity within the organization and the local public institutions: *There is a grand spacious piazza in front of a huge compound. There are many people lining up for some sort of examination. They all look very phony, as if they are dressed and made up to look 'acceptable': Africans with peroxided hair, Slavs dressed Mediterranean-style ...*

They enter a grand hall and find themselves in front of a long high rope, like a laundry line, to which are pegged numerous paper forms to be filled out, but the forms appear incomprehensible even to those who formulated them.

Then there were dreams referring to **masks** and **appearance**: *In some of my dreams I am myself, but I look like someone else; I am aware of being myself regardless of my different looks.* These were followed by associations to prejudices and the need to transform oneself.

The hanging forms of the dream were associated to photos pegged on a line in a darkroom, waiting to dry before they can come out into the light. Attendance to our matrices had been low, so we hypothesized that the SD project may have been prematurely proposed. The municipal promoters of the Project, whose presence, we had insisted, was essential in order to recruit participants for the SDMs, helping them to overcome their fears of exposure of illegal status or of breach of privacy, had been unavailable to collaborate, caught up in internal politics. Consequently, to promote attendance and increase interest and understanding, Dr. Mukamitsindo organized a Conference re-launching the Project.

The first two SDMs after the Conference therefore hosted **Italians, especially social workers, in the field of immigration and education**. The same themes formerly reported in relation to the dream of the pegged forms (identity, **insecurity, incomprehension**) appeared again. Many dreams offered by the Italian social workers or staff of Karibù reported: *feeling suspended in the air, unable to plant one's feet on the ground.* These feelings are in fact what the director of Karibù described as those oppressing the persons waiting for the legalization of their status.

Other dreams referred more specifically to **roles** and the Dialogue that followed offered an eye- and heart-opening experience with regard to the delicate task of welcoming foreigners, especially those seeking political asylum who due to their initial dependence and strong attachment to the social operators, evidenced the need to better define personal and professional boundaries.

The Italian participants expressed their strong need and desire to know more about the culture of the foreigners ('We cannot expect them to integrate into our culture unless we first know about theirs') and insisted on the support of cultural mediation. The matrices that followed were dedicated to the foreigners, the immigrants and refugees, separately, and then together. The dreams and themes that emerged registered the initial shocking impact with the alienating world of our cities and the stress of our style of life. The first dream from Rumanians' first Matrix was full of anxiety.

> *After 10 hours of work and one and a half hours in the car to pick up my son from school, I dreamt of my mother. She was trying to cross the street, frightened amidst all that traffic ... worried she might get run over.*

The Dialogue revealed the Rumanians' nostalgia for a more humane life which 'accepts mystery' and 'proceeds at a slower pace'; their insecurity in a style of life which has 'lost its values and is headed towards natural and social deterioration'; their effort to find a lost authenticity and truth in their actions; and to give greater meaning to the use and quality of time, how it can best be invested while commuting to work and school, so as to take one's life in one's own hands.

This produced a very positive reaction on the part of the Italians present who, with new awareness, expressed their surprise and admiration for the wisdom of those immigrants, who, contrarily, are usually judged as having come to our country with greediness for our standard and way of life. And the Rumanians seemed gratified to have received attention and respect at a time when they, as Rumanians, were receiving very bad press due to crime episodes caused by their compatriots in Sezze and in Rome.

In fact, another element which surfaced in these matrices of Rumanians and Italians was a rising premonition relating to dramatic TV news tied to immigration, which, it was acknowledged, were subtly inducive to prejudice and suspicion of the unknown stranger. One Italian young man narrated this dream: *I was lying in bed. I heard voices under my window. I was afraid that those people intended to break into our house but then realized that I had badly judged them. We spoke with them late into the night and thought they were really nice people.*

The association which emerged was to the 'darkness' of the night as a form of ignorance which can be overcome in the 'light' of reciprocal acquaintance and respect and it encouraged a dialogical, rather than dialectic, discussion about rising violence and insecurity.

The matrices shared by **Rumanians, Africans and Italians together** were more tied to universal themes (pregnancies, births, children, parents, ancestors, rituals, country life, food and meals, sowing and reaping) and referred to their new daily life of the present (city life, means of transportation, daily schedules).

One dominating theme in one such Matrix related to meals and food, more specifically to **bread**, the taste of which Dante Alighieri indicates as one of the principal pains of exile ('Thou shalt prove how salt the savour is of other's bread', *Divine Comedy*, Paradise, XVII, verse 59), and to **apples**, as a symbol of **family** shared by the different nationalities present.

The following dream, which also indicates the search for **authenticity** and the importance of **family ties** and **cultural traditions**, was centred on a Rumanian death ritual which involves the Church offering of a *cozonac* (a ring-shaped loaf of bread) for the deceased before burial.

> *I dreamt of my dead husband, who asked me for a cozonac, adding, 'It's important that you prepare it yourself.' I had this dream three nights in a row until I finally baked it. In fact, when he died here in Italy, the loaf I brought had been bought at the bakers ... .*

In the associations and the Dialogue, the importance of sharing meals and food was stressed as a main vehicle for developing a sense of belonging as well as social integration and community spirit. Western style fast-food meals were a shock to those whose cooking is based on slow sedimentation, and amalgamation, and for whom the consumption of meals is a time for sharing. The Africans were especially keen to explain that an African woman would never eat alone, that all homes are open at meal times for anyone to join in. Furthermore, as evidenced in a Matrix centred on children, African women, used to sharing the responsibility of child rearing with the entire community, are shocked by the need to recur to public or private institutions for childcare.

One particular Matrix, where there was a majority of Italians, including Sezze's Mayor and Social Affairs Director, mixed with foreigners, began with the following dream: *In a big hangar my cousin was preparing an infinite number of* frittate *(omelettes), as if she were at an assembly line. Her husband (who in fact is a surgeon who often volunteers in Africa) comments, 'How many are you making? We don't have to feed an entire continent!'*

The associations to the word *frittata* were multiple and one in particular referred to integration: 'Eggs must be well-mixed before transforming them into an omelette.' But also the association to the concept of number and quantity was dealt with at length. The Rumanians complained about the unfair speculation of the money exchange into Euros and referred to the Rumanian film *4 months, 3 weeks, 2 days* (2007) as measure of time in pregnancy and abortion. The Italians associated to hunger in Africa and the Western world's responsibility to fill the gap between the land of plenty and the land of want.

At the time there was a national transport strike, and in synchronism, the Matrix was jammed with dreams about cars, buses, and trains not reaching their destinations. But there was a difference in attitude in reporting the dreams. While the Rumanian expressed anxiety in her effort to be punctual—*In my dream when I got to the parking area, I couldn't find my car; I was stressed because I wouldn't be on time*—the dream of the African woman—*I dreamt I missed the bus. The next bus would be only two hours later, so I missed my lesson*—was narrated with amused resignation.

It was an occasion to discuss the different value and concept of time. Africans rarely even know their birthday and have a fatalistic relation with time, which accounted for the fact that they often showed up at our meetings over an hour late (or not at all). By the end of our project we had finally caught on to what was explained by the Polish journalist Kapuscinski (2001: 16): 'The European feels himself to be time's slave, dependent on it, subjected to it [...] time annihilates him [sic].' For an African: 'It is man who influences time, its shape, course [...] time is a subservient, passive essence, and, most importantly, one dependent on man.'

The site of our **last Matrix with the African Karibù guests** was cancelled at the last minute and it was improvised on the floor of the entrance of the Karibù office headquarters. The room was swarming with hyperactive children to whom we handed out pencils, crayons, and paper. The dreams flowed in: departures and separations, the distance separating them from their dear ones, the absence of men *a groom without a face, an unidentifiable dance-partner whose face is turned, two children on a river bank who say they are waiting for a man to come to retrieve them.*

Our association outspokenly revealed ('just like here at Karibù: many women and children, but no men. Men are absent'), received an immediate forceful reaction. There was a strong desire to set things straight: 'It's not a question of absence, but of distance,' the women argued.

In the Dialogue that followed there was much talk about the self-esteem connected to the African woman's role, with particular reference to her backbone, which is her pride. It was emphasized: While working the fields and carrying weights, she is capable of also carrying on her back her child, and if necessary, her husband, whom she is happy and proud to serve to the end. At this final Matrix, the vivacity and spirit of those women seemed to have been awoken to new life.

Also the last and **final Matrix with the Rumanians** was an improvised gratifying experience thanks to the efficacy of SD itself. A first dream was offered by a strikingly alert Rumanian eight-year-old boy. With a luminous/transparent expression, in a clear/quiet tone of voice, in perfect Italian, he narrated: *I dreamt that I wanted to plant some seeds, but I never had time and I didn't have the soil. One night I dreamt that I had finally found the time and the earth and so I planted them.*

In association to this dream one of us recalled a dream which she had associated to the child's efforts of sowing and our hope of collecting the fruits of Social Dreaming in Sezze: *Our grandparents had a house in the country where all our family would gather briefly every summer. I dreamt I went back there off season. The house was empty but outside the farmer's son was planting long rows of seeds. And I thought: when I come back in the right season, I will find that the seeds will have grown into plants.*

From that moment on, there was a flow of dreams and associations rich with plants and trees (apricots, citrus, olives, apples) as well as with animals (snakes and wolves) all projecting us in some sort of Garden of Eden, compliant with the setting of our Matrix, the headquarters of the Environmental League. That first dream of our last Matrix offered by that radiant, gifted and well-integrated Rumanian child gratified us with the hope that already a seed had been sown with the younger generation.

By introducing SD with the adults we, in turn, feel we may have sown a seed of tolerance and understanding, the fruits of which we hope to reap in a more favourable season, that is, if the Sezze community will invest in the needed care for the grafted plant to grow. A first token was offered by the initiative of the African, Rumanian, and Italian participants in the SDMs, who organized a very successful Christmas feast for families of all nationalities now living in Sezze.

Conclusions

It is with a certain disappointment that we regret that not more members of the Sezze community have benefited from the SD experience which we feel proved its positive function for the integration of immigrants. The problem of poor attendance, which never amounted to more than 50 persons, was due to the fact that the SD meetings were optional and located in different sites, anonymous containers, which were also difficult to reach and to schedule for working people who live scattered over a vast territory. As many of them agreed: 'We see how SD can be a good tool but it does not coincide with the primary needs of most of us immigrants whose priority is finding and keeping a job and a house, in order to guarantee a dignified life for ourselves and our families with whom, in fact, we need to spend the very little spare time we have available.'

By contrast, the SDMs later conducted by Eleonora Planera with Cultural Mediators at a regular site, where attendance was obligatory and strongly motivated by future professional acknowledgement, always registered a full-house. On the whole, besides its utility as action-research, the *Sognando & Sognando* Project proved the power of transformation and of creative thinking offered by Social Dreaming. Through a non-judgemental, dialogical form of communication, SD offered a dissipating effect on shared anxiety and allowed the open acknowledgement of prejudices based on fear and ignorance, confirming Professor Claudio Neri's hypothesis that SD could help immigrants to relate to the welcoming country. The matrices offered a supportive environment of connectedness for the foreigners' assessment of the new Italian lifestyle in the light of expectations which had motivated their emigration and of the positive and negative consequences of their present and future choice to either adapt or return to where they had come from.

From this SD experience what emerged was that the difference between the African asylum seekers and the Rumanians is due also to the motivations which have brought them to Italy. While the African women seeking political asylum escape from their country suddenly and rely on the Shelter Home for refuge and protection, the Rumanians who emigrate have long-planned their departure, induced by economic necessity, and immediately join the rat-race to achieve their goal.

In both cases, at the mercy of bureaucracy, they live their different precarious status in **fear** and in **search for security**: the Africans, as a guarantee of survival and freedom, escaping from wars or oppressive political regimes; the Rumanians, as economic guarantee and upgrading, with nostalgia, however, for the economic security granted by the past Marxist regime, and for the tranquil life of their villages. Both lament the insecurity of life for their children.

The SD experience also had a beneficial effect with Italian social workers in the field of immigration by stimulating the participants to analyse the multiple points of observation ('the multi-verse of meanings' according to Gordon Lawrence) offered by the dreams. Especially in the case of the Karibù staff, it brought to light that shadow dimension between the organization's primary task and the personal perception experienced by its members as operators: it allowed the awareness of the confusion generated in defining responsibilities and tasks within given roles. Many of the issues that emerged had been dealt with in the social workers' training, but this was the first time, we were told, that theory and personal/emotional experiences were addressed together, soliciting personal resources as well as those of the organization.

We can sum up our SD experience with the image of a bridge: a bridge connecting the past (to which one's identity is anchored) and the yet nebulous and insecure future; a bridge connecting one's country of origin and Italy, the new-found land of the present; a bridge connecting different cultures, still unknown to each other; a bridge which allows constant passage from individual to collective thinking, where the individual does not only coincide with a single person, but also with a cultural dimension of shared values and social norms.

While Social Dreaming requires of individuals an ego-lessness, in this particular case, it also imposes the abandonment of ego-centrism by any specific ethnic/cultural group, be it native or immigrant. The SD favours the emergence of contingency and relativity as essential for the understanding of the new cross-cultural reality, and it can allow the recuperation of subjectivity and identity through the encounter with *diversity and with otherness, in that third sphere sometimes called 'the between'. Such was the Social Dreaming experience for the Africans and the Rumanians in their retrieval of dignity and pride through the sharing of their own personal values with the native Italians, hence contributing to the building of an 'intercultural' rather than 'cross-cultural' or 'multicultural' society.*

In fact, the transformative power of this particular SD experience with migrants was most effective with the shifting of focus from the presumed requirement of foreigners to understand and adapt to the new socio-cultural context, to the necessity also of the native Italians to acquire knowledge of 'the other' in order to achieve an interactive form of integration. This amplified, symbiotic approach may allow the integration process to assimilate and metabolize the polarities of foreigners and natives and to overcome the gratuitous implications 'diversity = inferiority' and 'diversity = threat', by opening to what Gordon Lawrence (2003) advocates as multiversality and the exploration of *caritas*.

CHAPTER EIGHT

Selection of cadet pilots

Tiziana Liccardo

The intervention of Social Dreaming, as described here, has been carried out with a specific group of young people who are finishing a concourse, by which pilots are selected for the first year of regular courses for cadets with the role of Military Academy Pilot.

The selection of pilots is particularly complex and thorny, both because it exposes candidates to considerable strain for a long period of time (about 45 days) and because it represents an important experience on an emotional level, since it's the experience on which their identity as military pilots is based. The time spent in the military airport is characterized by a double purpose: selection, but also training. The candidate has not only to demonstrate his ability for the role of military pilot (selection), but also to acquire, mission by mission, the steps required to reach his suitability to piloting.

The thirteenth mission represents an important developmental moment, as it is the first mission without an instructor, going solo as a pilot. At the end of it, the candidate who succeeds in the test attains his "baptism' as a pilot. He's no more a candidate now, but a real cadet, and during a day in December he is thrown by his colleagues into a swimming pool.

The phase of selection for pilots is really crucial because the candidate while learning has also to cope with his expectations of himself and those from his loved ones (family, friends, and, possibly, partner). Moreover, the piloting not only implies specific abilities, but also activates emotional factors, which can interfere with examination performance. Moreover, the relationship with the instructor represents an opportunity for shaping self-identity as an air force officer.

The cadet's internship is also important because the cadets all live together at the time in the military airport, where some time is devoted to theoretical training and the rest to practical training. Some accommodation has been allocated in the air base, where the candidates reside. In this situation, relationships between the candidates and the higher-rank officers are characterized by a high level of confidentiality and empathy.

Purposes

The purposes of the psychological residence in the military base are, first of all, to contain and, as a consequence, to reduce, selection anxiety by mobilizing the personal resources of each candidate, to help them to recognize their own difficulties, and to tolerate limits by promoting awareness of their own abilities and interests.

Intervention methodology and its evolution

Since the first years the accustomed educational interventions are based on group methodology, and psychodynamic group counselling, which are used to encourage participants to change, by promoting experiences of sharing and communication. The identification process of the individual with the group of which he is a member and the recognition in the other candidates of feelings similar to their own ones are also facilitated. Candidates have been divided into groups of 10/12 persons. Three meetings of an hour and 15 minutes each were held.

Despite previous positive results, a modification in the selection planning (candidates' presence on the air base for a shorter time) induced us to consider the possibility of modifying the methodology of the proposed intervention by introducing the intervention of the Social Dreaming Matrix working technique (Lawrence, 2001). This was hoped to improve creative thought development and to increase the value of dreams contribution to the comprehension of the institutional social reality in which they live. Considering the short time available to us, we thought it could be useful to propose the use of Social Dreaming, since it allows for the activation of powerful psychical energies in the Matrix and to mobilize these energies for new possible solutions to problems. Another peculiar aspect is represented by the possibility of immediately detecting the complexity of the field in which we intervene. In the end, we felt sanctioned to work in a more extensive, articulated, complex, and profound way, with a particularly high number of participants.

Intervention description

Before starting the Social Dreaming Matrix session, we briefly introduced the technique, in about 10 minutes, and also the Psychological Consultations activities carried out in the Academy. After that, we referred to the working programme, accurately defining times and the planned activities.

The meeting has been divided into two parts: the first is called **Social Dreaming Matrix** and lasts about an hour and half. The Matrix task is to transform thinking processes through the exploration of dreams which become available during the Matrix. This is to be done by using free associations and images which allow for links and connections between dreams to be made and, as a consequence, new thoughts to be generated.

After the Matrix, there is a second event, realized in small groups, called **Creative Role Synthesis.** During this step a participant identifies and introduces to the group a theme or a dilemma to try to identify new solutions.

In the end, candidates are, once more, brought together in a big group to start the **Dialogue.** That is a method which uses dreams that have emerged during the Matrix which can be integrated also with new dreams, in order to identify feats which participants have to face in their life and which are linked to the role played by each of them inside the organizational system. During this last step, the focus is on what participants learned during the previous events, by thinking about how to transform their own role performance inside the organizational setting. Once the introduction ended, we finally started to work.

Social Dreaming Matrix

The Host who starts Matrix gives the purpose, or task, inviting participants to offer their own dreams and to propose free associations. The stimulus is taken up immediately by participants, who narrate many, some of which explicitly refer to the act of flying: *I dreamt to borrow an airplane. I went to Bologna (I went home), then I said goodbye to everyone and I went back with a borrowed airplane. I took off. The instructor wanted to make a panoramic tour. I took many photos. I printed them.* Some other dreams specifically referred to the act of taking off: *I dreamt to fly. I had to jump off. When I dreamt about taking off, I didn't make this dream any more. I was able to fly, I was in my town, I marched and I took the 'foot launch'.*

> *I make nightmares. I fall down. I remember that it's a dream and I say that I can fly. I have the sensation I'm falling down, then I wake up roughly and I dreamt my body was flying. I dreamt to fall down in a ravine, then I stood up and I continued walking. I was immortal.*
>
> *We are flying. I forget about the cart. While I'm crashing, time unblocks. The instructor tells me off, the plane crashes, I light a cigarette. I blow smoke in his face.* I go to the accommodation. Other dreams refer to the Academy: *I dreamt that we were marching and it was like when they do the parade on the second of June in Rome. At night I found myself lying to attention in the bed and I woke up.*
>
> *While we were going back to the Academy, me and him, we had to be cadet and vice-cadet, but, in order not to do it, my friend left me alone.* Dreams referring to the relationship between Officers and the Selected are referred to: *I dreamt that the captain punished me, because I didn't give my availability and he gave me three turns of confinement. In the Academy I was always scolded. There was always something wrong. Here, in Latina, I dream my family.*

It has been interesting to notice that some of the referred dreams have been made during childhood and the produced associations have showed their various facets and, in particular, the attempt to control the anxiety and the anguish of falling down and precipitating. Moreover, many dreams have **sexuality** as a basic theme: *I dreamt that I was in a supermarket with a friend of mine. I met a beautiful girl, the most important girl of my life. (In a shopping centre I've really seen a girl, she was with her father and I didn't have the possibility to speak to her.)*

> It happens to me to think about girls in intimate situations …

Once this session ended, we fixed the appointment for the next event. After a short pause, in which we restructured the setting, candidates were divided into small groups in which they would work during the second event.

Creative role synthesis

During this event, participants have the task to try to create a system whose purpose is to develop learning of the 'not-conscious', starting from the experience. Participants are free to think and organize themselves in the way they believe is most opportune in order to realize the purposes of the event.

Group 1

Having arranged the little sofas in the classical circle-placement, in a very big room, participants take their place. They seem to be curious. The trainer gives the task: 'We are going to think together about a theme that we want to face and to which we want to find a solution with the contribution of the group.' One of the participants poses his question.

The trainer asks everybody if they agree that he will expose the problem he has identified. Everybody agrees. The one who proposes to expose the problem has 10 minutes to speak about the theme, after which he will silently observe and listen to the colleagues who will bring their remarks about it. About 10 minutes before the session is scheduled to end, he will speak again to try to put together thoughts which emerged during the event.

The cadet begins to speak and to expose the situation: 'I think that the problem I would like to face together with you concerns almost everybody of us and it's about the qualifying flight. By now we are very near to it. Tomorrow we'll make the first flying experience. It's a difficult moment, a dream that which can come true. At the same time, it's difficult, maybe we won't succeed, we are too strained and there are many things to do, too many. Among us there is also somebody who, during the past year, didn't succeed and is now helping us, but if we won't succeed, we will have to go back home and so it means we have wasted a lot of months and a dream, all in all it will be a tragedy. Well, I would like to think about it.' The introduction ends with these words, catalyzing participants' attention, probably because the chosen theme involves everybody.

The discussion starts. During which it appears that the emerging points of view are many, and some also opposite to others. A part of the group affirm that they are not thinking too much about what will happen if they fail to succeed: 'I urge myself not to think about it.' One of them narrates a dream—*I dreamt to be dressed with a flight suit and I was really stressed, very much stressed*—while another participant begins from an image evoked by a dream which came out during the Matrix: *When I was a child, from my house window, I saw planes. Now I often find myself as I had that window in front of me, but there's nothing out of it, I see nothing.*

Another participant says he had an excessively optimistic dream. He dreamt to pilot the plane and he was *really skilled, too skilled*. In reality, he was wrong during his test and then, in consideration of it, he prefers to approach the experience of the first flight with prudence. 'If it will go the right way, it will be wonderful; otherwise it's not useful to be catastrophic, because it simply means that he doesn't have the required skills.

As the discussion goes on, the position of those who circumscribe purpose to the here and now comes out: 'Now we have to think about the test, then we go on, mission by mission. It's not useful to have too high goals and to think about the party for the cadets from the first months of courses or about the oath, because those stages are too far; it's better to concentrate on the single targets, as they come up.'

Candidates go on with their interventions, speaking about attainable targets and about fear as a motivation to do better and not as something paralyzing the execution of activities. One of them underlines his idea in a very strong way: he really wants to succeed in the selection because it has always been his dream and obviously it will be upsetting if he does not succeed. However, it won't be a tragedy; outside of the Academy there are other opportunities, there are ties of affection, and there is his own world.

Not succeeding in the selection can also represent a resource, because, in this way, it's possible to realize that they didn't make the right choice and so even if they experience sorrow, they will never be completely overwrought. This intervention seems to confer the chance to find a point of view that, until now, hadn't been taken into consideration, because the possibility of not succeeding was felt exclusively as an unhappy tragedy, a catastrophe.

That is also supported by a dream from the Matrix, which was recovered by one of the participants: *We are flying. I forget about the cart. While I'm crashing, time unblocks. The instructor tells me off, the plane crashes, I light a cigarette. I blow smoke in his face. I go to the accommodation.*

Thinking about this dream, they also discussed the fact that, even if it was a difficult dream, the pilot saved himself, but the airplane was destroyed. Talking about tragedies, it seems that the death of their own project is not properly equated to the end of the candidate himself. Cadets seem to be a little bit comforted after this discussion. There is the sensation that they really assumed a new consciousness.

We are about 10 minutes in and the candidate who presented his question now synthesized some of the points that had emerged: they should not have long-term targets and it's always positive to be supported by colleagues as they sometimes have opposed solutions to ours and so always provide a contribution. Also, it will always be unpleasant, if it won't go the right way, but it won't be a tragedy. On the contrary it means that they had the chance to confront themselves with the others and to understand that, even if it was their most important dream of their life, they are probably not made for that kind of work. The spokesman seems to be really comforted and, after having synthesized the numerous proposals, he remarks that, 'Perhaps, after, it's also possible to appreciate the failure, because outside from the Academy you can dedicate yourself to something else without any regret.'

Group 2

Some minutes before the fixed time, cadets are already waiting outside the room. Somebody loiters to smoke. One of the candidates approaches the trainer of the group. He is very strained, rigid, and in a clear condition of anxiety. He asks if it is possible not to participate in this session because he feels that it's a waste of time. He comes from *Nunziatella* (a military school for adolescents) and he knows everything about how these things work and that it's better to use the time to study.

Some other candidates standing near to him are clearly showing their dissent from that idea, but they don't intervene in the discussion, because he doesn't give them any possibility to. The trainer gives the task. The problem on which they focus is about the difficulty of choosing if it's better not to think, to saturate with study every space to think, or if it's better to leave some free spaces to keep in touch with these, essentially sorrowful, thoughts, because they are linked to life outside the Academy, to their beloved, to how the return home could produce the perception of a, by now overwhelming, gap with the outside world after the experience of the Academy.

The theme of the fear of being washed up and not knowing how to face this eventuality is linked to that. Solution production takes place in a prolific and serene, emotional climate, by continuously linking them to the previous solutions to integrate, contradict, and replace them, also promoting an enlargement to other points of view of the problem.

First of all, some dichotomies come up: 'You have not to think.' 'You have to save your space to think.' Then, some efforts to integrate different aspects, which compose dichotomy, emerge: 'There's a moment when you have not to think, otherwise you can't stand the situation. Then there's a moment to begin again to think, otherwise you are a machine, not a man.'

At the end of this work, the candidate who, before entering the room, had affirmed that psychological work is, in general, useless, asserted that he had found the work with role really stimulating.

After a 15 minutes pause, which allowed the unification the two subgroups, the third and last event started, Dream Reflection Dialogue.

Dialogue

During the third event, which was also the last one of this day, participants are invited to connect the themes on which they worked, by finding links and patterns which connect them to the content of dreams which were related during Matrix. The two spokespersons coming from the small groups introduce to the big group what happened in the subgroups. Immediately after, the group is invited to link the emerged problems to the content of the dreams narrated during the Matrix, by individuating their connections and facets. The work carried out showed the various facets of flying, as an activity, but also the effort to control the anxiety and anguish of falling down precipitately.

However, what seems to have excited participants was the chance given by the aspect, which had never previously been considered, of not succeeding in the selection to piloting, of recognizing that not to be skilled as a military pilot can also be a resource. There was a dream narrated during the Matrix and then retrieved during the reflection session which seems to have given a meaning to the fact that the death of their personal project is not necessarily equivalent to a tragedy: *I dreamt to fall down in a ravine. Then I stood up and I continued walking. I was immortal. We are flying. I forget about the cart. While I'm crashing, time unblocks. The instructor tells me off, the plane crashes, I light a cigarette. I blow smoke in his face. I go to the accommodation.*

Considerations

The realized intervention seems to have freed a high quantity of psychical energies, which have been appropriately used by the group, by creatively applying them to the identified problems, immediately finding the complexity of their chosen field. In fact, the methodology allows the realization of concentrated and intense work and to bring into play psychical energies, not fully active at the moment, with a high number of participants, in a short time, reaching a target which would be unthinkable with other techniques. Moreover, work has been made on two-levels, because, on the one hand, it seems to map the field surface, but, on the other, it catches extremely deep elements which would be hardly evoked with other methodologies, at least not with the same immediacy.

It also seems useful to us to indicate that, during this experience, there was one aspect which seemed to us to be particularly remarkable. In our opinion, it needs to be carefully considered and could also be a target of the next examination and research.

In fact, as it is possible to highlight dreams narrated during the Social Dreaming Matrix session, some dreams come out which have a, sometimes explicit, sometimes indirect, connection to the anguishes referred to. It seems to us to be particularly remarkable that all of these dreams have been referred by participants, in absence of a stimulus, which directly orients in that direction, in part as produced during childhood and, in part, reproduced, in more recent times, through infantile dreams.

Considering the setting in which the Social Dreaming experience took place—a group of young people involved in a selection process to attain the role of military pilots—we asked ourselves if this copiousness of dreams of that kind isn't something more than a coincidence. Anyway, the elements we have at the present time do not allow us to do more than highlight their peculiarity, which could be perhaps deeply investigated, in a future research work, in order to find a meaning and a scientifically valid explanation to it.

On the basis of a careful and in-depth analysis of the produced material and of the dynamics, structured during the Social Dreaming intervention, we believe that a working hypothesis can be formulated. This hypothesis is surely innovative and stimulating, both from the theoretical point of view and from the one of the consequences on an operative level. This is the possible presence of a contraphobic mechanism, which could represent an *attractor*, that is, the strong nucleus able to support the unconscious aspects, the motivation to fly, as an attempt to put the above-mentioned anguishes under control. It's clear that, at the present time, it's not more than a mere hypothesis, which, to be validated in a scientific unimpeachable way, would need a complex and articulated verification, which should be realized with specific instruments and with an intervention expressly oriented to it. However, the particular importance that would be assumed by the confirmation of the existence of a similar mechanism, in terms of evaluation and previsions, leads us to consider it useful to point out.

CHAPTER NINE

The training of family mediators

Francesco Tortono

The experience I will describe in this chapter concerns the use of Social Dreaming in a training course for family mediators, organized with the Neapolitan University (Università degli Studi di Napoli Federico II). This training activity, which lasts two years, is part of a course established 12 years ago and accepts people with different academic curricula and professional experiences (lawyers, psychologists, social workers, sociologists, and so forth). Since planning the course, we have privileged participants' acquisition of a wider ability to get in touch and cope with emotional aspects and the complexity of relationship dynamics.

The difficulty of realizing this in a training setting, which is geared to provide competences and abilities based on cognitive-type aspects, has been increased by participants' non-homogeneous working experiences and cultural backgrounds. The greatest problem was their different psychological knowledge level and, for many of them, the lack of a psychotherapeutic experience, which could have given them a better contact with their internal world. That was the reason why, from the beginning, the interventions have been aimed to privilege participants' ability to get in a more direct touch with their own internal dynamics and with relationships and, at the same time, to understand the complexity of group dynamics in the here and now.

About four years ago we succeeded in introducing the Social Dreaming experience into the training activities planning, even if there was considerable resistance by the staff, composed of the course director and those responsible for the didactics. The initial resistances, which came out of a fear of the new and the unknown, have been justified with the fear of possible superimpositions and interferences between the experiential group dimension, already scheduled in the training planning, and the Social Dreaming one. Their intensity was amplified by the presence of two institutions, the University and the association, understandably desirous to protect their own image and, as a consequence, reluctant to launch an innovative activity which did not have recognized academic credit.

Another critical element was represented by the fact that the theory of the course—its psychological and relational aspects—was absolutely predominant compared to the others, both in quantitative terms and in terms of importance attributed to them by the staff, embracing the classic, psychoanalytical model.

The fact that Social Dreaming was requested by people who attended a psychoanalytical training and possessed of professional experience in this field didn't lessen other staff members' resistances, but, on the contrary, was felt as something worse, an intolerable treason. So, it was difficult to launch the first testing session and to evaluate, in concrete terms, the opportunity to introduce this activity in the course planning.

We organized this new intervention, with the preoccupation, not so much about the results in themselves, which we believed would have been almost surely positive in consideration of our previous experiences realized in other settings, but primarily because we were constantly under observation. The persecutory fantasy was that even the possible participants' dissatisfaction could have been registered by the institution as a failure of the intervention, consequently causing the rejection of this activity from the training activity planning. For the first experience, we chose an already structured group of learners from the second year of the course, because we thought that a more amalgamated group would have better grasp, compared to a recently formed one. The group is made up of 25 persons who have been placed in a room with a snowflake chair configuration and two hosts.

After having introduced Social Dreaming and its task, we worked with a Matrix lasting one hour. Then, the group was divided, in a random way, into two subgroups, which worked separately, in different locations, with the Creative Role Synthesis technique, for 45 minutes. In the end, the group was built up again in its integrity and the spokespersons of the two subgroups referred a brief description of the experience they made in subgroups. The remaining part of Dialogue time has been used to try to identify links between what emerged in the two subgroups and dreams, which came out from the Matrix. Dialogue lasted 60 minutes.

The experience has been repeated with the same conditions the day after, by using the night-break to promote the production of new dreams, which could spur new creative thoughts. Having succeeded in coming out of this experience without any problems and having shared the positive results of the work we made with the other staff members, we felt ourselves entitled to repeat the same experience again with the learners from the first year of the course, achieving once again gratifying results.

Therefore, even if only experimentally, we introduced this activity the following academic year for both the course years, always working during an afternoon and the following morning. Even if in an empirical, limited, and subjective way, we have identified a positive return in the fact that learners from the second year, who, during the previous year experienced the Matrix and the Creative Role Synthesis work, came across as particularly motivated and desirous to repeat the experience. The confirmation of the good quality of the intervention made with learners from the second year, made it easier to us to obtain, this time, use of this technique also during the following academic year.

Probably, it was this reassurance, coming from the Institution through repeated confirmation, which allowed us to embark on an unknown journey. The idea came from the desire to allow the whole group to make this experience in its entirety, while the Creative Role Synthesis, even if it was realized at the same time by all the group members, represented a *tranche* of individual experience.

Moreover, another reason which induced us to consider the possibility to propose and realize something different, is identifiable both in the course structure and in the type of intervention that mediators have to realize during their professional activity. In fact, Family Mediation, whilst considering psychical dynamics of every relationship, is characterized by working on a concrete level, in consideration of the need to realize an intervention which is not tightly psychological, but which aims to restructure individuals' perception of the field of the relationship. Thus, the intervention is often oriented towards concrete and cognitive aspects.

We put ourselves out to realize a different approach, which used Matrix, applying it to something different from the Creative Role Synthesis. We were, at least in part, supported by the consideration that, if, in more than ten years, we succeeded to match a tightly psychoanalytical model with an intervention modality operating on a concrete level, probably the feat could have been tried again, in order to channel the powerful psychical energies activated by the Matrix towards a more cognitive kind of application. Then, we considered that, in this way, it was possible to give learners a chance to concretely experience how psychical energies, activated by Matrix, can promote the emergence of new thoughts and release creativity, producing solutions that, most likely, wouldn't have been normally either seen or hypothesized as possible.

Then, we experimented with the possibility of associating the Matrix to a Brainstorming session, cognitive technique *par excellence*, to experiment the possible results of this union, apparently difficult to realize, at least on a tightly theoretical level. In fact, on a practical level, during the first experience—realized with anxiety, because it brought into question the still limited credit we obtained—we immediately realized, by comparing the results we noted down on the blackboard, that we had achieved total success.

In fact, apart from the high quantity of solutions proposed to the problem processed during the Brainstorming session, we were affected with the quality, the innovation, and the creativity provided by them. Even more we were astonished, amazed, and also excited because we realized that the stream of proposed solutions had links and roots, clearly recognizable to us, in the dreams produced during Matrix. It was also exciting to see how people with only a scant knowledge of psychology and little acquaintance with dreams quickly learned. A few times after the beginning of the Dialogue, which followed Brainstorming, during which we as hosts tried to underline the first possible links between proposed solutions and dreams coming from Matrix, members started to propose references and links, as in the game of dominoes. Apart from the obvious gratification, it seemed to us particularly useful and profitable that somebody among the participants referred to the possibility of using, in a creative way, some of the associations, hypothesis and/or formulations, with reference to mediators' work, for which they were training. From that moment on, we decided to customarily apply Brainstorming after Matrix, considering it more acceptable to our training requirements.

Now, it is useful to propose some considerations. The first one is about the possibility to channel, by using a cognitive instrument such as Brainstorming, to the psychical energies activated by Matrix, by applying them to problem solving. In the specific case of learners from the Family Mediation training course, we think it has been particularly useful. Another consideration concerns an element that emerged as a form of serendipity. In a teaching staff reunion it emerged that learners who made the Social Dreaming experience at the beginning of their training seemed to be, during the experiential group work, more able to intuit emotional dynamics than learners from past years, when Social Dreaming wasn't used.

Our hypothesis is that learners of this course represent a temporary organization, one which is contained within the permanent one. Then, the construction of learning spaces to promote wider creativity, realized through Social Dreaming itself, could have expanded, like a fractal, also in the dynamic identifiable to the staff, of allowing in the training an implantation and consequent hybridization produced by this technique. As a consequence, at the present time Social Dreaming has not only found its formal acknowledgement and its definition, but is now also given credit to for its function of activating and accelerating the procedure of group amalgamation.

The knowledge of the Social Dreaming technique, of its potentialities and functions, allows me to highlight the reasons which are, in my opinion, at the base of that. In fact it is enough to consider that Matrix spreads its feelers in the organization's unconscious dynamic (we think that the course, with its structure, fully represents an organization on its own, different and separated from the institutions which organize it). It also easily put us in touch with deep aspects of the organizational and institutional dynamic. That also has a structuring function for the group, reducing times, in comparison to classical group work, which normally allows for interpretation of the group dynamic, but not the deep ones of the organization. In the organizational frame, used by us at the present time for this training course, the energies produced by Matrix find their use towards the construction and conservation of a group arrangement. That also promotes learning, considering that the training experience is based, for a large part, on experiential aspects.

This last consideration seems to us to be particularly important; in a particularly careful orthodox setting it has been possible to access diversity and uniqueness, as well as the validity of Social Dreaming, by not opposing it to the group work but by considering it as what it really represents: a different technique which can match it and creatively produce new and positive results. Now, the Social Dreaming event is described and realized following the guidelines described above. This is chosen among the many realized until now, because it is particularly remarkable, both for the themes which emerged during the Brainstorming and because it allows, in my opinion, the immediate detection of the evolutions produced, in a very short time, by the Matrix work, on the structure of the temporary organization constituted by participants.

The experience has been structured in two parallel sessions, like the ones described above, which have been realized one in the afternoon and another during the following morning, following the standard times of the course planning. During the first part of the experience 17 persons participated out of a total of 23, and during the second part, 19. Some of them who participated in the first part haven't been present to the second one due to certain commitments which couldn't be deferred. Everybody had already taken part in a Social Dreaming experience during the previous academic year.

The first dream of the Matrix follows: *I was in a room, by myself. I felt an incumbent presence on me. I felt a non-material load; it was something that was incumbent on my shoulders. I'm left-handed, with the right hand I moved it apart three times, but when it arrived to my hand, it clung to it again. The third time I woke up terrified.*

During the Matrix, which lasted 60 minutes, 53 dreams and an association have been referred. Seven of them have been referred as dreams of other people. A characteristic of this Matrix is that, in most cases, dreams are very short and there are lots of recurrent dreams. This Matrix climate is serene, even if the dream contents highlight, sometimes, critical dimensions. I think that the following dreams could represent the most important aspects of Matrix work progress: *I went to my mother's house. There were three cats, as big as dogs, in front of the door. One of them was white. I have got a white cat, but I was not able to understand if it was mine or not. My white cat falls down from the balcony. I arrive below the building and I see many white cats, identical to mine, and I can't recognize it. Many cats come in from the window; I can't recognize my cat any more.*

It seems that these dreams refer to a possible loss of identity, which activates feelings of anguish, connected to dangers, with the consequent desire to escape. We can see this in the following dreams:

> *I dream to kiss a very beautiful boy, I feel a strong attraction. He isn't my boyfriend. I'm anguished.*
>
> *I had to go out from my home from the balcony, by going down a wall. I was preoccupied I could fall.*
>
> *I had to escape, too. The banister was the only way to escape; I was scared I would hurt myself.*
>
> *I went down from the balcony and I had to jump. I was scared I could fracture something.*
>
> *I was at home with my mother who said there was a seaquake. A wave reached my home, on a hill. Then fortunately it receded.*
>
> *I found some snakes in my bed. I woke up to check that. I knew it wasn't true, but the anguish wouldn't have decreased if I didn't check.*

Almost at the end of Matrix, some dreams in which somebody cheats on their partner appear in succession:

> *My girlfriend dreams that I cheat her and gets angry in the dream. The day after she gets angry with me, as I really did so.*
>
> *I always dream to kiss one of my ex-boyfriends. My boyfriend cheats me with a person I know. I'm disappointed for that, also because I know that person.*
>
> *I dream I cheat my boyfriend. I don't feel serene.*

The emergence of these dreams resulted in a condition of anguish, which is possible also to notice in the following dreams:

> *I dream to be chased and to be kidnapped.*
> *I found myself in a labyrinth, from which it was difficult to come out. There was an ogre who wanted to catch me. My brother saved me, taking me into his arm.*

Matrix ends with this dream, which seems to indicate the need to shut oneself away in order to find a sense of protection which placates the narcissistic wound produced when somebody is cheated:

> *I was in very small places, like cages. I was happy. The smaller they were, the happier I was.*

Once the work had ended, and after a short pause, we went on with the Brainstorming session, asking participants to identify a problematic area to process, to verify the possibility to detect, if possible, a broad-spectrum of creative solutions.

The theme, immediately proposed by one of the participants and accepted straightaway by everybody, was the following: how to cope with a partner's ascertained infidelity. A short discussion among participants highlighted that infidelity should mean betrayal, not only on a sentimental and/or sexual level, but also on the level of betraying confidence and expectations.

The production, during Brainstorming, of possible solutions is particularly plentiful, which also means an intense emotional participation of these people, as it is possible to understand from the following list:

> Beating him very hard.
> Dropping him off. Punish him/her.
> Cheat on him.
> Trying to understand why he/she cheated me.
> Hating him. Showing rage. Thinking of something else.
> Preparing to face him.
> Having friends' support.
> Making somebody beat him very hard.
> Wanting to know everything.
> Analyzing the story.

Taking my time.
Listening to him.
Making him understand what he lost.
Making him burn by guilt feelings.
Trying to restructure confidence.
Defining separation terms.
Addressing to a familiar mediator.
Beginning a couple therapy.
'Abandoning the field' temporarily.
Trying to understand who the partner is.
Trying to understand where I was, when he cheated me.
Trying to remember his positive aspects.
Analyzing changes in the couple.
Regaining self-confidence.
Confronting other people.
Healing the wounds.
Trying to understand until a point when the story can go on.
Regaining own life.
Understanding what makes you really happy, coming through infidelity.
Giving to the partner and to myself another chance.
Ensuring about partner's feelings.
Understanding where he wants to go.
Making some changes in the relationship.
Going back to the origins of the story.
Tolerating disappointment.
Making partner's qualities express themselves.
'Channelling' rage.
Assigning the appropriate value.
Finding new common experiences.
Opening ourselves to new situations.
Discussing more.

During the Dialogue, it was possible to detect and highlight the links between dreams emerged during the Matrix and the solutions proposed during the Brainstorming, pointing out the existence of a kind of polarization between a proclivity to shut oneself away and another to reinvest in the relationship. Moreover, it has been possible to highlight connections with the task of a familiar mediator who, not by chance, has to cope with these themes during his/her professional activity, often having to confront himself/herself with couples in which critical consequences are determined by many different ways of cheating, not only in the couple relationship, but also in all the familiar dynamics.

The following day Matrix started with this dream: *I'm at school, the secondary school; there are my real mates and my brother. The teacher is my hairdresser. He's a psychologist too. He convenes students into a room. I call my brother. I think it will last an hour. I go out. I meet my cousin who tells me about his marriage crisis. He asks me to write some numbers out from a sheet to another. I can't, because they are deformed. In the end, I write them out, but they're not clearly readable. He gives it to somebody who is on the lower floor. Then, I realize that an hour passed and so I had to go to the psychologist.*

Since the beginning, the climate seemed less charged with depressive elements. During the Matrix, 37 dreams were narrated. The first interesting aspect, which differs from the experience of the previous day, is that many dreams are complex and articulated. If that obviously influences their number, for a matter of time it also enriches the Matrix with more complex and articulated elements. The most remarkable dreams which characterize this Matrix are the following: *I dream a person I was trying to approach since a long time. In the dream, finally he approaches me, but I feel anxious. I don't know how to come out from this situation. I find myself in a situation of danger and anguish. I need to phone. I've got the number, but the telephone roller rolls without stop and I'm not able to stop it. I try to block it to compose the number, but I'm not able to. I need to phone, but I don't know how.*

> It was my wedding day. I had to get dressed in my partner's house. Every thing I did was wrong. I thought I wasn't beautiful. I lock up my room, then my partner's mother arrives (she's actually dead) and she gives me some advice, she helps me. I calm down and I go out.

The referred dreams seem to indicate the desire to restructure the relationship and the anguish implied by it, even in consideration of the presence of inadequate feelings.

> *In the house-garden there were many Chinese people. One of them was lying down, blood-soaked, on the floor. I call for an ambulance. I say that it's about a 30 years-old person blood-soaked. I ask if I can open the breastbone to make him breathe. The lady on the phone asks useless questions. I say that the breastbone is getting bigger and I ask her if I could open it, as I watched it on TV. She tells me not to do it. I'm frightened. With his eyes he tells me, 'Help me, open my breastbone.' But I can't do it.*

The link with things from the past coming up in new relationships emerge from dreams such as these: *I dream to go back in the house where I lived during the first 10 years of marriage. In the house there are some women gathered around a table, in black dresses. They prayed or spoke. They weren't happy. I see, in a corner, my children's toys. I move them and I find the duplicate of my car keys that I hadn't found for years. I'm astonished by this fact and I say it to my mother. When I dream about my home it's always about the one I lived in since the age of 18 and never about the one I have lived in for 10 years. The first one is tied to familiar affections.*

Matrix ends with this dream: *One of my husband's aunts invited many people, among which there was also my family. My husband couldn't come, because he had working problems. I felt it was a lie and so I phoned him continuously to control him. After lunch, I helped my husband's niece with her homework. Then my husband arrived with a very old car. A little girl was with him. He said she was a friend's child and she had to take care of her, because his friend was busy. I was sure it was a lie to meet another woman.*

During the Brainstorming, once again immediately, it has been proposed the following theme: how to trust one's partner. Once again the production of possible solutions was very plentiful, complex, and articulated:

> Listening to him.
> Believing what he says.
> Making questions to acquire knowledge about him.
> Seeing how he behaves with other people to know him better.
> Trusting more in ourselves.
> Putting ourselves in the hands of instinct.

Putting him on probation.
Tolerating to suffer.
Accepting sorrow.
Getting information about him.
Engaging a private investigator.
Being less rational.
Letting yourself go into relationships.
Putting self in the partner's shoes.
Bringing ourselves into question.
Putting ourselves in partner's hands.
Observing him with attention.
Accepting diversity.
Analyzing people who surround him.
Trying to understand our past.
Understanding what's behind partner's behaviour.
Opening ourselves with partner.
Learning from disappointments.
Coping together with problems.
Making partner trust us.
Detaching ourselves from our past experiences.
Accepting mistakes in evaluating partner.
Modifying our way of interpreting partner.
Being less distrustful.
Observing partner's gestures.
Analyzing his past.
Understanding that partner is different from us.
Being more fatalist.
Listening to him narrating his past.
Taking our time.
Knowing family culture.
Knowing his/her political orientation.
Knowing religious choices.
Knowing sexual orientation.
Eating with him.
Going to bed with him.
Listening to him judging people.

During the Dialogue, it became possible to put in relation the existence, in the Brainstorming session, of a polarization between a persecutory dimension, which makes difficult the construction of a relationship, and a depressive one, from which a new thought can originate in respect to the relationship and the possibility to structure it. Once again, the reflection on the meaning of 'trusting partner' becomes profitable, linking all that to the specific professional activity to which they're training and, in particular, how trusting one's partner can mean to have trust, apart from a new person, also a person who has become 'something else' in respect to the image we once held of him/her, breaking all previous relational schemata when, by splitting up, the other, from husband/wife, becomes father/mother. In particular, what is highlighted here is the presence and permanence of persecutory elements linked to the critical experience of the relationship with partner as husband/wife, which could also degrade the image of father/mother, pouring over it all the feelings of persecution and linked aggressiveness.

Considerations

Among all the experiences now realized in the training for Family Mediators, I've chosen this because it seems to me that it realizes a remarkable point, one which highlights not only the utility of a similar intervention but also the potentiality to make more profitable and faster the training process through the deep connection that it allows between emotional elements and cognitive elements.

As said before, the training course represents, in consideration of its duration and of the dynamics which occur between participants, a temporary organization, which has a 'self-mind' and its own unconscious dynamics, which the Matrix realizes. In this working session, all that was clearly highlighted was the creative aspect both in the problems chosen to be processed through the Brainstorming and in the proposed solutions. Moreover, as we already verified in previous experiences realized in other settings, in the following period it has been possible to detect an improvement in the group to use the available resources to participate in the training. In the end, it is important to make a notation about the hypothesis that creativity, activated by Social Dreaming work with participants (temporary organization), also reverberated in the staff (permanent organization), through deep channels, allowing not only the acceptance and institutionalization of this work, overcoming the initial rigid resistances, but also the acknowledgement of the function of deep activation of cohesion, both inside the learners' group (temporary organization) and inside the permanent organization one. The reverberation between the two, temporary and permanent, organizations, in my opinion, has been surely facilitated by the fact that intervention potentialities were in hosts' minds, which represent the nexus of continuity and connection between learners and staff, of which, as said before, hosts themselves were a part.

CHAPTER TEN

Social Dreaming with lawyers

Mattia Tortono

The experience to be described here originates from a wish to explore the effects of Social Dreaming on people who, professionally, are inclined to use a pre-structured vision of the world, one which reduces the potential for creativity. The people who participated in this experience are mostly lawyers. Their profession normally leads them to put all information into specific legal knowledge, focusing their attention on judgements passed in similar previous cases, and leading to conformity to pre-structured thinking. The experience has been conducted only once, but a new session has already been programmed for the future with the same group of people, as a consequence of the interesting results achieved in the first *tranche* of work.

The first interesting peculiarity of this experience is represented by our interest in discovering what effects would be produced if we, the three hosts, slept in the same house the night before the experience of the Matrix. In particular, we were interested in evaluating the effects of the function of holding the Matrix, performed by the hosts, in order to allow participants to have a worthwhile experience of Social Dreaming. Our hypothesis was that sharing the dimensions of sleep and dreams, which represent the basis of Matrix functioning, would improve the holding function. The peculiarity of our testing was that the sharing was only between hosts before the creation of the formal setting.

The results achieved during this experience allow us to believe that it is very likely that it has been possible to create a stronger link between the hosts, specifically on the aspects of sleep and dream. It's likely that this has made us more cooperative and more able to accomplish together a useful function of holding a stimulating Matrix.

For these reasons we think that the Social Dreaming experience made by the participants is characterized by the real possibility to establish a deeper and closer touch with the dreams. This is, I think, also detectable from the very high number of dreams narrated during the Matrix. The number of dreams and associations referred in just an hour was 58. A fact made more important if we consider that only two of these were associations. Moreover, the production of dreams and associations reached not only a high level of quantity, but also a very high level of quality.

At the beginning, there was resistance by the participants to start the Matrix, because their fantasy was that they would be interpreted. As a consequence, we wondered if the Matrix could move from a condition of strong resistance to a valuable production of dreams.

Another characteristic of this experience is represented by the fact that the purpose, or primary task, was always respected without the hosts having to bring the Matrix back to its task. In fact, there were only a few instances when participants needed to be brought back to the task to avoid the Matrix moving from dreams to any excessive form of rational thinking, which is most typical when the Matrix strays from the matter at hand and loses its function. Anyway, in these rare moments, it was enough to bring back participants' attention to the task, to allow 10–15 more dreams to come out, without other interruptions.

Considering the very encouraging results, we asked ourselves if it could be connected to the fact that the three hosts had slept in the same house. In fact, we considered it useful to give to every participant a text containing a brief description of the Social Dreaming technique. This initiative had a promotional purpose. If the SDM was experienced by them as a positive happening, this could become a vehicle for similar experiences. So, we faced the preparation of the event in a condition of excitement, but also one of strain in organizing the room, chairs, and welcome to the participants.

Moreover, the situation was also complicated by a problem occurring while we were printing the text. The printer toner suddenly ran out, just a short time before the shop's closing hour. After many phone calls, we realized that the spare part was not available in any of the shops near us. We also realized that we needed to search the shops outside the city centre, but once again to no avail. In the end, we understood that the only way to solve our problem and complete our work was to buy a new printer in a shop located out of the centre of the city. So, we moved together to reach the shop and buy a new printer, and having done so, we went back home and finished printing and preparing the material we had to give to participants. We ended our work just a few minutes before going to sleep.

In my opinion, this event is as important as the fact of having slept in the same house, because I think it represented a way to take care and dedicate ourselves to welcoming and hosting the Matrix. Therefore, the hypothesis is that the high level of activity we required to finish the printing, because of the difficult situation we faced, represented a further investment of time and attention in the creation of the pre-setting, insomuch as it provided an even bigger ability to hold the Matrix.

Aside from the three hosts, 17 persons participated in this event. They were almost all lawyers, with the exception of three people who had different job titles; but two of those still worked in the legal area. Moreover, almost all of them are very accomplished in their field, which is almost exclusively represented by the area of family law. Everyday they experience strong resistances to coping with problems arising from the changes happening in their work because of the traditional deep-rooted ways they employ.

Notwithstanding this, during the Brainstorming and the Dialogue, their ability to involve themselves was apparent. It represents one of the other elements that aroused our interest as hosts.

In this publication, I think it is important to focus our attention on the following aspects:

a. Matrix composition is essentially homogeneous, being almost solely made up of lawyers, who obviously have the same working identity, with the exception of three of the participants.

However, one of these exceptions graduated in the Economy field and now, in his work, deals in economic and legal aspects, as he emphasized during Dialogue, while another one works as an intercultural mediator dealing in mediation between different legal orders and different cultures. Only the last one of these three people, a biologist, deals in totally different things.

b. This person, who was a complete stranger to the law field, openly asserted during the Brainstorming module that she didn't feel comfortable because she didn't share with the others the proposed solutions. This was the reason that made her also feel a condition of total emotional non-involvement towards the other participants.

c. The last interesting characteristic of this experience is represented by the use of Brainstorming in place of Creative Role Synthesis. We have already used this module in other experiences, because, even if we considered the Creative Role Synthesis profitable, we realized how strong the potentialities of Brainstorming were, especially if used in a Matrix with a homogeneous composition of participants.

The Social Dreaming experience

We now describe in more detail how this experience unfolded. It took place in the office of a Neapolitan professionals' association, which deals in consultancy and training courses in the legal and psychosocial areas. The room, which hosted the participants, had been chosen as suitable for the Matrix size, being neither too large nor too little. We used the snowflake pattern (Lawrence, 2005: 96) of chair placement, because it is nowadays considered as useful for Matrix activity and its appropriate functioning. Every participant chose his or her place, in consideration of his or her own preferences. In this situation, it was necessary to answer a participant's question about the fact that it's not necessary that hosts sit on the chairs placed at the centre of the room, as they thought.

Before the Matrix started its work, we dedicated some minutes to introducing Social Dreaming. In particular, one of the hosts gave some information about the technique and the second spoke specifically about the Matrix, highlighting its functioning and potentialities. In the end, the third one, following the others' speeches, introduced the purpose, or primary task. We decided to divide our tasks because our previous experiences made us believe that it's useful to participants to perceive the hosting function before the Matrix starts by individuating those who undertake this function.

After we asked, 'Who has the first dream?' a sequence of dreams started. I refer here to the first of them, because it represents not only the Matrix beginning, but also indicates the profound observations the participants came to as they addressed problems during the Matrix. The dream is the following: *Somebody tied my wristbands. I felt a strange sensation; I was not comfortable. I asked myself: Why he ties my wristbands? I didn't dream since a long time before that moment.*

After the first dream, the whole Matrix voiced a long concatenation of dreams (to which two associations were added as well), which came one after the other very quickly. Moreover, participants narrated similar dreams, which was surprising. Suddenly a participant gave one, premising, 'I narrate this dream, even if it is not a recurrent one.' I was immediately surprised by this participant's premise while the whole Matrix was working, in a recurrent way.

In fact, the recurrent seemed to be, in connection with some of the other elements, a very important theme in reading problems which came out in the next few working modules. Another interesting element is that in the whole Matrix it is possible to highlight the existence of sequences of dreams concentrated, in the same moment, and characterized by common basic themes, which differ from previous and following passages, by virtue of the different theme by which they are characterized. In fact it is particularly difficult to notice the presence of dreams with the same basic theme in different moments of Matrix work.

Then, one of the peculiarities of this experience is represented also by the location of a basic theme inside the space and time of the Matrix condition, unlike what normally happens, when there is a continuous recurrence to previous basic themes. Moreover, Matrix has been characterized only by three interruptions of the stream of dreams. These moments have been particularly rare and characterized by the transition to a condition of rational thinking.

Notwithstanding, these interruptions have been very short, because, as the return to dreams was stimulated, their stream resumed immediately. Moreover, in my opinion, the fact that some erotic dreams came out shows how participants engaged in Matrix work. In fact, more than any other kind of dreams, erotic dreams are very intimate and represent total openness to other participants. This openness is even more remarkable if linked to the initial difficulty, explicitly referred to by some of the participants, to entrust their dreams to the Matrix.

Once this work module ended we paused for 15 minutes before commencing the Brainstorming event, which lasted for 45 minutes. The use of this technique was born when we verified that, in situations like this one, participants who have the same identity (professional, institutional affiliation, and so forth), arrive to find a high incidence of hypothesis to the identified problem, always maintaining a high level in their quality.

In fact, the possibility to individuate a common problem promotes all participants' cooperation and contribution. As a consequence, it is possible, in my opinion, to consider the basic themes contributing to the valuable results of the Brainstorming.

The problem chosen by participants was: changes in our profession. It represents a very big problem for them, because, as I said before, currently they experiment difficulty in leaving behind their old working model, which allowed them to work in a completely autonomous way without needing to find a connection-point between their work and that of others. For these reasons, they find it difficult to integrate much of their professional work, bearing in mind internationalization and comparison with different legal orders.

The strong emotional strain produced in the participants by this basic theme has allowed them to find as many as 44 different possible solutions to this problem. It has also been possible to highlight a thread which crosses all the possibilities suggested and which is represented by the idea of, while always strongly keeping their professional identity, integrating it with innovative aspects linked to the cooperation with other professionals and to the international dimension which is nowadays required in the field of law.

So, it becomes clear that participants have succeeded to move from a dimension in which opposites cannot co-exist (access new, by dismantling old, or preserving old, by refusing new), to assume a modality in which a concordance between these two aspects is possible. This kind of choice is very hard, because, as mentioned previously, they normally use, in their work, very precise schemata to interpret reality. As a consequence, having been able to realize integration between old and new represents a very remarkable step forward, also considering that it happened in just one Social Dreaming experience.

Another very interesting aspect is that lawyers are used to representing their clients' positions by opposing themselves to the counter-party lawyer's position. So, during their work, they are sometimes also compelled to assume some extreme positions. That makes us understand even better why it is so difficult to them to realize integration with other professionals, especially if he/she is another lawyer.

During the Brainstorming module, instead, participants proved to be able to cooperate in a very useful way, not only finding solution hypothesis oriented to solving problems, but also trying to make them all go towards the same direction. **So, given solutions aren't set one against the other, but rather are oriented towards a common dimension.** Moreover, by always adding new elements, which consider different facets of a problem, **an integration of the innovation in the old scheme has been proposed.**

So, it is impressive the double work of integration made by participants: on the contents level and on the personal one. In fact, even if they are used to polarizing differences and to 'clash', in this situation they have easily shared the common problem. As a consequence, work has seemed particularly worthy because it aimed to **reorganize the old, rather than cleave the old from the new**, and because it has produced useful results for formulating hypothesis to improve working activity.

In my opinion, it could be helpful to refer some of the solution proposals highlighted during the Brainstorming:

> Studying in a different way.
> Comparing with the diverse.
> Intercultural relations.
> Expanding our horizons.
> Being concrete.
> Courage into changes.
> Daring.
> Breaking 'schemes'
> Network.

Construction and conservation of social relationships.
Construction of priorities.
Knowledge and use of new technologies.
Ability to adapt.
Continuous comparison with other professionals.
Balancing profession and private life.
Teamwork.
Resources and time optimization.
Taking risks.
Continuous reformulation of the 'scheme'.
Bringing ourselves into question.

At the end of the Brainstorming session no more breaks were allowed as we believed that we would work more appropriately on the basic themes which had just emerged by using the Dialogue module. Some interesting results emerged, especially about the intersection between the aspects that characterized the Matrix and the ones that were highlighted during the Brainstorming. About that, some dreams are very interesting, particularly the ones in which the theme of *sons with Down's syndrome* emerges. Among them the most relevant is surely the following: *I suddenly discovered that my son suffered from Down's syndrome. I asked myself why I didn't understand it before. My son was 7 and I had never noticed the problem.*

This specific dream, and others referring to sons with Down's syndrome, led to some observations about fears linked to professional problems experienced by participants. It came out from the Dialogue that the sons with Down's syndrome, represented in dreams, could be linked to their ambivalence in respect of the innovations they have to face in their working field.

In fact, if, in a metaphorical sense, on one side they are able to tolerate giving 'birth to a new child' (in other words, adopting a new working modality and identity), on the other side the fear of giving birth to a child with troubles seems to be too strong. **This fear, and the possibility of facing it, represented the real intersection-point between the Matrix work and the Brainstorming.**

The second dream narrated during the Matrix is also very interesting: *It is a recurrent dream. In this dream I'm in a house made up of pieces of all the houses I have lived in during my life.*

It has been noticed that there is a resemblance between this dream and the recurrent dreams which dominated the Matrix, and, lastly, some dreams which, following what the participants who narrated the dreams said, were interrupted by their awakening and which then began again when the person returned to sleep from the same point where they were cut off. All these elements seemed to acknowledge the existence of past aspects in common (the dream which repeats itself; the house filled with the old houses; the dream which begins again from the previous point), which present themselves in the course of the Matrix.

During the Dialogue, all of these dreams allowed the need to square with elements which often appear deeply problematic and which, unfortunately, generate a condition of deep annoyance, introducing themselves in the present in a compulsory way. There are also other dreams which refer to the same theme; for example, the following is very interesting: *It is a nightmare. I have to get engaged again with my first boyfriend. I think my life is really busted if I'm compelled to do it.*

There are also dreams in which the anguish due to the cancellation of some important exam comes out: *They phoned me from the University and they told me they cancelled the exam I did to become a lawyer.*

Another significant theme is the one about accidents: *This is a recurrent dream. I'm in my car on the highway A3, on the Castellammare di Stabia crossroad[1]. In the curve I find an obstacle and I hit it. I dreamt this scene a lot of times, as far as I had a real accident, in which I was almost dying. From that moment on I never dreamt this scene again.*

Ultimately what seems to emerge in this module is the fear to lose the identity as lawyers, which has to be considered more as a part of personal identity, considering the importance given by these people to their work. Anyway, the choice of integrating old with new has seemed to be potentially very worthy, because it allows innovation while retaining identity.

---

[1] The A3 is a highway which goes all the way south from Naples. The place indicated corresponds to an exit of this highway.

Conclusions

We can come to some brief conclusions on the experience performed:

a. About the Brainstorming module, it's important to say that it is a way of working that, in this case, like in all the other experiences in which we used it, has always provided very worthy results.
    In fact, in the presence of a Matrix with a particular composition of participants, like for example Matrix with a homogeneous composition, Brainstorming revealed to be very useful to channel—in a very strong way—all of the energies activated by the Matrix itself, creating the possibility to a lot of solution hypothesis to the given problem to emerge, in consideration of the essentially similar abilities of the participants.
b. Another aspect that has been highlighted is the ability of the Social Dreaming technique to create cohesion among participants. In fact, even if Matrix doesn't work on a group level, it produces deep effects on relationships and dynamics between participants, as it is possible to discover after the Matrix work.
    In fact, in this experience, it has been possible to observe a strong cooperation between participants in order to identify hypothesis to a common problem, even if, in their everyday work, they normally work in conditions of contraposition rather than of collaboration. A hypothesis we formulated is that, especially in case of repetition of the experience, some of the effects of this cooperation can be experimented by them also outside of this setting, by trying to integrate their working modality of contraposition proper to lawyers' work with a network modality.
c. In order to confirm the hypothesis that Matrix has cohesive power towards people who have the same professional identity, it is also useful to repeat that the participant who had nothing in common with the other participants (because she was a biologist) expressed her discomfort during the experience in which she felt herself to be a stranger.
d. The last element to add is the very strong innovative potentiality of this technique as it comes from the opportunity to find possible solutions, which does not eliminate any of important evidence. Moreover, this technique makes possible to accept that which is really negative, allows progress, and tolerance of that which is

ambivalent. In fact, on many occasions, the solution was exclusively represented by this possibility to accept what is negative. As, for example, coming from the first dream, *tied wristbands*, from a simple *link* (especially with the past) which forbid development, is the possibility of transforming it into a link between old and new, assuring a deep innovation. As a consequence, the *wristbands*, which, at the beginning of the Dialogue were associated also to *handcuffs*, in the meaning of a constrictive link, have been, in the end, recognized as *useful handcuffs*, in other words as the possibility of liaison between past and present.

In the end, the promising results achieved in this experience which was led by us, made us hypothesize that, in the following experiences of the same kind, these people will be able to reach an even higher level in creativity and integration.

CHAPTER ELEVEN

Totalitarian toddlers: Consulting in the mental health service

Franca Fubini

'The work of the Matrix mirrors the functioning of the mind!' says a participant at the end of a Social Dreaming program, with a great deal of satisfaction at his discovery; understanding that the Matrix mirrors in waking life the 'Matrix of the undifferentiated unconscious' that operates while we are asleep and dreaming. It is quite extraordinary when actually experienced in reality. Unconscious and conscious contents can be seen, multiple strands of dreams/thoughts/discourses coexisting simultaneously in the continuous waves that at times coalesce as particles.

One way of regarding consciousness in relation to the unconscious is to imagine the world as a psychic pond. This is the Matrix of the mind through which everyone is connected ... the universe is pure mind. Thinking and thoughts can be likened to pebbles thrown into the psychic pond, setting off waves radiating from them. When two or more sets of waves of thinking coincide, going forward and backward in time, an event is likely to occur. The phrase 'shadows of the future cast before' takes on a new meaning. The shadows—subjective memories and dreams, cast before and backwards (for time is relative)—bring about events and happenings that exist in real time and that are objective. This is an example of reality being both 'out there' and 'in here' (objective and subjective) ... Dream has an important place in determining what takes place in day-to-day life (Lawrence, 2005: 85).

Every Social Dreaming Matrix engages with how dream and reality relate to each other; how boundaries between the two can be crossed; how one person can dream the dream of another person; and how dreams/minds can probe and anticipate future events.

In the Matrix there are many points of resonance, each dream and association resonating with some other in the room; each setting off a variety of responses. Some stand out more than others and might determine the flow of the discourse. In reality all of the strands are simultaneously present and move at their own pace, contributing to creating the whole picture.

I shall write about a piece of consultancy work within a mental health service where adopting the methodology of Social Dreaming was an essential tool for managing the complexity of reality and for transforming the institution's rather pathological state of being. Multiple dimensions were present from the start, in spite of the massive attempts to level everything to a two-dimensional and comfortable reality.

'Totalitarian toddlers' is the expression, or the image, evoked soon after meeting the team. I hope that in the course of reading these pages it will become clear why.

The consultancy

In the course of an exploratory meeting with the chief psychiatrist consultant of a psychiatric unit and his head nurse, I get two rather different pictures of the state of their department and of the possible causes of its difficulties. They agree only on the fact that it is dislocated/dispersed over a large territory and that the team is rather fragmented. There are 25 of them: nurses, social workers, an occupational therapist, and doctors. Women are in the large majority, aged between twenty-five and fifty-five years. Tensions and disagreements seem to be the daily nourishment of their interactions. Common is the recognition that it is necessary to do something about it by improving the climate in the department, wounded by a history of frequent turnover of chief consultants, each one with a very particular, and conflicting, model to shape the life of the unit.

In that first exploratory meeting I feel a certain degree of despair and a sense of a culture of dependency which could not be explained solely by the turnover of consultants. No mention is made about the nature of the work and how difficult it might be to be in close touch with mental illness. These are accepted as 'given' and both the consultant and the head nurse can only look at the functioning of the team isolated from a wider context.

In time we agree on a series of interventions every two or three months for two years with the declared aim of:

> Facilitating a more tolerant culture within the unit, where people may experience the possibility to move from static opinions and rigid interactions to a somehow more vital and creative position.

The interventions, called supervisions, for the clinical work involved, are designed to last one afternoon and the following morning. The approach is systemic as well as psychodynamic; Social Dreaming is chosen for its capacity to entertain the unknown, so that thinking and the availability for new thoughts are particularly activated. Moreover beyond tolerance of the unknown, the SD facilitates diversity, modeled on how in the Matrix dreams and associations coexist in a multiverse of meanings—a real foundation of the sense of democracy which seems to be sadly lacking in the team. The design of the two half-days combines Social Dreaming Matrices (SDM), Dream Reflection Groups (DRG), and Creative Role Synthesis (CRS). I shall explain the format of the DRG and CRS, as it is a little different from the original one: it has been modified to fit the context and the circumstances of this work.

Dream Reflection Group

The task of the DRG is to identify themes and patterns which connect the dreams of the Matrix, in order to disclose the thinking of the dreams and what it reveals about the shared reality. DRG in the context of this consultancy project lasts two hours with the break of a night in between: after the identification of the themes of the Matrix, the team splits into small groups, each working on a chosen theme, and at the end of their elaboration they draw a group picture.

When the whole group meets again, rather than reporting back, each small group lets the others put in words that they see in each of the pictures. It is very effective: cutting through intellectualization and didactic attempts to say the 'right thing', people are able to plug straight into the emotional quality of the information offered by the pictures and they can see at the end a first elaboration of what the discourse of the Matrix might be.

Creative Role Synthesis applied to clinical cases

Following the intuition that CRS could be extremely useful if applied to clinical cases, the event has been used in this particular context by explaining that the task of the CRS is to present a clinical piece of work in the following way:

1. One person presents a piece of clinical work for 10/15 minutes, providing the relevant information and possibly dreams of the patients, of one's own, and of the dreams that emerged in the Matrix that might relate to the chosen patient.
2. The rest of the group free associates for 30 minutes to the material, with the task of creating links and connections and advancing hypothesis so that the situation of the patient as well as his/her relationships with the members of the staff might be illuminated.
3. The last 15 minutes are a reflection and a synthesis of the work done, with the last word to the presenter.

As there are 25 people and only one consultant, the group is divided into two, one group working on a chosen case, sitting in an inner circle of chairs; the other observing in an external circle.

At the very end, the external group that has been observing the work of the inner group reports on how the process has developed, commenting on where it has been more effective or where it has hit a dead end. Two cases are presented each time so that the two groups can work in both the inner and in the outer circles. It takes a great deal of discipline to stick to this model with the curiosity of revealing the 'unthought known' (Bollas, 1987: 101ff), that which an individual, a group, or an organization knows, but has not yet been consciously thought. (And, if actively recognized, could make a substantial difference to the appropriate lives.) In this project one difference is to the life of the patient and team. A well-rooted attitude of, 'I *do* know what is really happening with this patient (and *you* don't)!" would block any access to any unthought known and hence to the real communication between the patient and the staff. However, slowly as the work of the Matrix develops and people trust the containment of the dream discourse, so does also the creative role synthesis connected to clinical work, which is not surprising as the latter is the direct application of the former.

The first meeting

The first meeting with the team is described in detail.

After an introduction to the work in general, we start with an SDM; such an unusual and novel experience is accepted without questioning. The first dream, often the fractal of the discourse to come, is: *It is a recurrent dream. I have the feeling of being sucked inside a dark space, in the shadow towards the evening. I was inside, with the sensation of being sucked like a funnel upside down.*

My (FF) silent and fantastic association, full of wishful thinking, goes to the birth process, but in fact as I listen better it is not so, quite the contrary: the dreamer is sucked inside, she does not go anywhere, she stays in, it is upside down. The following dreams illuminate even more the landscape of the first one:

> *A patient is stuck in the library; she is blocked and doesn't know which direction to take.*
>
> *I was in a hotel—it was beautiful—but suddenly I realize there is no way out.*
>
> *I was in a castle, in one room; there is beautiful big table: it could sit many people, but it is empty. I don't want to be there, it is too empty, lonely, but nothing can be done about it. It could be of use, but unfortunately it is not: it is of no use to anybody. It is sad.*
>
> *The water is all dirty.*
>
> *My mouth is full of water and hair.*

Another cluster of dreams voice anxiety about not being up to what is required by one's own role:

> *I dream that I have to repeat my high level exams.*
>
> *I dream that my degree is not valid and I have to repeat each exam all over again.*

> *I dream that there are exams to pass.*
> *My therapist is arguing with me about a geography exam.*

And finally there are dreams, which speak about the patients, and the fears related to their presence:

> *All the members of the M. family (patient) are in the room, so many that it is overwhelming. There is no room for me.*
> *P. (a patient) has taken a whole dose of Trilafon. I am scared and it is like falling down into emptiness.*
> *I keep dreaming that a patient is killing me, over and over again.*
> *In front of a hut there are two people, one is a patient. A dog, an Alsatian, attacks and bites them. There is blood everywhere. But I go in the hut unharmed by the dog and find much money. I call the police. They come but they don't believe what I say and don't do anything.*

There is enough in these dreams to declare that the department is not in work mode; that the people are mostly scared and they don't feel up to the job. Thinking of Bion's basic assumptions, my first intuition of a dependent group is confirmed, in the literal sense of feeling still incapable of fulfilling the requirements and expecting a parent/consultant/institution to provide comfort (Bion, 1961: 81ff).

Frustration and resentment belong to the dependent culture and, unsurprisingly, the following dream reflection group doesn't go anywhere: after I state the task and talk about the themes which have emerged during the Matrix, tensions and conflicts within the team explode, giving a real sense of how communication can break down far too easily and I get a glimpse of how unmanageable that group can be.

When communication breaks down, it looks as though each member of the staff becomes a small totalitarian unit, contemplating only one's own view and attempting to impose it on all of the others; like small children crying for attention all at the same time and without interruption: the ones with a louder voice believing that this might get them what they want more easily and ignoring the presence of others.

It is a loud and solitary isolation which brings to mind the state of the basic assumption of Me-ness:

> Our working hypothesis is that baM occurs when people—located in a space and time with a primary task, which is to meet and do something in a group—work on the tacit, unconscious assumption that the group has to be a non-group. (Lawrence, Bain and Gould, 2000: 100)

During the clinical case supervision/CRS, two patients are presented: a man and a woman, who have become a couple after entering the department. The fact of being a couple has split the department in two, between the ones who support them and see their relationship as a proof of vitality and hope within the unit and those who are against and relating to the pathology of their situation.

The first program ends with an SDM with few dreams:

> *I ask a friend, who lives in Berlin, how is his son; the son arrives in front of us and commits suicide.*
>
> *Our consultant carries many sheets of paper in his hands, some in the right way, the readable one, and some upside down; I fear he might not be able to put all of us together.*
>
> *The lawn mower is cutting the grass and dividing neatly one line going up and one going down. It is neat and they never overlap nor meet.*

I go away exhausted, puzzled and rather disturbed; by the end of the day I become sick, literally sick, and I wonder how much of the indigestible material present in the unit has been internalized and become a somatic statement.

Trying to make sense: Tentative hypothesis

The material can be read from various angles: I can identify at least three, relevant for the task of this consultancy:

One deals with the here and now of the Matrix and of the whole program, which is after all called 'supervision' and can easily be associated with past supervisions, with being observed, judged, and put on the spot. The uncertainty of being in touch with an unusual task becomes manifest. And so does the paralyzing fear of swimming in the unknown, which is particularly menacing in a department that deals with mental illness, far too close to the danger of evoking psychosis. It is important to keep the 'here and now' vertex in mind, even if it is equally important not to focus on it explicitly: In the SDM if the transference issues are addressed by the host, or participants, directly in the 'here and now', the Matrix is robbed of the opportunity to dream about it (Eden, Chapter 14 in this book).

Another angle deals with the institution: as I was told in the first meeting the team had to adjust to three different ways of managing the unit by three different consultants in the space of two years. A bewildered, tired group is facing a 'colander-like' structure. The dirty waters and the dangerous whirlpool talk of the liquid quality of an organization perceived as unsupportive and uncaring, in relation both to the patients and to its own employees. The staff can only reply with paralysis, the most primitive of the responses to the fear of dissolving into a puddle. Individuals become entrenched. There are hints of the political turmoil that is sweeping the National Health Service: it is becoming a service to numbers, balance sheets and cash flow rather than people; and, in turn, the main concern of the employees is whether they can keep their job, not whether they are really capable of taking care of the patients. The anger against the consultant is the anger against the one person identified as the institution, but who in reality is the only one in the room who is truly concerned with giving space for reflection and training to the staff. But he is both a 'democratic' and 'patronizing' consultant, who cannot shift the incapacitating dependency of his team, and in some ways—like a mirror of his team—is asking someone else, the consultant/supervisor, to do it.

A third strand is related to the primary task of the unit: they are there to treat people with mental illness. In the dirty waters which speak of leaking containment, there is a traumatized group, traumatized not only by the turnover of consultant psychiatrists, but by the fear of incompetence and by incapacity to give meaning to their work experience. It is a group in the mist of a sea of uncertainty, overwhelmingly evoked by a leaking container, mental as much as institutional. It is a group in search of a psychic envelope which might allow the encounter with madness to be safer.

The couple, represented by the consultant and by the head nurse, could well be the messenger of hope and of the capacity to generate. In reality, however, the couple is seen as pathological. If they ever were a functioning pair, they still would have to be kept in a state of separation, as the split between them seems to be the most accessible way to voice fragmentation. Even the hostile feelings expressed against the consultant appear to be the more visible, and accessible, manifestation of the deep impotent discomfort in the team. The despair is also that of mental illness, of the staff reproducing the same state that their patients are in, of being so identified and scared that their capacity to really work and help is absent. The staff seem to mirror and mingle with the mental anguish of their psychiatric patients.

Having said all that, I also perceive the vitality of their survival instinct: like a suffering child, the group has very clearly, loudly, managed to communicate the state of unease and to test whether the new supervision/Matrix can contain it.

In that complex state of being, I trust that the generosity of the Matrix will make room for the multiple dimensions and the many needs of the team, by giving the dreamers the authority to unravel the thread of their discomfort in a constructive way.

Making use of the Matrix

In the course of the next months, most of the material points to the fact that it is a priority to create a holding space so that the staff may start working with patients more efficiently and fulfil the primary task. Turbulent waters are still very present, but already in transformation, elaborated with some vital contents.

> *In the river a van is carried away by the stream. Nobody helps. I call the 118 (emergency number) so they can save the people from the water.*
>
> *There is an enormous waterfall, but in the water there are packets of pasta, snacks and much food.*

Needs can be met:

> *I have to go to the toilet for a 'big' need. The toilet is not normal, but I manage to do what I need. There is a warm fireplace in the room.*

Maybe there is even a warm place where to take one's needs, one's own and perhaps those of the patients; but needs are still rather toxic:

There is a beautiful little girl less than one year old. I take her in my lap and she pees. Later in the same dream, men put toxic substances in the water; it is menacing.

In the first meeting toxicity was just evacuated, now the team has grasped how to make use of the Matrix and through dreams and associations it manages to articulate what is toxic in the work environment. There is no separation: patients and staff seem to share the same mental space—that of madness—which becomes the explosive quality of being blown apart, staff and patients together:

I was in the van with patients; the engine doesn't work, the windows are blocked, we are suffocating, but we cannot release them. A small person arrives and throws a match in the petrol tank: the whole van explodes like a bomb.

The cruelty which puts victims and executioners on the same level:

... dogs hang from poles, handicapped and mentally ill people are ridiculed and tortured. I don't understand who is acting with such cruelty, who is the victim there and who is the torturer: I cannot reveal the secret of the two black spheres because there is too much evil around.

The simple fact emerges that perhaps neither patients nor staff have sufficient space or nourishment:

... there are two plants; they are both ill. We need to put each in a bigger pot with some food and closer to the light, but it is a bit as though the man who is saying this feels ashamed, something illegal ...

In the course of those first months people mostly learn how to make use of the supervision as a space where thinking is encouraged and consequently they start to function better in their role. What I see is that more dreams and associations are told; there are less occurrences of conflicts and meaningless arguments; the consultant and the head nurse start collaborating (they both say so and it is visible); a few members of the staff are actually able to integrate the experience of the Matrix into their work; and some new thoughts appear.

A totalitarian-state-of-mind

I put forward the hypothesis that a culture of dependency, vulnerability and isolation facilitates the growth of totalitarianism: a mental state of unhealthy ego centeredness where the vulnerability of the singletons provides the foundation for a social system ultimately based on the lack of recognition and concern for 'the other'.

Such a state lives within the individual as well as the institution at large, and in fact the two mirror each other. *The totalitarian-state-of-mind may seem an exaggerated working hypothesis but I think it fits the reality of the unit as I experienced it. Fear is overriding the actions of the staff. In such a state the wish of the staff is to have a management that will provide certainty to overcome their fragmenting, and psychically disturbing, experiences. The staff are driven into a dependent mode and, correspondingly, so act with their patients for they do not feel that they have the authority to act in their roles with compassion, care, ruth, or just with their wits.*

The second hypothesis is that the Matrix works through that danger, by facilitating a culture of connections, equality and, I would dare to say, freedom. As the paralyzing culture of dependency decreases, the dreams of the Matrix deal with the themes of work, profession, institution, and, in a larger sense, what to do when the 'new' is released.

> *My grandfather was dead and my two years old daughter was dead too. They were rigid. I was trying to put clothes on them by pulling arms and legs, but it was impossible.*
>
> *My father-in-law has died at one o' clock. I get angry because now it is ten o'clock and it will be very hard to dress him, by now he must be rigid.*
>
> *One patient has hanged herself. Nobody had understood her pain.*

The lack of emotions connected to those deaths, particularly that of one's little daughter, is very disturbing. Associations talk of how often one needs to cut off from emotions in order to deal with patients, otherwise their pain would come too close. Unfortunately by doing so one is also banished from the 'warm fireplace' of a previous dream, where needs could be met and the experience of being human could become meaningful.

> *There is a bus full of people and it has to cross a stone bridge. Somebody warns the driver not to cross because the bus is too heavy for the bridge. But the bus goes anyway and the bridge collapses. The roof of the bus is of the same length as the bridge so it keeps out of the waters, whitish and a bit muddy. People stay where they are without shouting or trying to run away and the bus becomes the bridge.*

At this point associations explore how the bus might be the administration levels of the service imposing impossible workloads which the staff have to bear without crying or running away—and possibly even losing their lives in the process—but who cares as long as there is a way to keep some kind of bridge going. It is the starting point of an elaboration of the 'institution within'; not only do dreams and associations start an exploratory process on that theme, but also the pictures drawn during the DRG, where in most of them is recognizable a sort of bigger entity ready to squash individual vitality.

> The-organization-in-the-mind has to be understood literally and not just metaphorically. It does not (only) refer to the client's conscious mental constructs of the organization: the assumptions he or she makes about aim, task, authority, power, accountability and so on. It refers also to the emotional resonances, registered and present in the mind of the client. This is the equivalent to Larry Hirschorn's graphic phrase 'the workplace within'. (Armstrong, 2005: 7)

A context larger than the team has come into consciousness.

It is also the beginning of a phase when the theme of the 'new' which has to survive the attacks of the 'old/dead' emerges and is worked through; in parallel with the well known tendency to project one's discomfort on the head of a 'guilty' party. In fact the team once more falls into the culture of dependency. It is difficult to be aware that the rigidity of death could well be connected with an internal rigid system of defenses, with one's own fear of being freer and consequently responsible for one's actions and choices.

The manifest content has moved from the internal conflicts within the staff and against the chief consultant—who by the way is always bravely present in the meetings—to a menacing institution, ready to squash any attempts to innovation. It is a paradox: the uncaring institution exists; the policies of the government are indeed dismantling the remains of the Welfare State (the little one that existed in Italy) and yet to have awareness of the level of personal responsibility is essential and of the utmost importance for one's psychic maturity as well as for a mature society.

The Third Reich of Dreams by Charlotte Beradt illuminates this point with extreme clarity: in the book hundreds of dreams collected in Germany between 1933 and 1939 demonstrate the overbearing influence of the political climate on the psyche of the dreamers, the mind's destruction by the hand of a totalitarian regime. But not only: as Bettelheim writes in that same book:

> ... this is a collection of warning tales ... warning of the inner pulsions which force us to believe in omnipotent external powers when we are torn by anguish. (Beradt, 1968: 143)

In 'Thoughts on the Meaning of the Word Democracy' (Winnicott D.W., 1950: 546–557) Winnicott relates the natural development of an innate sense of democracy to the unimpeded development of the human being towards his or her emotional maturity.

Deadness and rigidity are passed on from the government to the local authorities, to the National Health Service, to the consultant and so on until reaching the members of the team and from them the patients and their families.

But there is the other direction as well, that most of the role holders I am working with seem unable to bring into consciousness: one's inner world is constantly construing an outside reality which is based on subjective perceptions. Dead areas inside oneself (the rigidity of those dead people in the dreams) are projected onto the 'mad' patients, onto the 'cruel' staff, onto the 'bad' consultant, the 'bad' institution, and so on.

In a continuous stream of reflections, inner and outer reality mirror and shape each other; keeping alive the space and the movement which connects the inner and the outer reality with the play of dreams, associations, questions and discoveries, seems to be one way of not falling into the black hole of a rigid world. In that 'potential' space, so well defined by Winnicott, lies the possibility to give one's contribution to the creation of a flexible breathing world. The Matrix seems to offer that space, where the major questions could be dreamt and elaborated, not only in relation to the workplace, but also to existence and life in general.

Dreams actually dealt with this complex puzzle.

First by voicing the danger of thinking with one's own mind, surely one of the big fears of the group, which is paradoxical as the 'no-thinking' mind, is the major obstacle to any real work and to collaboration of the team:

> *There is a man who has been sentenced to death by his colleagues because 'He doesn't think like us!'*
>
> *In order to enter the hospital I have to go through a tunnel and a kind of door, very, very narrow ... in order to come out I have to go through an even narrower door ...*

Then there are glimpses of change and of the possibility to be freer:

> *My cat is dead: I hope I will be given one of the kittens which have just been born.*
>
> *I was going to the hospital but it is no longer as it was before. They are restructuring everything. I don't know if I like it.*
>
> *I open a drawer: there are jewels inside.*
>
> *My car has no doors, nor boot, but it works well anyway: the inner structure is sound.*
>
> *I meet a man; we like each other. He says: 'I am married!' 'Me too!' I reply, then we can relax and be together. I see myself relaxed and beautiful. We don't need to think about a permanent relationship, just enjoying the moment ...*

CRS was the complementary space where in an even more essential way this elaboration could take place.

It looked as though the same revealing potential usually carried by the first dream of a Matrix was present in the unconscious choice of clinical material. The two cases that each time were brought in the CRS represented in a nutshell the dilemma, the puzzle that the team was trying to work through, torn between the discovery of one's own responsibility for keeping mental freedom alive and the fear that 'the dead institution' could take over.

For instance, at the time of the dreams of the rigid dead to be dressed, one case was dealing with a catatonic patient who in time was helped to get back to a normal life by activating a wide web of connections with the staff and with her family; the other case presented (the other side of the dilemma) an elderly woman who, against her will, had been put into care by the institutional procedures and was slowing letting herself die.

Another example at a later stage dealt with Angela, a young woman who was extremely vital but much of which had to be denied because neither her family nor the unit nor her environment could support her and the fear was that she might be acting out dangerously. The second case presented Maria who curtailed her life potential in a series of wrong decisions and the team felt that more than filling up an existential void, it was more appropriate to create a containing space for her to be able to think and regain some of her own authority.

And to stress the point even more, in another CRS, one case dealt with the necessity to act very cautiously because facing reality might release a suicidal depression: it is useless to free much creative potential if the environment is not supporting it.

The other case explored the massive support needed in order to help a patient in the discovery of her creative and maternal role, in spite of an environment which had deprived her of her own child.

Two years have gone by, the unit works better, with greater satisfaction; it has been decided to carry on the supervision, with a different format and focusing on understanding systems and roles, which is one way of declaring the maturity to articulate differences, diversity, and interdependency.

Matrix, group and work group

I attribute great force and influence to the work group, which through its concern with reality is compelled to employ the methods of science in no matter how rudimentary a form. I think that one of the striking things about a group is that despite the influence of the basic assumptions, it is the W Group that triumphs in the long run. (Bion, 1961: 134–5)

This piece of work supports the working hypothesis that the Matrix fosters development and evolution—like dreams do and like Bion's work group does.

Social Dreaming in the context of an intervention which lasts in time offers very interesting points of reflection, as the work of the Matrix and the work of the group become clearly intertwined and visible, stimulated by the element of continuity. Transference and group dynamics can be seen. The experience of a reversible perspective becomes very real. As a host I focus on the Matrix; the other perspective exists in the background.

The team/group at first was mostly and clearly in the grip of a culture of dependency and me-ness. It is quite extraordinary how, in line with the task of the Matrix, that element was known, present and yet never focused on, but nevertheless effectively worked through in the dreams.

Keeping to the task of the Matrix, people learnt at their own pace—in reality quite fast—how to make use of the dreams, of the associations, of the freedom of expression offered in the Matrix, until most of them could germinate seeds of authority 'in role' and move on from the dependent position. Along with this process the mental envelope, or membrane (concept borrowed from psychoanalysis), which is the emotional base for the possibility to think, started to be perceived and the SDM revealed to be a true crucible for creative thinking and the playground for a feared experience of mature freedom. Like poetry, the Matrix reached the depths without disturbing the surface.

CHAPTER TWELVE

Dreaming to emergence in a general hospital

Lilia Baglioni

This experience took place in Rome, Italy, in a medium-sized general hospital designated by the Ministry of Health as a centre for the reception, assessment, and second level treatment of victims in case of macro catastrophes that would generate a large flux of intakes. In accordance with the Ministry's guidelines, the management had to develop and file a detailed plan covering both the technical and the administrative changes to go into effect in case of what was called 'Maxi Emergency'.

The process of finalizing the emergency plan was neither short nor painless, and brought about much turmoil and anxiety as the General Manager and the Heads of Departments negotiated the required changes to the routine of their wards and services and to the chain of command. The need to reorganize the hospital was because of the extraordinary dysfunctional problems faced by all role holders. These had conveniently slipped out of every formal discussion, or had been addressed, but with the solutions repeatedly and ritually being postponed.

The Service of Psychology could count at the time on only one member, the Director, who had been appointed six years before, to design and develop it. This first building block of the new service had stood ever since alone, a monument to the chronic lack of economical resources and possibly to the unconscious ambivalence of the medical culture *vis-à-vis* the introduction of psychological elements in the organization. The seemingly impossible, paradoxical challenge of designing a plan to cope with psychological distress of uncommon magnitude with resources not even sufficient for the day-to-day needs of the hospital was accepted by the Director of the Service, who produced a detailed document, based on state-of-the-art understanding of the psychodynamics of trauma and group psychology and its applications in institutional contexts.

The services to be provided included: assistance to the victims (in accord with the Psychiatric Consultancy Unit); assistance to their relatives; monitoring of the psychological conditions of the personnel; assessments of risk of breakdown; and debriefing of the personnel.

But who was to perform all of this? The Director searched the hospital for possible unacknowledged resources. Graduates and senior students of psychology already employed by the hospital in a different professional role, and psychologists who were doing an internship in the hospital as part of their post-graduate courses in clinical psychology, were found, selected, and recruited to be employed as consultants on a provisional basis. This creative *excamotage* (clever device) might provide the maxi emergency unit with some twelve additional potential members. This task force would remain dormant, so to speak, but ready to be activated if needed.

All its members would have to attend a training course on emergency psychology that the hospital would organize on a yearly basis. As the emergency department was foreseen to be in the first line of fire, medical doctors and nurses from that department would also be invited to join.

The four-days course, which was entitled 'Elements of Emergency Psychology', featured a short (one half day) and compacted theoretical part, managed by the Director of the Psychology Service, comprising lectures on psychological trauma and first level treatment given by herself and two outsourced psychologists who had been interns at the hospital in previous years. A video presentation on emergency procedures would also be shown during the class and commented by the head of security of the hospital. To this, a longer experiential part was to be added.

I (LB) was called in as an external consultant to devise an appropriate experiential activity and to manage it. I was the only element in the course that had no previous professional contact with that hospital. I decided to consider my 'ignorance' actually an asset, to preserve it as much as possible, and build on it.

On being given the background information that I summarized above, I imagined the institution already facing an emergency. It had to address, all of a sudden, some long, unattended realities of its organization and regroup in order to take immediate and effective action and answer sensibly the requests of the Ministry.

I also reflected on the fact that the theme of macro catastrophes and related annihilation anxieties seems to suffuse the atmosphere of our contemporary Western or Westernized society at large, and to be mostly entertained by its members through images endlessly replicated by the mass communication systems, which tend to have a standardized form. These images don't allow thinking, or learning from experience, and do not bring about change, but seem akin, at the large system level, to the nightmare in traumatized individuals and possibly should be regarded as failed attempts at dreaming.

I proposed that the experiential programme would consist of a set of four Social Dreaming Matrices (Lawrence, 2005), three Dream Reflection Dialogues (Lawrence, 2007) and one Creative Role Synthesis (Lawrence 2007; Biran, 2007). During the experiential programme, the participants would have the task of exploring their personal experience of emergency and trauma through their dreams, in order to flesh out the notions learned through the lectures and relate them to their role in the work place. Each Matrix was to last one hour and fifteen minutes; Dream Reflection Dialogues and Creative Role Synthesis lasted one hour.

My choice to use the Social Dreaming Matrix methodology was motivated by the following hypotheses:

1. Social Dreaming focuses on the knowledge contained in the dreams and not on the relationships among the dreamers. This provides a safe holding environment (Winnicott, 1971), minimizing individual and group defences.
2. Spontaneous unconscious sense-making processes will be activated and facilitated by the technique, and will liberate and

increase 'Emergence', which is a natural endowment of all living complex systems, influencing favourably the intelligence of the organization (Lawrence, 2007; Briggs and Peat, 2000).
3. Since Social Dreaming strengthens the capacity of collaborating in the presence of the unknown (Lawrence, this volume), it would have been a very appropriate training instrument for an emergency task force, that would have to accommodate recurrent and substantial change of membership and unexpected environmental conditions.

The material I shall discuss in this paper refers to the first two courses held, that were considered to be pilot experiences to test and refine the format before definitively adding it to the hospital protocols. I shall report the first in full and add some notes on how the process developed in the second. I shall describe the workings of the Matrix and report dreams and associations, keeping close to the meaning-making process the way the Matrix members themselves noted it, voiced it, and negotiated it through the different events, to allow the reader to make also his or her personal associations and hypotheses. My writing style will thus mirror my mental and factual posture as host in the Matrix, during which I refrained from intervening, except to facilitate and model the primary task. I shall leave some of my afterthoughts for last.

The setting

The course was held during regular work hours at the Nursing School of the Hospital. The first three matrices, Dialogues and Creative Role Synthesis were scheduled on a once-a-week basis for three consecutive weeks; the last Matrix and final Dialogue took place after an interval of two weeks. Twenty-three participants attended the first edition. The Matrix membership included: the hospital employees who held a degree in psychology and the interns, the director of the service and the lecturers, one social worker, the head of security, one surgeon, and five nurses from the emergency department. Since the psychology graduates otherwise employed worked each in a different department, including the administrative offices, we unexpectedly ended up with a fairly complete sample of the professional population of the hospital and of its different work environments.

The first Matrix: Earth, and the 'void and formless infinite'

After a brief introduction aimed to explain my role as Host of the Matrix, state the purpose of the work, the few basic rules we would follow, and the primary task of the Matrix (1), I invited to voice the first dream, which readily came: *A friend gives me a small terracotta box that contains salmon-pink sand. She tells me that I can use it to orientate myself in the desert, in the Valley of the Kings. She tells me she knows I am leaving on a journey to Egypt. I am surprised because such trip is not in my programmes, although I always wanted to visit that country. I am happy and scared at the same time, because the huge pyramids and the tombs of the pharaohs make me feel uneasy.*

A second dream followed immediately: *I am in a spaceship or shuttle that has two windows. I am the pilot, sitting in front of a console full of control instruments and blinking lights. I turn to the right and I see a totally black space; then to my left, and I see an infinite number of stars. Without knowing how, I find myself out of the spaceship, among the stars. I fluctuate with great ease and pleasure in the void and the stars seem so close that I feel I can touch them. I extend my hand as if to try, but I find I am back into the spaceship; intense frustration.*

Since the dream has been told by the Head of Security, somebody notices it seems quite appropriate he should be concerned with control panels in his dreams too. An association follows that links the uncanny feelings in the first dream and the strangeness of being in a medium unfit for human life in the second: How can one survive without oxygen?

The third dream: *I associate a macabre dream to the black space. It is a recurrent dream: in the middle of the street I see a black cat. It is dead; a large amount of blood has come out of its mouth. I recognize it as my cat. I feel an unbearable pain and wake up.*

The macabre dream abruptly gives a name to the anxiety in the Matrix, and it is clearly difficult for the psychologists to observe the rule of not engaging in a direct conversation with the dreamer. The dreams and associations that follow bypass the dark dream, and link back to the second, elaborating on the pleasure of moving freely in a vast and unbounded space. One association brings back the black cat into focus: *Cats have seven lives, they say ... but seven is a finite number anyway.* A silence ensues.

And the fourth dream comes: My dream too has something North African in it like the first dream, but it was the cat in the last dream that triggered the memory: *I am sleeping in a blue Berber tent. I wake up and move towards a group of houses that look like products of a northern culture, maybe Scotland. I have an appointment there. I realize I left my backpack in the tent and go back to get it. When I come close to the houses somebody points to one and tells me it is my new home. Next to the door, where the number should be, there are two small identical elongated solids that make me think of the twin towers. I go in and find out it is not void of living presences. There is a little cat there and this cheers me up. In the next scene I am at a busy restaurant. I dig into my backpack, pull out a pizza and start to eat. I realize that everybody is looking at me. I am ashamed and embarrassed because I am eating the food I brought with me from home, instead of choosing among the foods supplied by the restaurant, like everybody else.*

Somebody notices that the number of the Psychology Service room is 11. Associations on 9/11 and the Twin Towers follow: the pride of America; the unthinkable attack; the infectious spreading of terror; and clash of cultures.

Then comparisons are made between old but manageable living spaces and more modern, apparently more solid buildings.

In the last dream there is a back-and-forth movement between the two kinds of buildings: A hospital is a transitory home, somebody states, and the atmosphere is suffused with this feeling of impermanence—one patient comes, another goes, making the bed available for the next. The next association chain elaborates on the theme of desert and solitude. Lack of vegetation in the dreams is noted, many participants voicing their uncomfortable somatic states: I feel too hot. I have tachycardia. I feel tense.

As if to produce a first aid kit, the terracotta box was connected to the candy box that the Director of the Psychology Service always keeps on her desk, at the disposal of patients and colleagues who enter room 11.

Back and forth: being able to oscillate between the hurried rhythms of the wards where time feels compressed as in a tight box and the more relaxed rhythm of room 11, where time is supposed to be a time of pausing and waiting. It is noted that one should learn to go from one dimension to the other, to take a rest and a deep breath and dilate the time.

The Matrix seems now balanced enough to accommodate associations that, like this one, directly point to unavoidable vulnerability and again to death: dilating makes me think of uncertainty and death; the heart inside, so vulnerable, dilating and contracting.

The control panel and blinking lights inside the spaceship are now associated to the monitors in the intensive care ward, where vital functions are supported by machines and dependence is total. Sometimes we have to give up trying and disconnect the patient.

The tent is now the curtains that are pulled around a bed by the nurses when the patient is in a critical condition, or that are removed to show an empty bed following a death, but it also triggers the personal memory of a nurse. She recounts how happy and relieved she was to see the other patients when the curtains were finally removed, after a seemingly endless night in the emergency ward where she had been brought following a serious accident.

One participant associates the pink sand in the terracotta box to the death of her own father and the sand from Israel that is put in the coffin at Jewish funerals. The fourth dream comes: *I am walking along a road lined with trees and I am looking for something, but I don't know what. Eventually I reach a lake; the water is dark and muddy. I put my hand in it without seeing, touch something and pull it out. It is a person. I don't remember her face.*

And the fifth and last of the Matrix: *I know I am in a swimming pool, but it feels like the ocean: vast, dark and deep and I want to fly away from it. There are huge waves. I am scared and overwhelmingly sad. Then I put my head under the water and its colour changes; it is clear like that of a riff. I see something big moving, maybe it is a whale. There are also submerged tree trunks. An island can't be far, I think, but I cannot see it yet.*

Second and third matrices: Water and fire

During the second Matrix 10 dreams were told. Seven featured water, as if the Matrix had developed a common basic language, the language of dreams, capable as water is, of taking infinite shapes and penetrating every recess. The participants have also become aware at this point of the possibility to oscillate between two different mind–states or thinking modes and are starting to enjoy the process, a bit like the pilot in the first scene of the second dream.

I shall give a few examples:

> *A bizarre situation; I go back and forth between two tables without moving. Somebody tells me this is how things are according with the quantum theory.*
>
> *Labyrinths ... houses that open each into many others at the same time in an endless sequence. It is very beautiful. It is like being in a drawing by Esher; I am in no hurry to reach any specific place.*

Surrendering to unexpected and inexplicable situations can make one pregnant with new thoughts, like in a dream in which *the uneasiness generated by finding oneself on a strange ship at sea, while thinking all the way of being in one's familiar room turns to joy on encountering a pregnant friend.*

Or another in which: *I am swimming underwater and I am very curious of what I may find down there. I notice that the water has different depths in different places. I enjoy swimming where the light of the sun reaches the bottom. Where it is deeper and I cannot see anything, I keep swimming, but slowly and with caution.*

Going slowly is enjoyable and is a good protection, one you would want to carry with you all the time, like in this dream: *A small turtle jumps on me. I think it's ok to take it to my garden and keep it with me.*

Then two almost identical dreams are told: *I am walking on a pier going towards the land. I watch my grandfather coming towards me, going in the opposite direction towards the water ...* The other, mirroring it, has *the old person going in the direction of land, and the young in the direction of water.* In the dimension of dreams, time flows in both directions, I think silently, but the first associations that come are with the death of an old person and the acceptance of death as part of the natural order. But what then when the unexpected, unthinkable, and unforgivable happens, when the young or the ones in our charge die before their time, when we fail to protect them, as in the dream that follows?

> *My beloved nephew, who does not have a driving license since he is still too young, is driving the car. I am sitting in the back seat*

> with his two older brothers. We all have safety belts on. All of a sudden, at a turning of the road he loses control of the car that jumps off the cliff and ends up in the water. I and the older boys survive, but he is dead. I was not able to save him; I feel I cannot go on living.

In this Matrix the emotion of curiosity appears and is not so inhibited by the terror of the unknown like in the first Matrix and thus the thought of death and humane vulnerability can be addressed more directly. The associations in the Matrix and the thoughts shared during the Dialogue point to an oscillation between feelings of confidence and power and feelings of utter impotence.

The dreamers start to associate cases of patients, mostly victims of accidents. Survivor's guilt is mentioned. The case of a young man, the victim of an accident at the workplace who was taken to emergency recently and did not survive surgery, is recounted. The nurses discovered that while he was dying his unaware wife was delivering their first child at the same hospital. Many members know the episode only too well, because they were actors in it, and have now a chance to voice their emotions and reflections.

The nurse who told the dream of the black cat relinquishes her remote and tense posture, then loosens up a bit and shares her story. She confides that she has been having this dream since the death of her sister, whose care she had been involved with until the very end. She participated in the decision of disconnecting her from the machines when there was nothing more that could be done.

It is the first time that she has talked about her feelings and thoughts in the presence of her colleagues. In the beginning she was afraid that 'the shrinks' would want to psychoanalyse her and had felt angry and had withdrew.

An association links now the space shuttle dream and the frustration of the pilot at not being able to dwell among the stars for long, to the inability to accept impotence, the desire to feel and be always at the top or on top of things. (The Italian word for shuttle is *navetta* which sounds just like *una vetta*, a mountain top.)

Taking a risk to save a life is discussed, and also risk-taking because of greed, like in playing the stock market. The head of security, a retired fireman, shares traumatic experiences that have to do with putting one's colleagues at risk and causing their death because of a poor capacity to foresee consequences and because of excessive self-confidence. Risk is also exciting and addictive, like strong emotions are. A participant admits that when she puts on the TV set she looks for catastrophic news.

During the third Matrix six dreams were shared. The first was associated to performing surgery on an unknown patient in the emergency operating theatre, but also to the hospital itself, that now looks like a much more complicated, multiversal animal than before and with the problem of using or wasting its resources. *I have to cook a strange kind of sea creature to feed a large number of people. I am in a hurry and start to cut it as I would a common fish, but I realize that in so doing I am wasting a lot of meat. In fact its shape is difficult to tell. It is all protuberances and crannies and seems irreducible to a simple geometric form. I stop and start to imagine how this animal is made in the parts I don't see, before cutting it in pieces.*

The absence of familiar points of reference in the anatomy of the unknown sea creature was connected to the experience of looking up at the sky in the other hemisphere and not recognizing the constellations, or to the experience of not recognizing the faces of people one is supposed to know.

The four dreams that followed all featured close encounters with something strange, excessive, unexpected, and capable of engendering terror and an impulse to flee.

Everybody was impressed with the many evident connections between these dreams and especially with their common high-energy emotional atmosphere. An association was made with a chain reaction.

> *I stop at a red light and spot the police chasing a strange man with a bat in his hands who is smashing the car windows. When he reaches mine we look at each other straight in the eyes for a long moment. He spares my car and goes away.*
>
> *I see an airplane with a bush growing out of it, which seems on the verge of falling down, but eventually lands. A red huge monster comes out; he looks like a skinless man. Terror spreads, people run away and so do I, in the beginning. Then it dawns on me that maybe he is like King Kong and that he is himself running away from something that scares him to death.*

I am at the base of a volcano; hot stones and lava are bursting out of it. I run towards the sea, jump in the water and the image of the volcano disappears.

I am in a classroom. I open the door to go out at the end of the lesson and I see a parallel universe where a volcano is erupting fire. I turn and see that my colleagues are very alarmed. They are shouting at me: 'Shut the door! Make sure you shut it for good!'

I shall report the associations that followed in some detail; they poured out one after the other, like the dreams. The man smashing cars was associated to the recent tumults in the French *banlieues*, to ethnic discrimination, and to isolation. To the colour red, the reassuring Red Cross was associated. Red, it was noticed, is nevertheless a colour often associated to something malign, and volcanoes were also believed to be doors to the underworld and to the territory of the dead and spirits.

The light of the stars the sailors followed in order to not get lost in their journeys is also the result of a chain reaction, it was noticed. But the light of the stars is yesterday's news when it reaches us!

Would it be possible to read the signs—the traces of things to come—in advance? Maybe the dreams give us a pre-alarm: wake up to reality!

'But one has to be able to hear … But one must be able to listen,' another participant adds. 'There is always too much light, too much noise to hear the soft sounds or see the dim lights.' A participant mentions the newly opened Museum of Silence: 'There is very little silence during our working hours and in general in our day,' he complains. 'We are bombarded with stimulations of all kinds and in turn we bombard the others. I am stressed out!'

A participant says that what strikes her is how aggressive the personnel are with each other: 'Maybe the work we do makes us have adrenalin rushes,' she says. 'We are hyperactive and over-reactive. I am stressed out. Bat, beat, sound—the man in the dream has no skin, I remember reading of music as a second skin of sort … sound reaches us even in the womb.'

There is music that the human ear cannot capture; maybe the silence is not silence for other creatures though, and it is just a matter of what we can register. The bats are sensitive to ultrasounds and, like the dreams, they are nocturnal animals. I associate thinking of the English word 'bat'. There is a limit to what we can tolerate to receive! One participant says: 'Until recently I worked as head nurse but I changed job. I had started to feel like a living target and a disposable commodity. I had built my role with love and pride, but I could not survive in it; I felt like they were eating me to the bones. I had to shut the door. Shut the door ... shut up ... for us as firemen silence is a clear signal during an earthquake. It means that the next shake is coming and the animals feel it. Some animals are more sensitive than us, we lost that sense ... how can we recuperate these more primitive capacities and educate them?'

Creative Role Synthesis

This time we did not have a Dialogue after the Matrix but, after a short break, I introduced the new event: Creative Role Synthesis. The former Head Nurse volunteered to be presenter: 'Since,' as she said, 'I already started.'

The seats were rearranged in two concentric circles. Ten self-selected members sitting in the inner circle would be consultants to the presenter while the others would listen and think quietly.

The former Head Nurse's insoluble problem has to do with 'the paradox of investing a high percentage of my energies in my work, that I expect to grant me a meaningful and creative life, and getting just more frustration out of it the more I try to have some satisfaction. I thought of solving the problem changing my role, taking up teaching at the Nursing School, but it did not work. I had lots of ideas and plans, but when I tried to put them into action they always turned to nothing good or could not be supported by the organization and were terminated. I feel deadened and, what is worse, sometimes even feel rejection for the work I love; another paradox. I cannot think of a personal dream to recount. In fact, I don't remember my dreams.'

The consultants seemed to resonate intensely with the material presented. In their associations, they also lent the dreamless colleague two dreams from the Matrix: the one about the blind searcher, which ends with a person being pulled out of the water, and the dream of the space shuttle. The dreams were then connected to her two roles and work tasks—the old and the new—and also to two different mind-frames. One controlling, focused, and highly goal-oriented, the other relaxed, receptive but not at all passive; in fact there is something reminiscent of a skilled midwife in the act of pulling the person out of the water.

Some consultants contributed personal memories of when they had to choose or accept a job, the conflict between the pull to fulfil family expectations and the desire to follow personal inclinations was recalled with feeling. At this point, a movie was associated: *The Story of the Weeping Camel* (2004). In this movie, the whole Village becomes concerned for the survival of a newborn camel that the mother refuses to feed. A shaman (musician) is summoned from far, who attaches his sensitive instrument to the flanks of the mother camel so that the strings, solicited by the vibrations of her breathing, shall produce a simple musical pattern on which the shaman shall elaborate making it into a melody that all the villagers shall sing to the animals while they help them take and hold a correct nursing position.

The colleague (a consultant) made the hypothesis that the natural match between the highly experienced Head Nurse and her new job, which involved feeding her experience to the younger professional generation could be re-established only if education, that is feeding the heads of the young nurses, was recognized by the organization as a matter of survival. The consultants also hypothesized that, like the mother camel, the teacher-nurse too had suffered too much in delivering her services in the previous job and was still digesting that experience. Maybe her emotional reactions were not inappropriate in her situation, maybe more time and less action was needed to resettle and re-orient in the new situation.

The presenter, who had the last word, said that she had found the intuitions and hypothesis of the consultants very helpful and to the point; she said she felt 'rebalanced' and more relaxed at the idea of reframing this troublesome moment as a period of transition and not as the ominous sign of a new professional catastrophe. She also thought, now, that maybe she contributed to the chronic ineffectiveness of the communications between herself and the management. Some of the consultant's associations had made her think of the fact that she had been the first female child in her large family to challenge its culture and circumstances and win her right to study and work outside of the home. Maybe this was relevant. She would reflect on it.

Last Matrix and synthesis

Six dreams were contributed; five had been dreamt during the two weeks interval between the third and last matrices. All had something to do with encountering, communicating, or exchanging. Some featured familiar situations or objects found in unusual places or vice versa. For the first time some of the colleagues appeared as characters in the dreams: *R. had given me a valuable present. I knew that it had been bought at dear price. It was a radio transmitter that was capable of connecting me with everybody.*

> *I am enjoying a stroll along the Appian Way (a major ancient Roman road) with L. We notice a movement in the thick vegetation and have a glimpse of something red. We pause, and soon a red fox appears, sits down in front of us and stares. She is not scared. When she is tired of staring—or maybe her curiosity is satisfied—she moves back into the thicket. We are surprised and delighted and continue our stroll commenting the unusual encounter.*

A male nurse, who had never uttered a word during the entire programme, associated another 'Red fox dream', almost identical to the other. He felt doubly surprised and somewhat mystified because not only did his dream happen to be prophetic (if he could believe these things), as he really did come across a fox during a walk with a friend the day after dreaming about it, but also, and unexpectedly, he met his fox again today, in somebody else's dream!

There was a dream in which *a strange cat, red and blue and possibly sick and contagious visits the room of two sisters during the night engendering, at first sight, panic and efforts to avoid contact. Eventually it conquers some space under the covers, close to the dreamer. The intimate contact, in turn, allows the dreamer to appreciate some other features of the cat, for example its softness and warmth, its fragility, and its sociable nature. Her emotional reaction changes …*

Not only animals were encountered and entertained in the dreams but also bizarre and whimsical objects that seemed to have come out of a science fiction novel: *A gadget that captures the satellite signals. It does not look very technological and polished; rather it seems made by assembling miscellaneous pieces of common use objects. It has a light bulb sticking out of it and it moves like an organic creature.*

We stare at each other. I go: 'Boy, are you strange!' 'Hearken, who says?' it retorts.

Many associations picked up the 'staring' element which was first connected to the dream of the strange man smashing windows and then, through the common element of violence, to the red, skinless King-Kong in the third Matrix. The terrifying monster is pushed (Bushed?) to attack by his terror. It is a vicious circle.

The terror attack to the Twin Towers, the bombing of Afghanistan, the war against Iraq, and the refugees fleeing to other countries were associated. Looking at the face and establishing and holding eye contact was associated to the capacity of receiving and communicating emotions. Curiosity for who and what is different was also in the dreams: not an inquisitive curiosity, like when one looks for specific signs or symptoms, a participant said, but something more diffused, global and not goal-oriented, at least not consciously. Examples from work experience were added.

The red fox was also associated to the Director of the General Medicine Department by many because, somebody said, he behaves just the same: like the red fox he is everywhere and nowhere. You never know if you shall find him; he appears and then as quickly disappears.

The blue and red cat dream triggered some stories of domestic animals that were thought lost, were looked for everywhere, only to discover that they had been all the time in the vicinity, locked up by mistake. The animals locked in without realizing it and the animals found in unexpected places were connected to the story of a distraction that almost killed some new born black kittens who were thrown by mistake in the washer with the dirty dark coloured rags among which they were sleeping.

The first and last dreams were associated to the Matrix. The bizarre object was also associated to the Internet: it is wonderful, strange, and scary. One can find all kinds of things on the net, the best and the worst and even the unconceivable.

Finally, a joke was told about a psychotherapist being asked by an ashamed compulsive chatterer if the inability to engage in a conversation, except with a computer, was a very serious symptom. Not yet, was the doctor's response, but make sure to come back if it starts to answer!

During the final event, the participants tried to make a synthesis of what they had learned and had a chance to share their thoughts about the experience. I shall report some ideas that were voiced. Disoriented and scared is the state of mind of a patient or relative getting to the emergency room minutes after a serious trauma: the known constellations have disappeared; he or she is lost in a strange world. Even the world of the hospital, which should be reassuring, is mysterious; only the local inhabitants, nurses and doctors, understand it.

But nurses and doctors too are scared: scared of making mistakes in the triage; scared of having to deal with the anxious relatives; scared of being bombarded with questions and having sometimes scarce answers to give or none at all; and scared of having to admit impotence. Scare and frustration surface as violence, not necessarily against the patient, but maybe against a colleague or a relative of the patient. Terror is highly infectious. It is not only the quantity of patients that matters, but the intensity and quality of the emotions that saturates the air and the absence or presence of effective communication.

Managing difficult, dark emotions or thoughts of 'a different race' by locking them up or wanting to bleach them may result in adding a risk factor and may even kill the germs of new and vital thoughts. Life needs diversity to carry on.

The theme of isolation was considered paramount: Isolating from the colleagues or isolating from the patient was seen as a defence that transforms the context in a desert where nothing can grow. The theme of isolation was also elaborated by comparing dissecting a corpse and isolating the pieces, like in an autopsy, and performing surgery in a live body, which involves first of all having an awareness of an uninterrupted whole, a complex system of processes. Both procedures are useful but they should not be used unskilfully. They are in the mind when the patient is referred to with the name of the affected organ (for example, a patient with breast cancer is 'a breast'); and when a patient is moved from one department or service to the other and they disappear from awareness. The only trace that remains, the sign of continuity, is the clinical records with their name on, but often they are not read in full. What is a name, a face, after all, when in immediate and present danger of death? This culture of emergency pervades the hospital and justifies many absurdities, just like it happens in a country under martial law.

It was noted that the space-time of the hospital is not homogeneous under the surface, it is perceived differently in the different departments, and it is construed differently by the psychologists and the medical personnel. The different perception of time even modifies the language and sometimes makes communication impossible.

What is homogeneous is the quality of the emotions: they do not seem to have fixed boundaries. Death was present in every Matrix, it was noted, and so were the emotions that the awareness of the reality of death engenders. Boundaries are important, it was said, especially in an emergency situation, but they should have emergency doors: easy to open, easy to close, and subject to ordinary and not just extraordinary maintenance.

A major catastrophe, it was noted, would also break boundaries between professional and private domains, since the population at large might be affected and the personnel of the hospital may end up receiving wounded or traumatized relatives, or would be concerned with their safety and unable to make contact for some time: in the dream, the dead cat is *my* cat.

Nobody is immune to death or to the danger of psychic deadness. The oceans, the volcanoes, are macro elements of nature which command respect; it is like the dreams were also saying: you cannot do everything only because you can think of it, look at how small you are, you depend on circumstances. Dreams seem to have their feet well grounded in reality, more than our waking thoughts.

The second experience

The second experience took place after four months and was identical in design but the participants now numbered 26. The Matrix included all the old members minus one, two new nurses, one new intern and a 'special guest', a military doctor holding the role of coordinator of a similar programme at another hospital who had heard about Social Dreaming and had asked to participate in order to have a first hand experience of the technique.

In the first dream of the first Matrix the desert was portrayed and the main question that the Matrix was seemingly formulating and trying to address was: Why does nothing grow here? Or, as the song has it: Where have all the flowers gone?

In the second set of matrices, four months later, the first dream even had too much vegetation in it. The first dream was: *I am in an arid field but I find some seeds in my pocket and sow them. I find some water, sprinkle the soil with it and the grass begins to grow fast, abundant and tall, and it is like a tumultuous sea. A strong wind starts to blow as if the grass movement had been communicated to the sky. A storm is created and the uninterrupted rain destroys all the crops. I see on one side a patch of short grass, like Irish grass and go sit there and wait. After a while the storm subsides and the grass starts to grow again.*

In all the dreams of the first Matrix there was something green growing inside the most unexpected containers. So much so that the associations started to voice concern for the mental conditions of the Matrix: one association referred to the grass of the *Matto Grosso* (the South American immense pastures, but also, in Italian, the big loony); another was to the tropical jungle that is to be kept in constant check, lest it invades and eats up all human artefacts. Paraphrasing Bion (1987), one might say: when two (or more) dreams meet, a storm is created; nobody can predict beforehand what shall emerge out of the turbulence, one can just sit back, and try to make the best of a bad job.

A dream arrived, in fact, to point to a more benign possibility: *A number of people are having a picnic under the shadow of a huge and ancient tree. The dreamer notices that its roots are growing in every direction and are becoming longer and longer. They look more like rhizomes than roots. On turning to the others to check if they also noticed the awesome phenomenon she realizes that as the roots grow long, the hair on the head of the people is growing long too.*

A hypothesis was that the dreaming intelligence of the Matrix was growing and reaching out of the grounds of the hospital and that the hair represented individual dreaming thoughts. The vegetation that appeared in the dreams that followed seemed to be less obtrusive and left some room for other details to come into focus. There was, for example, a dream in which the woods surrounding a model jail were hiding Che Guevara guerrillas (El Che was a medical doctor before becoming a commander).

There was a dream that seemed to complement this one, in which *the dreamer was with her colleagues outside a castle reminiscent of the hospital buildings when she discovers that fresh vegetables are sold there. She wants to stop and buy artichokes, since they are in season but is ashamed to divert from the group's course. On second thoughts, she boldly does it, only to find that the heart of the artichokes has turned to paper. Too late!*

If not now, when? was the association of a participant, that introduced the ethical dimension and the unavoidability of personal choice and responsibility. The revolutionary dreams in this second set of matrices questioned all sorts of taken-for-granted assumptions and allowed the dreamers to venture into new dimensions.

Many of the themes present in the first edition were revisited from new perspectives, like the theme of using/wasting/sharing resources. In the first set of matrices this had been explored in the sense of a waste of emotional and intellectual resources, but in these matrices was related also to concrete aspects of the organization.

The participants could not only address some of the unthought known (Bollas, 1987) of their hospital, but could also connect their personal experiences, thoughts, and feelings to a larger, non-local social reality. Once reset into this larger and multifaceted picture, some more local troubles that everybody knew about, but nobody would discuss in public, could also be directly named. These, formerly taboo, pieces of knowledge filled gaps, and once linked to other available information allowed the participants to formulate more realistic hypotheses on formerly inexplicable and therefore terrifying facts. For example, there was a Matrix in which *deceased fathers appeared in almost all the dreams. They would come back from the great beyond and deliver ambiguous messages or patently false reassurances. One was walking on stilts like a clown.* Political leaders Italian and from other countries were associated at first; in time, it turned out that, in the last five years, five different general managers of the Hospital had been appointed and had all 'disappeared'. Each had initiated changes of different kinds that their successor did not foster and complete.

Aside from generating administrative chaos, this state of affairs added to the emotional atmosphere of instability and diffidence and maybe increased a tendency to resentful isolation and hostile dependence in the staff (Stapley, 2006). As it seems, the little sample of the organizational Matrix, inseminated by the dreams, watered by a self-regulated flow of associations, and sticking to the Matrix mode that involves tolerance of the unknown without reaching out for premature conclusions, created the right conditions for the silent self-organization of a learning system and the emergence of a new wider angle perception of the complexity of reality.

In a dream of the last Matrix, *there is a group of people all dressed up for an important meeting. The journey to reach the meeting place is long and difficult; their clothes become muddy and ragged. They get to a pond of clear water, stop, undress completely and jump in. They come out rested, put back on their rags and start off—but in another direction.*

Future developments shall tell if the 'out-of-the-box' dreaming thoughts helped to re-orient the intelligence of the Organization towards the place where its rich, creative resources and more favourable, temperate climatic conditions are.

Some participants commented on their experience of the Matrix

- This was my first experience of a psychological course: I lived it as a moment of introspection; it was like looking at my thoughts and emotions for the first time as if, like the domestic animals in the dreams, they had always been there and visible, but I did not pay attention.
- I was struck by the vitality of our exchanges; I understand that what deadens me most is that my social skills are devitalized at work. I open a patient, close it … I am happy if he survives, disappointed if he does not, then they take him away, and another comes. For me it was like treating the asphyxia of my mind and soul—giving it a larger space to expand in to.
- For me the experience challenged the belief that I know who we are and what goes on here. The white uniform is no more a reassuring, homogenizing shell. Under it there is an ocean of diversity. This is scary and comforting at the same time.
- I was impressed at how my attitude changed during the experience. I was very defended in the beginning—this felt like too much intimacy—but it changed in time and I relaxed and started to enjoy playing. Then the dreams and associations started to sound related to many things that are part of my everyday life here. I only shared some, many more I did not but I have a feeling that others here had my very thoughts.
- I think this work should be steadily done in our department. It was valuable, but I wonder if the results are going to last now we go back to our usual rhythms and tasks. This we should do with the patients too and more doctors.

- I was impressed by the fact that we could abandon our roles so easily and be open and intimate with strangers. The emergency department is like a seaport. Here you meet the stranger without filters; this was a good training.
- I recuperated some anxieties that I had lost sight of, but strangely enough I feel better, not worse. I feel more alive, more awake to reality.
- It was a surprise. At the beginning this group seemed to me like an odd, forced assembly of people who did not have anything to do with each other and I did not see the point of it. I ended up feeling proud of us, I thought: look at us, what a wonderful *equipe*!

CHAPTER THIRTEEN

Social Dreaming with black rappers in New York

Wolf Werdigier

As a painter and conceptual artist the Social Dreaming Matrix is, for me, a wonderful access to the unconscious of target groups and a rich source of metaphors to be represented in paintings.

In my projects I very often start by organizing groups for Social Dreaming Sessions. While people are sharing their dreams and free associations I make notes, writing them down afterwards. Then I start reading all the notes and recordings made. During the following months I crystallize the most important dreams, themes, metaphors, and images to be transformed into paintings.

During 2005 I was invited to Castillo Theatre, a centre for performing and fine arts in Manhattan, to present my Israeli-Palestinian paintings project, parallel with paintings on African-Americans and Whites in New York.

There were no further explanations as to why these two themes were chosen to be shown together in one exhibition. It was clear that the riots following the Crown Heights incident (Orthodox Jews *vis a vis* African-Americans) and the theatre play based on this had anticipated this exhibition.

In contrast to the already existing paintings of the Israeli-Palestinian project, the paintings on the relationship between African-Americans and Whites in New York still had to be developed. Therefore, I was very happy to have an opportunity to invite people in Manhattan to participate in Social Dreaming workshops.

At the same time I had been invited also to Erasmus High School in Brooklyn to do a project with Social Dreaming matrices and paintings there. In both places I had the chance to do Social Dreaming Matrices with African-American people. It was an interesting experience to see how age groups behave completely differently.

Erasmus High School, Brooklyn

At the Erasmus High School students who participated in the Social Dreaming Matrix were aged between 15 and 18. The situation of the school was rather unfriendly. Not only was the building huge, in fact there were several buildings, much like a university campus, it was also completely barred off from the streets around. With all the security installations, iron gates, and wires it looked more like a prison than a school. There were only African-American students attending the Erasmus School.

On the other hand, once inside together with the young people the atmosphere was very warm, very bright and the young students were dressed more fashionably than those in other schools and universities. I was surprised to see African-American students in these buildings dressed in an Armani-like style that I knew previously only from fashion journals. Obviously there was a big contradiction between my comprehension of security, and wealth *vis a vis* the situation in a poor living area.

To add to these contradictions, the head of the school and all his assistant staff were white and reminded me less of school directors and more of military personnel in their gestures and way of speaking. This contrast between the beauty and aesthetics in behaviour and dress on the one hand and the brutality of the actual life these kids are confronted with, reminded me of the many very beautiful songs and texts of their rap-tradition.

> You got whites killin blacks
> Cops killin blacks
> And blacks killin blacks

> Shit just gonna get worse
> They just gonna become souljas
> Straight souljas
>
> (Tupac Shakur)[1]

After introducing my project to a group of students, explaining my interest in the dreams and free associations of African-Americans in New York, and that I elaborated on these subjects in my paintings, the students started to immediately tell their dreams in a rush, like a water cascade. Dreams almost exploded out from them. We were sitting in a very small room and everybody was very near to the other. Everyone was speaking very, very fast and, at the same time, the others were listening with great attention. It was the atmosphere of an audience, sometimes even with acclamations and applause. Sometimes the fast rhythm of telling was just like rapping, but always very short, as if nobody wants to be exposed for more than a few seconds.

The dreams

I always dream. I'm on the top of a mountain.

There is a beautiful landscape around and in the middle there is a huge waterfall. I stand on the hill and I am looking back and forward.

No matter where I go I find myself being chased by Freddy or Jason (these are virtual film characters, monsters, to create fear and death).

I always dream that I am a small little thing between all the others being large size. It is as if I am an ant.

In my dream there are the two characters: Tina and Tamara—just like in TV. But in the TV show both characters are good; in my dreams always one makes me good and the other makes me doing bad things.

I had a very violent dream. I was walking in a wild landscape. It was like in a violent maze. I tried to find a way out, but I did not know where to go. I could not find the way.

I had a wild dream. I hardly dare to tell. It was really wild. I dreamed having sex with the devil.

When I have been a baby I dreamed of being killed.

Someone wanted to stop me. This person was trying to kill me.

---

[1] Tupac Shakur, American Rapper 1971–1996.

Several times I dream someone is shooting me when I am walking in the neighbourhood.

When I wake up, the area of my body wherever I was shot, it feels hot.

This is a violent dream. I dream myself standing on top of a roof and falling down. I fall and I try to stop desperately during I am falling, but it goes and goes on. I want to control my falling but I cannot. But I never reach ground and it is as if I start falling again from the roof top.

I fly always uncontrolled. Not levelled. I try to control, but my arms, which I use like wings, are bubbling and I have no control of my flying.

I am always building a house again and again. It is my dream house. I start from bottom and build it up. Then I build the windows. Then the roof. At last my house is finished. Next time the dream starts from the beginning again.

I always dream of a man dressed in black. The man, he is a really big man, I do not see his face. When I tell the dream to my mother she says, 'He is Jewish.'

The man is not doing anything to me. He is just watching. In the second part of the dream I am sexually aroused and touched by fairy-like women and having sex with them.

It is as if I am watching this happen to me. I am in and out of the dream. After the sexual part of the dream, I end up being very small. I am a small person and everybody around me and all things are very big.

I dream from school. I see my class friends. I see Madeleine. I see all the other school mates.

When I was young I always dreamt being in a forest.

The landscape is full of snow and a bear is chasing me. Then two years I had no dream. Afterwards this dream started again.

I had a similar dream: There were big trees, a forest but no snow. There was a noise in the forest. I was not sure whether it was a bear or something else. But it was chasing me. It started running and I kept running away from this noise.

Social Dreaming Matrix at the Castillo theatre, 42nd street, Manhattan, New York

This place is designed to be a cultural centre for African-Americans coming together with white people. The participants of the Social

Dreaming Matrices were between 20 and 40 years of age. The way of talking was much more elaborated, people really telling dreams in detail and also making their associations. It was not at such a high speed as with the teenagers, it was slower and very well elaborated.

> *I am in my kitchen together with Muhammad Ali.*
> *But he starts strangulating me. I could not help anymore, so I tried to reach out for a knife and all of a sudden I cut off his head.*
> *When I was working in a deserted area in the Bronx, two rats came like they were to bite me.*
> *In my dream I was in a dark alley downtown, underneath of Manhattan Bridge.*
> *Two huge black cats were running towards me and I was scared to death. They were like tigers. But they did not attack me, they passed by. Then they laughed at me. Then I got into a crowd of people. Suddenly a man looking like a Joker from the play cards, was looking at me. He smack up on me and startled me and made me scream.*
> *When I was a child my parents have just immigrated back to Trinidad. And the first time I had my own room; it was the only bedroom. I have a recurring dream when I was much younger; I have been together with my grandparents in their big house.*
> *At night always somebody was walking in the corridor. I woke up and could hear it. I dreamt it will be coming in my room. I would dream the ticking get louder and louder, so I knew it will come in my room.*
> *I was sure there was somebody or something. It lives in the living room only at night. I had no sense how it could look like. I had always this threat. I woke up and I did not dare to open my eyes.*
> *I had a dream last year. I was together with a volunteer from 'Castillo Theatre' at my parents' house (she is white, he is African). She said something which made me mad. So I started screaming on her. Then I walked out of the room.*
> *Later I came back and apologized. She was hugging me. Then she would not let go and these two guys came in. One was her husband, a big guy. The other was a little guy, a midget. The big guy gets me in a headlock, so I struggled to get out. The small guy got a razor, to cut me. So I kicked the razor out of his hand and I got the razor. I took it and cut off the big guy's arm, to get out of his headlock.*
> *I saw they both were on the floor, maybe dead.*

> *Then I got upstairs to find my friend, but she was gone. When I went downstairs the two bodies where gone as well. I run out of the house and I kept running. Then I woke up.*
>
> *After the dream I run into the same volunteer and I hugged her. Yes, she let go.*

Association

There is the character of the writer Richard Wright, called Thomas. He grew up in Chicago. He was dreaming of a better life. All things he would like to have he struggled for. This character also had a dream of being in this violent struggle. I wonder if Richard Wright is transferring his dreams into this character, into his writings.

Association

Last time I was in the Social Dreaming Matrix, I cut Muhammad Ali's head: I had a lot of violent dreams.

Heroes, mentors, and idols of identification

Two years later I did a project to investigate the ideals, mentors, and idols of young immigrants in Vienna, Austria. I was interested in their inner pictures, the horizons of their aspiration and identification and I also asked them why they find these heroes so impressive, so fantastic. The result of this project has been exhibited under the title 'Africa' in January 2008.

The interesting connection between these three investigations is an overall picture emerging, which starts with wonderful nature and landscape, lyric environments, and goes on with threat and being chased, on to killing, shooting, and fighting.

Of course the role identity of African-American young people is very much linked with the struggle for freedom. They identify with people like Tupac Shakur and other militant rappers.

Interestingly enough these 'Gangster-Rappers' are idols for teenagers from Serbia and other nationalities on the Balkan as well. At the same time the ruins of the Balkan war mirror the burned-out houses in the derelict areas of the Bronx.

Even more surprising to me has been the very distinct identification between male and female teenagers. Males dream, as well as of idols, of being connected with fighting, killing, and war. Women much more identify with the beauty of the body as well as with the beauty of male film stars and singers. And it also was the female dreamers who dreamt of wonderful landscapes and of building houses rather than male dreamers who reported shootings and killings.

Adult African-American participants of Social Dreaming Matrices had much more dreams associated to family and history, very often experiences of arriving in New York following migration from other parts of the United States.

Teenagers and High School students Social Dreaming Matrix metaphors have to do much more with: landscapes, woods, waterfalls, and hills; chasing, shooting, and violence; and sexuality.

Does this mean that our society, in a genealogical sense, is still linked to the pastoral landscape (female) and to chasing, hunting, and killing (male)?

Appendix

All the paintings mentioned can be seen at **www.paintings.at**

The paintings were shown at Castillo Theatre, New York, 2005.
The Austrian Cultural Forum, Washington DC, 2007.
Cleveland State University Gallery, Cleveland Ohio, 2007.
Spektakel-Theatre, Vienna, 2008.
Spittelberg-Gallery, Vienna, 2008.

CHAPTER FOURTEEN

Learning to host a Social Dreaming Matrix

Angela Eden

This chapter traces the development and implementation of a training programme to host Social Dreaming events. It will cover the development of the programme, the role and function of a 'host', the learning experience, as well as some practice development ideas for people who host a Social Dreaming Matrix.

Background

Gordon Lawrence has worked with SD since 1982 and has hosted innumerable Social Dreaming matrices all over the world. As he experienced the richness of Social Dreaming, he also established some principles and practice for holding the Matrix in mind. The function of 'host' became clearer as an important role to contain the Matrix during Social Dreaming.

Now in 2008 there is the phenomenon of a third-generation of people who contribute to Social Dreaming, with hosts and participants who have had no direct contact with the origins of Social Dreaming, and may not know its original aims and values. This means that there is an expanding group of individuals who participate in SD, and who run matrices in a variety of contexts.

As this interest in SD has grown, so has the style of hosting. Some people have worked directly with Gordon, and so with the experience of 'Elijah's mantle' consider it a mandate for taking on the role. Gradually, as with all ideas, the principles and practice shifted to encompass the experience of the host. It is only recently that the provenance of Social Dreaming has been questioned and the need for training explored.

The Social Dreaming community realized that people may have detailed expertise in related fields yet may possess no 'training' in hosting a Matrix. Thus an intention evolved to create an educational experience of hosting SD which would expand the pool of hosts and the idea of Social Dreaming. This idea was explored by the Board of Social Dreaming, Ltd. during July of 2005, and was inaugurated in February 2007.

> The design of any learning experience to host a Matrix needs to pay attention to issues of quality in hosting and clarity about the intention of SD to honour the dream. Its intention is to open up the SD world via inclusion: exclusivity is seen as against the spirit of the work; this training is to enable colleagues to work with dreams in a different way. (Proposed by Ruth Silver in November.)

Requirements

The aim of the programme was specifically to learn about the role of hosting a Social Dreaming Matrix and thus consolidate theory and practice of Social Dreaming.

The design was for people who had experienced Social Dreaming and who wished to learn how to host matrices and develop the 'flow' of new people who might wish to do so in the future.

In the sprit of learning rather than teaching the event would not be a formal training, but an exploration of the experience in a Matrix. This implied a discursive experiential approach rather than lectures and instruction. The event would include a range of approaches to reflect the participants' differing learning styles.

It also had to include theoretical, conceptual, and practical elements, with opportunities for knowledge acquisition, concrete experience, observation, reflection, and further experimentation.

There was some discussion about validation, without having to explore the constraints of an external accreditation body. So the board recommended that part of the validation process for a new host would be to recognize prior learning. The content of the programme would provide underpinning knowledge as a foundation for acquiring skills and would be based on the agreed guiding principles of Social Dreaming.

The design

The board authorized a small design group (Angela Eden, Ruth Silver, and Laurie Slade) to develop the work. The Board's recommendations influenced the design to include experiential opportunities for all of the participants. The time and space consideration meant that the groups could not exceed 12 people. We wanted to include some input from experienced hosts and an opportunity to hear Gordon's perspective about the emergent theory and culture of Social Dreaming, the link from Social Dreaming to a reality context, and action-research applications. We wanted to include some thinking about the overall process of a Social Dreaming Matrix, for example: What constitutes a dream? What constitutes a free association?

Finally we had to create space for exploring practical issues concerning the setting; the way to introduce a Matrix and the primary task; and essentially the role and practice of a host.

The design solution for all of these requirements was a series of interlinked matrices, in order that each participant would have at least two opportunities to practice the role by hosting a Social Dreaming Matrix with a co-host, with observation, reflection, and then discussion of the hosting observed, with feedback provided for the participant. The structure was designed for 12 people and covered four days of working together as a learning community, over two weekends, with a month in between.

The structure

Each day followed the same pattern: a Social Dreaming Matrix followed by reflection and learning. Each Matrix was hosted by a new person, sometimes individually and sometimes in pairs. Each host or pair of hosts were encouraged to plan their session, to think about their introduction, the layout of the chairs, their understanding of the primary task, and their shared, complimentary roles. With this structure we were able to hold 10 different matrices, individual learning for each host and five theoretical inputs about Social Dreaming, its application, and possibilities.

Introduction to the day
- The purpose of dreaming in the Matrix free association.
- The primary task of the workshop, a place for learning, and establishing principles and practice.

1. **Social Dreaming Matrix and Learning Dialogue**
   - Reflection on hosting and the primary task.
2. **Social Dreaming Matrix and Learning Dialogue**
   - The experience of and learning from hosting Social Dreaming.
3. **Social Dreaming Matrix and Learning Dialogue**
   - Reflection on what the SDM tells us using amplification.
   - The experience of and learning from hosting Social Dreaming.
4. **Final dialogue**
   - Working hypotheses on Social Dreaming and hosting.

Within that structure each participant had two sections to consider about their role:

1. The hosting:
   - Prepare themselves and the room for a Matrix.
   - Introduce and host a Matrix.
   - Close the Matrix and introduce a period for participants to reflect on the experience of the Matrix.
2. Review and learning facilitated by 'programme hosts'
   - Facilitate a discussion involving session hosts and other participants regarding the manner in which the session hosts performed their tasks, and so forth.
   - Assist the group in identifying possible learning from the Matrix.
   - Assist the group in identifying possible theoretical perspectives.

The training experience

The experience of the four days was rich and complex. Each person learnt about their own style of hosting, the words they felt comfortable to use, and their particular style of associating and intervention. The central question was always about the role and task of the host. We worked on the following definition:

> The 'host', which is the name for the facilitator, has the role of managing the containing boundaries of the SDM—task, time and territory, but also has to be alert to the dreaming and free association. The content of the dreaming is all important, noting the themes and thinking about their significance, starting to connections between the contents of the dreaming, and free associating to provide a model for all the other participants. The hosts have to keep their wits, being vigilant on behalf of the Matrix to make sure it remains with dreaming and free association, which is the essence of unconscious<>infinite thinking and avoid group processes that are a defence, in the context of the SDM, against unconscious thinking. The host has to take on this role without Interpretation, which, though valid in the therapeutic situation, is always a rendition of past knowledge of the known in the light of current circumstances. In the SDM working hypotheses are the chosen tool for enlarging understanding. A working hypothesis a sketch of reality as it is understood. The less it fits the reality, the more working hypotheses can be generated to capture the feeling of that reality. The working hypothesis engages with the unknown.

Each Matrix used an introduction stating the primary task, ending with the question, 'What is the first dream?' This gives the message that the SDM has a purpose and is to be engaged with immediately. It was found that if the primary task was not stated, there always followed a silence because participants were not sure how to proceed. The precise wording was developed by each individual host to fit with their own style and learning.

Each session and each day discussed the experience of hosting and raised a series of questions, which were answered partly by the individual and partly by the group.

Questions for hosting a Social Dreaming Matrix

- What is the appropriate behaviour and stance as a host?
- How can we do it better?
- How can we help each other do it better?
- How can I listen to dreams, not as personal, but as a thread in the structure?
- How can I hear the dreams, notice the associations, and think about themes that are emerging for me?
- How, and in what way, can I add my thoughts?
- How can I try not to be envious, competitive, ego-led, and narcissistic?
- When should I hold back and let dreams tell the story?
- How can I learn to trust my co-holder to contribute in their way, with the best intentions?
- How can I develop the state of as if I was an interested stranger?
- How can I be uncluttered from knowing (including what I have been 'trained' to know—including 'psycho stuff'; even the very good concepts) and be there to try and serve the Matrix—a labour of interest and love?
- How can I remember there is no real seniority—the discovery can come from, and to, anyone?

Establishing the learning from the sessions

After each learning review the group defined their important learning, and at the end of the workshop we reviewed and agreed the following basic principles. The concern of the Board is not that these principles are fixed, or that the experience of an SD Matrix is the same, whoever is the host, but that the spirit of creativity and the dreams are respected and nurtured.

- The 'management' responsibility is to somehow monitor myself and others for directions which take us away from the level of discovery which the Matrix may privilege us with.
- Be aware that 'interpretation' can interfere with the unfolding of the Matrix.
- The work needs openness as to what and how the Matrix may be revealing, including our resistances to it.

- 'Acting out' and boundary management tends to manifest itself when professional skills are being used to take us *away* from discovery in the Matrix.
- Be aware that competent efforts to 'interpret' as an intervention can also interfere with the unfolding of the Matrix.
- Reflection freshly after a Matrix session may be valuable—though again we cannot be sure that we are not colluding and escaping into too conscious a kind of thinking. My experience is that it is the feel of it which provides the discrimination.
- Realize when thinking and feeling seem to come together to illuminate, which is how I think about being open to thought and discovering themes in the Matrix.
- Realize that if I 'think' about it, I can no longer understand. I can only 'understand' when in a state of mind which is different from that which I label as 'understanding' or 'explaining'.
- There may be an aptitude for this style of work that fits with the gentle, curious, enquiring mind.
- There are no RULES, just a set of guiding principles and an environment that will support a Matrix.

The future

There is only one way that Social Dreaming will develop, that is with more Social Dreaming. This model of learning to host can be adapted to suit any number of modules. The Social Dreaming Board have produced a certificate which names each participant as:

> Attending an advanced professional development course on the Social Dreaming Matrix and learnt about hosting a Social Dreaming Matrix together with the consolidated theory and practice to attain a level of competence accepted by Social Dreaming™ Ltd., London.

There are still questions of a 'probationary' period of supervision, with observation, grading, and coaching, by a Training Host supervisor, before validation is complete. Though the role of a training host has yet to be defined, the role may need to include ongoing mentoring support over a specified period and a review meeting annually with a supervisor.

What is clear is that the idea and appetite for Social Dreaming is alive. It has a number of appearances in different countries and cultures. Gordon Lawrence has given us a way to work, and we have to nurture and grow through Matrix.

Appendix

Hosting Social Dreaming

Principles and Practice developed from a professional development workshop with Gordon Lawrence. March 2007

Background

These principles and ideas about best practice are not written as formal guidelines. They emerged from the workshop which was run for four days over two weekends. Each participant had an opportunity to be a host, and reflect on the experience. The SDM is recorded to have available dreams and dream-thinking for subsequent creations of new thoughts.

This record is the output from those four days.

Preparation

- Coming to the role of host is directly affected by the style of 'entry'. The host might have asked to hold a Matrix, or have created the opportunity through marketing, promotion, or building a community of interest. However this happens the host/s will benefit from preparing themselves.
- **State of MIND.** Use oneself as a model for curiosity, creativity, and cooperation. Pay attention to your own dreams, being open to the process and open about the outcome and respecting the Matrix. Take time before hand to refresh yourself through reading about the concepts.
- **Working with a co-host** needs thought; time to share your experience and journey into Social Dreaming; expectations of each other in the Matrix; thinking together about the roles, boundaries, culture, gender, and ways of hosting
- **Ask rigorous questions of yourself and colleague.**
- **Agree the minimal conditions you need to host a Matrix.**

- **Signals for non-verbal contact.** How will you deal with the unexpected, as a team?
- **Knowing what the Matrix is**
  – For you.
  – For the participants and their context/language culture.
- **Practical management (dynamic administration)**; a way to ease the process without setting up obstacles. What will you send to participants? How much information will you send in advance? Can you prepare the newer participants before the Matrix? What is the space? How will you arrange the chairs? What theory could you use? Consider the context and any expectations of outcomes.
- **Plan the roles; the introduction; time boundaries.**

In the Matrix

- **Introduction**/Background **to SD**
- **The primary task of SD** (Gordon says elegant and parsimonious)
- **Define the time boundary**
- **Explore confidentiality**
- **Notes** explain that the role of the host is to record the dreams
- **Share the introduction**; include all the hosts as a way to identify the container
- **Think about the appropriate tone of voice**, that is, to ease into the process and prime the participants for the Matrix and the invitation to dream.
- **Work towards brevity of intervention**, allowing for dreams and associations, not disrupting the flow of the Matrix.
- **Work at making links.** (This can be less helpful to making associations and maybe sharing your own dreams in an inexperienced group.)
- **Temporary role.** Hold the possibility that the role can be redundant (except for opening and closing) as the group matures into a democracy.
- **To remind participants of the primary task** if they start interpreting the dream for the dreamer, or analysing contributions in terms of group dynamics.
- **For the host to offer working hypotheses** on the transference of the dreams to the Matrix may be helpful.

After the Matrix

- **Make time for the power of a dream reflection group, or dialogue.**
- **Build in time to share links with co-hosts.** (Have these ready in case the work needs a spark.)
- **Define the primary task.** (To think about the links people have left with in order to have new thoughts, and build a working hypothesis; a synthesis of the themes and patterns in the Matrix [unweaving the Matrix!])
- **Record new thoughts** for the individual and/or the system/community/society.
- **Record or find a process to share the new thoughts.**

CHAPTER FIFTEEN

Creative role synthesis

Halina Brunning

When the invitation to contribute a chapter to this book arrived I eagerly agreed to write something about Creative Role Synthesis, or CRS for short. My positive reaction to this invitation was based on past experiences of seeing and applying CRS in action. Yet, as weeks changed into months and the deadline for producing the promised chapter approached, and then passed, I found I was not able to put pen to paper or fingertip to keyboard, my discomfort and sense of 'stuckness' only growing. Then, one night I had a dream which seemed to have sorted both my resistance and doubts about writing the chapter as well as bringing to my conscious mind, upon waking, a well-ordered structure for the chapter. The next morning I was able to complete the work without delays.

There is no doubt that I had been thinking and planning this chapter both in my conscious and unconscious mind if there was no visible activity to show for it, but the final push towards completion of the task came entirely from within my unconscious mind.

The creative power of dreams

When humans are asleep and dreaming the neural nets and the unconscious mind is fully operating. The dream is imagery and relies on metaphor. Whereas consciousness is self-reflective, the unconscious mind is not, and is imbued with a sense of 'other worldliness'. The dream is surreal and images and ideas are juxtaposed defying everyday logic. The links and connections between the dream images are multi-branching and display lateral thinking that would be impossible in waking consciousness. Fewer words are used, and more metaphors and connections are formed between the contrasting worlds of consciousness and unconsciousness and between subsystems of knowledge (Lawrence, 2006).

Such moments of creative insight arise from the unconscious mind rather than consciousness. This is because ideas are free to recombine with other ideas in novel patterns. The unconscious mind is a storehouse of memories which cannot be readily recalled and which 'speak' to us beyond words.

And here lies the creative potential of dreams. Thanks to dreams and dreaming, old problems and conflicts and a frustrating sense of 'stuckness', as well as recurrent fears, anxieties, and doubts, various barriers to action and progress can suddenly be perceived differently, as if illuminated afresh by a different insight. 'Insight' is defined in the *Oxford Reference Dictionary* (1987: 423) as 'the ability to perceive and understand a thing's true nature, mental penetration, a piece of knowledge obtained by this'. This definition of insight seems to fit the purpose of describing the role of dreams in CRS as bringers of new thinking and new creative potential. It also helps to differentiate it from the customary use of the word 'insight' in psychoanalytic psychotherapy where 'insight' denotes emergence of conscious acknowledgement of psychic material that previously has been repressed, pushed into the unconscious due to its problematic anxiety-provoking nature that can be threatening to the equilibrium of the individual. This difference, as it were, in the understanding of the concept of 'insight' is the corner stone that differentiate the use of dreams in CSR as opposed to in psychoanalytic therapy.

The creative power of dreams cannot change our personality, remove old habits, or eradicate persistent dysfunctional patters but thanks to this new 'in-sight' the dreamer is offered a glimpse of new possibilities and free thinking on an old subject. What we do with this new affect and connected thinking will depend on many factors.

In this chapter I describe a new approach to using dreams called Creative Role Synthesis and propose a range of potential applications.

Creative role synthesis—the primary task

The purpose of CRS is to highlight a paradoxical puzzle/an existential challenge of a role by making use of creative unconscious thinking. This methodology was invented by Gordon Lawrence and Bipin Patel as part of experimentation with the methodology of Social Dreaming, now used worldwide. It is therefore appropriate to start with his own words to describe the rationale and the process of CRS:

The experiences of the Social Dreaming Matrix gave rise to other events that made use of the thinking processes that dreaming engenders. What Social Dreaming does is to excite, or agitate, unconscious thinking. At the private, individual level the Matrix will result in dreams being recalled from the personal past. Because of the primary task of the Matrix these dreams will not necessarily be used. They are kept private appropriately.

Nevertheless dreams can be used to illuminate the personal complexities that are experienced in carrying out roles in a system, for example, work and family. This evokes the parallel mental processes which sit alongside all the rational processes of executing a task in a system. This is the unconscious thinking which, metaphorically, becomes the 'white noise' that is part of the stream of consciousness.

Everybody experiences puzzles, or conundrums, in their various roles. Not being able to resolve the problem, or impasse, results in interpersonal difficulties of varying degrees. In the worst cases a mediator has to be appointed to help the parties to acknowledge their difficulties.

This attempt could lead the pair (the person with a puzzle and the mediator) to become isolated, split-off, in their interpersonal thinking from the system that contains them.

What is creative role synthesis: A definition

Creative Role Synthesis is a method of using dreams to achieve the following:

To identify a paradoxical challenge, existential puzzle, or conundrum, or problem, or living doubt—of role to make a synthesis of the systemic elements involved, so as to authorize a creative role reformulation.

This reformulation is based on the idea that the individual manages him/herself in his/her role which is determined by the nature of the relationships to the system in which the role is carried out and that this process can get stuck and become dysfunctional. CRS brings new elements into thinking about the challenge or the puzzle and can mobilize new resources (see below).

The following diagram captures the essence of CRS:

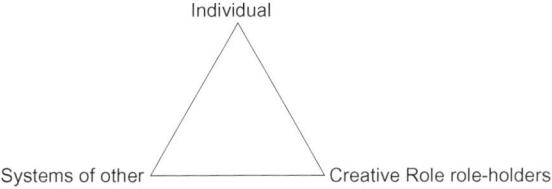

How to run a session of creative role synthesis

All participants have experienced the cultural dimensions of dreaming. After the Matrix the members will be convened in a large group. The task of the CRS will be given as well as the thinking behind it. Each participant will be given time to think of a private dilemma, a 'puzzle'.

A CRS is composed of, roughly, eight members in a small group. One of the host team for the SDM will act as chairperson of the group. The sequence of work has three parts:

1. Presentation of role puzzle—10 minutes
2. System synthesis—15 minutes
3. Role-System reflection—5 minutes.

Part one presentation of role puzzle

A presenter volunteers to present: a current life puzzle or issue that is unresolved, in which the presenter has a role and responsibilities and for which creative outcomes are important to the presenter.

This is followed by sharing a significant dream by the presenter of the puzzle. The only expectation is that the presented dream should in some way (it is not prescribed exactly how) be felt to be linked, connected to, or illustrative/illuminative of the presented puzzle. The dream offered could be taken from a recent stage of life, or could be an old or even recurrent dream, or be taken from the Social Dreaming Matrix.

Meanwhile, the rest of the CRS group will take up the role of facilitator by, silently at first, free associating to what the puzzle and the dream presenter is sharing, recalling their own relevant dreams, and formulating working hypotheses on the puzzle being presented.

Part two systems—synthesis

After the presentation the silence facilitators will be invited to speak, offering hunches, feelings, free associations, and intuitions in the form of working hypotheses. They may offer their own dreams to illuminate the puzzle. Free-flowing discussion is the aim. Interpretation has no place in the CRS, only working hypotheses and new thinking. The tone of the discussion is not directed at solving instrumental problems but rather exploring affective dimensions of the presenter's puzzle. The presenter of the original puzzle has freedom to reply to the hypotheses, or not.

Part three role-system reflection

This is an opportunity for all to manage themselves out of their temporary roles in the CRS. The facilitators talk about what they have learned of the existential puzzle with their feelings and thoughts.

The presenter has the last word in the session by summarizing their experience of the session and what they have learned.

1. Example of CRS in action

The presenter is a Psychologist and a Family Therapist from an East European country. The context for CRS is the second day of a Social Dreaming Matrix ran by Gordon Lawrence.

The presented puzzle

'I work in a variety of different professional settings but feel that my Family Therapy role seems very different and disconnected from all of my other professional roles.'

The presented dream

I have had this recurrent dream early in my childhood. There is a picture of a low, mountainous landscape with a low hill ending sharply and slopping down into the landscape. Visible only to the person from the other side of that landscape is a tree with exposed roots. The tree is growing on top of that hill but is cut in half. Nestling inside the roots of that tree is a dead baby.

The associations of the presenter

The landscape is cut in half, ruined and ravaged by the war. There is a train to Auschwitz, and my own daughter is inside one of the wagons!

Associations offered by the CRS group

The landscape described by the presenter is connected as the system of the roots of that tree by a common theme of loss: loss of daughter; mother's losses; loss of childhood; loss of innocence; loss of landscape; loss country; loss of wholeness; and loss of hope.

Associations of the presenter

Yes, I can now see three layers of loss: within my own country, intergenerational losses within my own family, and within my own work. I can now see that in fact my work as a Family Therapist is also connected with and not at all different from all of my other professional and private roles in life. Perhaps it would have been too daunting to also see my Family Therapy role as being connected to the same sense of loss. Indeed, this is my role in life: to be 'the memory candle' for others and to be open to the experience of loss both within my own family and amongst my own patients!

2. Example of the use of dream as part of team consultation

In their celebrated paper called 'A Search for New Partners ... or an Invitation to a Harem?' Ross A. Lazar and Mathias Lohmer (2000) describe how an accidental dream, offered rather unwillingly by one of the participants of a retreat organized by the consultants for the Firm in search of a new organizational structure, suddenly lead to unblocking communication within the team. The dream was unique, not as a dream per se, but by the opportunity to offer itself as an unexpected transitional object capable simultaneously of symbolizing the unspoken hidden conflict of connecting the conscious with the unconscious, the visible with the invisible, the resisted with the longed for, the unnamed with what needed to be named, the individualized with the group, and the feared with the desired.

This is an extract from their paper: Frau Z's reaction to what I said was both immediate and intense. Highly relieved and suddenly very communicative, she reported that she had not slept for three nights. Instead she had spent them pacing up and down, crying and worrying what to do. Finally, in the early hours of this morning, she had fallen asleep and had a terrible dream; a dream which she felt might be of significance in helping to answer the question I had just posed. Her dream went as follows:

She was in her bedroom at home, but it was not her house. It was a huge old mansion, spooky, dark and cold. People came (adolescents, perhaps). They tried to get to her, to get into the room ... wanted to do something with her ... something sexual she thought. She fled in her nightgown onto the street, but the people followed, keeping after her. She ran through the dark streets, the others in pursuit ... Cold with sweat and full of anxiety she awoke.

This disclosure shocked the group even more. In the interchange which followed each was able to speak more freely for the first time of the terrible anxieties they had been suffering and which they had felt unable to share with anyone. All spoke of feelings of being pursued and of being subtly forced to do something against their will.

At this point, on the basis of my counter-transference reaction and the evidence I had been gathering, I formulated the following working hypothesis: I said they appeared to me to be like candidates waiting to be admitted to a harem. To talk of equality or of freedom of choice seemed absurd. They all felt themselves compelled, forced under enormous pressure to agree to become something akin to subordinate concubines, to accept a lesser position in comparison to the original partners, and, above all, to submit to being under the aegis of the No. 1 Wife, Frau B.

Their conscious intention and wish had been to become at least 'partial' partners in a growing and flourishing company. Unconsciously, however, each had secretly been wishing, hoping, and phantasizing themselves in a unique and special relationship with the 'Chief-Founder-Father', only to have been brusquely rebuffed by him and attacked and/or snubbed by No. 1 Wife, Frau B (Lazar and Lohmer, 2000).

The consultant, Ross A. Lazar, who ran the retreat for the Firm identifies that very point when the dream is being offered as a significant shift in the working with the resistance and the unspoken fears generated within the Firm. The Firm's own understanding of its problems with the personnel and the planning of new strategy was helped by this new thinking that arose as a result of the transformational moment afforded by the dream.

3. Example of CRS in one-to-one coaching

Although the CRS is usually performed in a small group setting, where the other group members can also offer their own dreams, I have experimented with the use of dreams in a one-to-one coaching setting. Here is an extract (reprinted with permissions) from one of my coaching clients, Alexis Waitman:

I have been both a coach and a coachee for the past three years. During my period of being coached I discovered that the process and experience of coaching could be the most spontaneous, challenging, exciting, revelatory, mind-altering experience if I allowed myself to be spiritually and emotionally free.

Whilst this might sound a little grandiose to some I was truly amazed at both the process and the outcome achieved thorough utilization of my inner emotional/spiritual thinking as opposed to my outer, intellectual 'head' thinking. Being given the freedom of my creativity in combination with that of my coach allowed me to utilize dream material in an entirely new way: not simply by analysing the dream but by using it to see beyond the imagery into the role that I was finding so difficult. My role at the time was confused, complex, and chaotically managed by somebody whose incompetence was only just beginning to emerge. Through coaching I was able to see beyond the awfulness, the chaos, and confusion through to blue sky and transition. I believe that CRS, applied by a particularly creative and innovative coach, facilitated not only my learning about organizations and their leaders but about myself and how my own creativity holds secrets and stories that are in themselves able to provide the exploratory power from which comes strategic and personal change.

CRS may not be the perfect vehicle of discovery for every coachee, but it has to be offered and ideally experienced so that everybody has the opportunity to find for themselves that there really can 'be another way' to the freedom that we all seek through our work and personal lives. For this coachee the Organization in the Mind is more visible and creatively available when we are ourselves free to rid ourselves of the shackles of conformity or habituation.

4. Example of CRS as part of the group relations training

In Copenhagen, Denmark, in 2007, Birgitte Bonnerup and her colleagues from Group Relations Denmark, the OPU/IGA (Copenhagen) organized a training event for approximately 70 trainees. The conference was managed in a group relations format and the overarching theme was 'Coaching in Organizations'. The organizers, lead by Birgitte Bonnerup, used the CRS as the tissue connecting all parts of the programme. The invited guest speaker, after her introductory lecture on the theme of coaching in organizations, demonstrated the use of CRS in a fishbowl exercise within a plenary setting. This was followed by working in 10 small parallel groups where the use of CRS was key to learning about coaching.

Bonnerup explains the rationale: 'I wanted to explore other ways of using dreams, not necessarily in a Social Dreaming Matrix, not individually focused, but by trying to connect personal resources to working life. I was hoping to find passion not only in problem analysis and definition but also in problem solving. This stems from my research that in both individual and in working lives the choices we make arise from our sense of personal identity and are closely related to the very choice of a career. I believe that the use of CRS has helped the conference to achieve its stated goals' (Bonnerup, 2009, personal communication).

5. Use of CRS as part of teaching and training in systems-psychodynamic coaching

It strikes me that the CRS is most suitable to utilize as part of the 'here and now' experience of coaching within the systems-psychodynamic training setting. I usually include a session of CRS as a way of demonstrating the systemic and the creative possibilities that systems-psychodynamic coaching should encompass. Here is an example of applying a CRS as part of the training in systems-psychodynamic coaching.

One of the workshop participants presents her current puzzle: 'I am not sure whether I should stay with this job in this company or find a more suitable job for myself where I can be happier.'

She then presents a recent dream: *I dreamt of Frank Gardner the BBC war correspondent who got shot on camera whilst reporting from Beirut or another battlefield. He was shot and still worked! I could not believe it was possible! Even now, in reality, he is still working although he is paralyzed from his waist down, oh, what a sacrifice. In my dream he was laying on the ground and still holding a microphone reporting to the BBC when his blood was on the road around him!*

Dream offered by another workshop participant: *I dreamt that I was about to marry. I was on my way to a wedding, but looked at myself and could not believe it! I was wearing black dress, and, oh no, on my feet I wore some horrible old slippers not elegant shoes! What was I doing dressed like that on my own wedding?*

Another dream offered by a workshop participant: *I once dreamt that I was about to marry but when I realized that this wedding was just a scam. Apparently, I had agreed to marry somebody only just so that he could stay in the country, as otherwise he would have been expelled from the UK! I was also dressed so shabbily that this alone forced me, in my dream, to rethink my decision and I put a sudden stop to it!*

One more dream offered by a participant: *I saw a friend of mine, a tall blond woman very elegant and accomplished in her own profession. But I saw that she was wearing a blond wig and not just one but two! Every wig she wore was a shade blonder than the previous one! Why was she doing it when her own hair was already blond and pretty?*

Reflections on the dreams were offered. In all dreams, with the exception of the first, there was a central element of falsehood and pretence: a wedding dress that was more suitable to a funeral procession than a wedding; an illegal, scam wedding; and blond wigs upon the head of a naturally blond professional woman. The first dream was about the true and extraordinary personal price of sacrifice, blood spilt in the line of duty, a unique, heroic but painful and rather imprisoning position to endure.

Reflections of the original puzzle presenter: I can now see that I need to ask myself whether I can really stay much longer in a job that is not *me* where I feel that I sacrifice myself for no good. I pay the price of sacrificing my own identity and by creating falsehoods. Where has the passion for my profession gone? Why am I in this role? Where is the true me in this company? How long can I pretend to myself and even to my employer that I can be happy in this sterile role?

The strong emotions generated, the questions associations, and finally the reflections gathered, during the CRS lead me as the workshop organizer to open discussion on the role of authenticity in professional life, the role of falsehoods versus true selves, pretence and role playing, the role of passion and fulfilment and the various dilemmas and sacrifices women can experience in the workplace whilst undertaking challenging leadership and professional roles. This naturally leads to examining the role that coaching can play in addressing these issues.

Systems-psychodynamic coaching was framed by the attention that it pays to the three overlapping contexts: the personal, the role, and the organizational (Brunning, 2006). It also encourages the coachee to make synthesis and integration of all three contexts in a search for deeper meaning. It is likely that this discussion could have taken place without the help of the CRS but it might have been sterile, based on pretence and devoid of passion, all vital ingredients identified as essential by the participants, as their dreams attested to.

Final thoughts

Let me end by offering some hypotheses as to why CRS appears a useful method of enquiry.

First of all, by the very nature of how CRS is introduced and offered to the participants (by inviting volunteers, by asking for the sharing of recent or old dreams, and by offering a choice of how dreams can be used—not for therapy but to play with) dreams could be connected to the presented puzzle but do not necessarily need to be, resulting in a lighthearted and non-threatening atmosphere. The output of the reflection is in the shape of hypotheses and not interpretation. So, from the start, a divergent rather than convergent thinking is encouraged.

Furthermore, as no promises are made to resolve, dissolve, 'therapeutize', or eradicate the declared puzzle, the participants have no heightened expectations and are therefore more inclined to experiment with the dreams, associations, and new thinking.

To describe how CRS works, a metaphor of a broken mirror comes to mind: it does reflect reality, but in a different way. What it offers is not a one hundred per cent accurate full-size, copied version of reality, rather it is a myriad of new possibilities, shards of broken yet connected parts each containing similar elements of the reflected reality, but in a slightly new, oft unexpected configuration. Shards of broken mirror also offer a degree of distance; you do not hold the reflected reality as close as you do with an unbroken mirror. So that old reality can be deconstructed with a modicum of distance and playfulness and a collage of new possibilities can be thought of and this, once metabolized, can lead to potential new solutions and new meanings.

CHAPTER SIXTEEN

The priesthood of dreamers

Thomas A. Michael

> But you are a chosen race, a royal priesthood, a dedicated nation, a people claimed by God for his own.
>
> I Peter 2:9 REB

In 1520 Martin Luther cited this scripture to claim that the medieval belief that Christians were divided into two classes, spiritual and temporal, was a false teaching.

Since ancient times people had believed that an order of priests was required to mediate between the faithful and God. Following Luther, Protestants hold that the only mediator is Jesus, and that they constitute a priesthood of all believers. They maintain that all people can have direct access to the Almighty.

Gordon Lawrence has performed a similar, if more modest accomplishment, in his approach to dreaming. He suggested that we must move away from a politics of salvation, in which an expert mediates between the dream and the dreamer, to a politics of revelation (Lawrence, 2000: 165ff). A Social Dreaming Matrix, in which all participants are equal, functions as a priesthood of all dreamers. The use of such terms as 'salvation' and 'revelation', and the attraction of having no human mediator between the dreamer and the source of the dream, would resonate with modern-day Christians.

I started a Social Dreaming Matrix in a congregation of the United Presbyterian Church in the United States a little more than a decade ago. This Matrix meets once a month. In this essay I will describe some of the outcomes of this Matrix and its effects upon the life and mission of the church.

During our discussions the participants became curious about the relationship between our dreams and the dreams reported in the Bible. I searched the Bible to see if there were any themes that had also arisen in our Matrix. We also wanted to see if there were themes in our Matrix that are not reflected in the Bible. I have gone through the Bible and extracted out all of the dreams from Genesis to the letters of the Apostle Paul. In addition to the events that were specifically identified as dreams, I have included some visions that came in the night; however, I have not included those visions that appear to be more political or programmed. (These are located mostly in Ezekiel and the Revelation of John. The book of Revelation, the final book in the New Testament, is an elaborate cryptic description of the Roman world, in the manner of works written by novelists who must disguise their works because they labour in oppressive regimes.) What is left is a Social Dreaming Matrix with 33 dreams from the Old and New Testaments.

Martin Walker first suggested that all of the dreams in a Social Dreaming Matrix be thought of as a single dream. I decided to apply this idea to the dreams in the Bible. The result is a Social Dreaming Matrix that lasts for about 2,000 years, from the time of Abraham, who it is estimated lived between 2000 BCE (Before the Common Era) and 1700 BCE, and the Apostle Paul, who was an older contemporary of Jesus, and who is believed to have been killed by the emperor Nero in about 64 CE.

The first dream is recorded in Genesis 15:1–20. After a military campaign in which Abram, later to be called Abraham, helped some local kings, the word of the Lord came to him in a dream and said, 'Do not be afraid, Abram, I am your shield; your reward shall be very great' (NIV, 1984). God then promised that a son would be born to him even though he and Sarah were very old, and that he would be blessed and given land and his descendants would be as numerous as the sands on the seashore. God added that 'in you shall all families of the earth be blessed'.

In Genesis 28: 10–19 Abraham's grandson, Jacob, dreamed the well-known dream of the ladder. Angels went up and down the ladder from heaven to earth. Gordon Lawrence has written that:

> This dream shows Jacob that there is reciprocity between man on earth and the forces of creation. The dream is a ladder up and down which messengers (Angels) move, influencing both God and man. There can be communication between the God in the mind and man on earth. (Lawrence, 1998: 34)

In this dream the same promise was made to Jacob that his offspring will be like the dust of the earth; and again God added, 'Through you shall all the families of the earth be blessed.' Later, his son, Joseph, had dreams in which his sheaf of grain stood up and the sheaves of his brothers bowed down to it; and one in which the moon, the sun, and eleven stars bowed down to him.

The theme that runs through all of these dreams is that God has chosen certain people to carry out His purposes on earth. Even Laban, Jacob's father-in-law, when he realized that Jacob had fled with his flocks and wives (who were Laban's daughters), had a dream where God said to him, 'Take heed that you say not a word to Jacob, either good or bad' (Genesis 31:24, NIV, 1984).

In a similar vein, a boy named Samuel was servant to the Prophet Eli, and it was written, 'In those days the Word of the Lord was rare; there were not many visions' (I Sam 1:1, NIV, 1984). But the word came to this boy in a dream that God would punish Eli for the sins of his sons, and Samuel would take Eli's place as God's prophet.

An important feature of the idea that the Jews were the Chosen People of God is that they would be protected. But as this story of the accession of Samuel to be God's prophet shows, there is another element here. Soon after his first dream, Abram dreamed that the Lord said to him, 'Know this for certain, that your offspring shall be aliens in a land that is not theirs, and shall be slaves there, and they shall be oppressed for four hundred years' (Genesis 15:13, NIV, 1984). The reason for this is that the Amorites (a name that means, 'Westerners'), who already lived in the land of Canaan, were to be given 400 years to be straightened out or they would be driven out of the land that was promised to Abraham.

Of course, we know that this account achieved its final written form long after these events, probably about 400 to 500 BCE, so it may have been a literary device to explain the captivity in Egypt as well as the Babylonian captivity which occurred following the fall of Jerusalem in 589 BCE. The point is that though God promises to protect those whom He loves, he does require that they be ethical. It is not enough to worship. One must live a good, upstanding life. So the sons of Eli were passed over, and the children of Israel could be allowed to endure defeat and captivity.

But God is slow to anger. So Jacob could deceive his father-in-law, the Amorites could have four hundred years to rid themselves of evil, and earlier, Abraham was protected when he deceived Abimelech, a king, telling him that his wife, Sarah, was his sister. As a result, Abimelech intended to take her as his wife. However, God spoke to him in a dream and told him not to do so.

In addition to the dream given to Abimelech, there were other dreams attributed to kings and rulers. The Egyptian Pharaoh had a disturbing dream of seven fat cows that were devoured by seven thin and ugly cows and seven plump ears of grain swallowed up by seven thin ears of grain. Nebuchadnezzar of Babylon had a troubling dream of a great statue of gold, silver, and bronze with legs of iron and feet of clay, but a rock fell on the statue and shattered it and the rock became a huge mountain. In another dream a messenger came down from heaven and commanded him to cut down a huge tree and bind the stump and roots with iron. Then he was to live with animals and be given the mind of an animal. In the Christmas narrative of Matthew, the three kings were warned in a dream not to return to Herod to tell him of the location of the infant Jesus. And at the time of his trial, Pilate's wife told him to have nothing to do with Jesus, for she had had a troubling dream about him.

When Pharaoh and Nebuchadnezzar sought assistance from their advisors, they were not well served. These powerful rulers were forced to turn to Joseph or Daniel, who were known to be just men who spoke on behalf of God. It is ironic that the most powerful of men must be wary of entrusting their subordinates, so they must rely on their dreams. They have to rely on the un-thought known, since their advisors are likely to be self-serving, treacherous, or dishonest. Most humans can rely on those in positions of authority in our company or family or church, but when rulers look to someone above them in authority, there is no human being there. Rulers have troubling dreams and must rely on God. It is a theme that persists in the biblical Matrix.

Though the chosen people were expected to live exemplary lives and worship one God, they continued practices of primitive religion, including bloody sacrifices, even on occasion sacrificing their own children, cult prostitution, and worship of pagan gods.

A series of amazing prophets arose, describing their dreams and visions. Isaiah proclaimed this new vision in Isaiah 1:11–20 (NIV, 1984):

> The multitude of your sacrifices—what are they to me ... wash and make yourselves clean. Take your evil deeds out of my sight! Stop doing wrong, learn to do right! Seek justice, encourage the oppressed. Defend the cause of the fatherless, plead the case of the widow.

Zechariah, who lived two hundred years after Isaiah, had a similar dream: *There before me was a man riding a red horse! He was standing among the myrtle trees in a ravine. Behind him were red, brown, and white horses.*

A man standing in the trees said that they had gone through the earth and found it at peace. So God proclaimed that he would return to Jerusalem with mercy and would again comfort Zion. Afterwards, Zechariah dreamed that he saw four horns and then four craftsmen. The horns scattered Judah, Israel, and Jerusalem, but after seventy years the craftsmen built them up again. The prophets continued the theme that people chosen should be upright, but that God patiently forgives.

Joseph, the man who was entrusted to be the father of Jesus, was apparently a dreamer. First he was told in a dream not to divorce Mary. Then he was told in a dream to flee with his small family to Egypt to escape Herod's bloodthirsty slaughter of little boys, just as Jacob had been warned in a dream to flee from Laban, and Abraham to flee from his Aramean homeland in order that God's purpose for his people could be achieved.

Many scholars have suggested that the early Christians very conveniently read the scriptures to support their cause. These scholars suspect that the early Christians read into the events described in the Old Testament as prophesies that were fulfilled by the life of Jesus. It appears to me that what they were doing is similar to the process used in Social Dreaming. We hear a dream, and it sets our minds to thinking of associations and links to other experiences and thoughts. As different thoughts are expressed, we begin to form a shared perception of the dreams. What were formerly individual experiences hidden in the shades of night become open to everyone. From this we develop ideas about themes. We are developing our culture and directing our history of the future.

I have written about how Social Dreaming contributes to the creation of new cultures (Michael, 1998: 111). Three conditions must be met in order to make a change in culture: the change must be relatively enduring in order to develop a stable pattern of basic assumptions; there must be a shared experience and a shared pattern of perception; and there must be a means of uncovering unconscious processes to make them available for thought. These conditions are found in a Social Dreaming Matrix. I believe that these conditions were also met in the primitive Christian community. For the early Christians, it was a way to discern the word of God from all the words they had read.

They believed that the dream was from God when it was said:

> I have chosen you to fulfill my purpose on earth. You are to do justice and love mercy and walk humbly. You are to care for the oppressed and the poor and the widow and the orphan. Don't try to impress me with grand ceremonies. If you go astray, you will suffer for it. But I am a forgiving God, and I will forgive you.

They made links to Jesus, who taught these same ideas.

After the crucifixion of Jesus, this new approach to the faith of the people of Israel became embroiled in controversy. Paul was convinced that Gentiles could become followers of the Way, while Peter and James, the brother of Jesus, held that the only way to be a follower of Jesus was to observe all of the traditions of the Hebrew faith, including circumcision. Paul and Peter had a confrontation, and it was agreed that Paul should confine his efforts at proselytizing to outside of Israel. Then, as Peter was approaching the city of Joppa, he went up on the roof of the home where he was to have a meal, and apparently took a nap. In his vision he saw heaven open up and something that looked like a giant sailcloth was lowered to the earth by four corners. In it were all sorts of creatures, and a voice said, 'Get up, Peter, kill and eat.' He replied that he did not eat anything unclean or profane (he observed kosher laws). The voice said, 'It is not for you to call profane what God counts clean.' Soon after this dream he was asked to go the house of a Roman, Cornelius, and when he met him he said to him, 'I need not tell you that a Jew is forbidden by his religion to visit or associate with anyone of another race. Yet God has shown me clearly that I must not call anyone profane or unclean' (Acts 10: 9–23, NIV, 1984). Christians place great emphasis on Pentecost as the beginning of the Christian movement, but I believe that Peter's dream changed the Way of Jesus from a Jewish sect to a universal movement, and the early Christians could view their enterprise as fulfilling God's promise to Jacob and Abraham that through them all nations will be blessed.

The last dream recorded in the New Testament came to Paul when he was in Corinth. He continued to preach to both Jews and Greeks, arousing controversy among them. The Roman authorities were beginning to notice this, to them disturbing, movement. 'One night the Lord spoke to Paul in a vision. "Do not be afraid, keep on speaking, do not be silent. For I am with you, and no one is going to attack and harm you, because I have many people in this city"' (Acts 18: 9–10, NIV, 1984). The last dream in the Bible is like the first dream given to Abraham: do not be afraid. Keep on fulfilling the purpose of God.

I have identified three themes in this 'Bible Matrix', one is the theme that the dreamer is not to fear, because God promises to lead and protect him. The second is the universalization of God's purpose for the children of Israel. This universal purpose included a requirement that being merciful towards the weak, caring for widows and orphans, seeking justice, and being honest in dealings, were as important as proper worship. The third is the theme that kings and rulers cannot trust their own advisors. They are led to attempt to understand important issues by recourse to examining the meaning of their dreams.

Ancient rulers usually were afforded the status of gods. They ruled absolutely, capriciously, and ruthlessly. When their advisors were unable to interpret their dreams, the advisors were executed. These rulers were to be feared. They were not slow to anger. When the ancient peoples imagined what their gods must be like, they had as models their own rulers. Many of the Psalms speak of a God who could protect his people, and being victorious in battle, could command his armies to lay waste to the conquered foes and execute men, women, and children. He was a mighty ruler who was to be feared. The model they had was a god of fearsome wrath.

Yet 'Fear not' is a thread that runs throughout the narrative of the Bible. The God who was speaking through these dreams was not capricious and fearful, but one who encouraged the dreamers to live without fear of God or man.

Given the assurance of protection and the encouragement that they need not fear death, it is not surprising that a central tenet of the Christian message is the resurrection of Jesus and the promise to his followers of a similar resurrection. This idea did not originate with the Christians. Within Judaism, the two main groups were the Pharisees, who believed in a bodily resurrection, and the Sadducees, who did not. At first, the Christians were just another sect within Judaism. However, the crucifixion of Jesus struck great fear among his followers. It is easy to see why they would place so great an emphasis on the resurrection, and this could have enabled them to approach even death by torture with hope. The most succinct statement of this attitude was written by Paul in I Corinthians 15:55: 'Where, O death is your victory? Where, O death is your sting?' If we were to describe this change in attitude towards rulers and gods in terms of Social Dreaming, we could suggest that the early Christians made links and associations as they read the Hebrew Scriptures. It was not just a change in attitude, but a change in culture. Two questions arise in connection with the Social Dreaming in the Matrix I have been hosting in our church. First, do we find themes in our modern experience that can be linked to the Biblical themes? Second, have we experienced a culture change?

The greatest fear that humans have is the fear of death. The assurance given to Abraham, to Joseph, and to the Apostle Paul was that they need not fear death. Yet, of course, they have all died. Paul's death was particularly gruesome, and it is likely that he was tortured before he died. The death of Jesus on a Roman cross was the most horrible punishment they could devise. The cross was so horrifying that the earliest Christians could not bring themselves to depict it until the fifth century of the Common Era (Cahill, 1999: 285).

I have notes from thirty-eight meetings of the Matrix that has been happening in our church. Only one dream included an encounter with God: *I met God and he said we had it all wrong about Jesus and sin. I said, 'Well, Gee, Murray, that's a good idea.' He said, 'How did you know my name is Murray?'* (It might have been Marie.)

Our response was hilarious laughter. We had to encounter what might be a message from God through indirect means. This could be through dreams of friends and relatives who had died, or through other individuals who might be linked with the scripture accounts.

As I looked over the notes of the Matrix I was surprised to discover how often the dreams encouraged us to not be afraid. Most often these encouragements were spoken by recently deceased members of the congregation, or by family members: *I was back at work and a woman who had died brought a big pan of chicken and vegetables to take to a friend. I asked her if she was OK, and she replied, 'I'm in heaven,' and there was an unusual light.*

A dream reported to the Matrix from a young granddaughter of a beloved member who died unexpectedly was that on the night of her death the grandmother appeared to the girl and said, 'Everything is alright.' Another dreamer was in the church. He felt he had a sad place in his body, and four male friends were there. Three of these had died and he felt bad that he did not get to say goodbye to them. Then he dreamed *that his father-in-law, who had died four years previously, was there. He told him that it is good to see you; by the way, could you help me with a client?*

The congregation was shaken by the accidental traffic death of a very popular member. A dream had him in the church serving as an usher. *The dreamer was able to identify him because he was whistling in the same way that he had done so as he worked around the church as a volunteer sexton. The dreamer was initially frightened because he was dead, and another member said not to look at him. However, he said, 'Are you scared of me?' The dreamer answered, 'Yeah!' He responded, 'Come down with me.' And when the dreamer went down, there was an intricately carved pedestal (the dead man was a master carver), but he was gone.* The dreamer was aware that the deceased knew that he was dead. Another dream had the dreamer *in a great cocktail lounge decorated in the style of the 1950 s with aqua-coloured swivel chairs. Lots of people were there including her father and the pop singer Andy Williams.* All of them were dead, and all of them were charming and jovial. In all of these dreams the dreamers were helped to overcome fear by the deceased persons.

In addition to all of these visitations from the dead there were other dreams that suggested that there were no reasons for fear. There was a dream *of a huge, grassy field with a high fence around it. Everybody from the church was in it as if it were a concentration camp, but we were fine and nobody was trying to escape.* Another reported that *she was walking down slippery steps and her body felt as if it were shrivelling, but she was not afraid of dying.* Another dream had the person on a street with no sidewalk and a young friend teasing her. *A pile of gray gravel was coming at her but she was not all that scared and woke up pleased to have the inner power to face it.* One member summed it up by saying, 'I feel different when we do dreams here. I was here in the church this afternoon and I felt that I was not alone.' Another participant, who had once told of dreams of being stabbed in the stomach, reported in the Matrix several years later that he was no longer having anxiety dreams.

Though we never had a dream in which God said, 'Fear not,' it appears that we have absorbed this message. The dead are not so much frightening as friendly presences. We have no illusions that these are actual ghosts or visitors from beyond the grave. Instead, it appears that we have become participants in the culture that developed as a result of the Biblical Matrix.

This willingness to face death without fear found expression at the organizational level. A previous pastor had been told by a Presbytery official when he was called to the church that it would be his responsibility to help this dying congregation disband. By the time the present pastor arrived on the scene, the congregation had dwindled in size to just over 120 communicants. There was pressure to downsize the programme, dispense with parts of the music programmme, and try to live within the decreasing budget constraints. Church leaders decided instead to increase the programme and activities of the church. The congregation has increased in membership by adding numbers of younger families.

The second theme, that of the universalization of God's having chosen Israel so that all nations would be blessed, comes into play at this time. I have written previously about the Matrix that occurred just after the 9/11 tragedy (Michael, 2003: 142–156). After a period of several months the participants in the Matrix were able to 'move from a group to a Matrix in which it was possible for any one person to present a dream that could become available for all to own' (Ibid.: 152). Then a dream appeared to be related to the attacks on September 11, although it was set in Afghanistan: *The dreamer was running with a crowd of people. A man came by driving an ATV (All Terrain Vehicle). The dreamer got on, then got off in town, but realized that he should not have done that and began to run again. With that his feet lifted up behind him. He flew through a tunnel and ended up in front of the running mass* (Ibid.: 152). A link was made that 'We are dreaming for the Afghans,' who are so terrified that they cannot dream. With that we framed the hypothesis that the Social Dreaming Matrix was opening our eyes to the universality of the human experience. The statement by the Apostle Paul that:

> ... there is neither Jew nor Greek, male nor female, slave nor free was being enacted in our experience. The Matrix had from the beginning included participants of all ages, from people in their thirties to several past eighty. The men had come to understand the vulnerability that women live with daily. (Ibid.: 152).

A subsequent dream was about the church sanctuary. The Cross, which occupies a prominent place before an elaborate dossal, was replaced by the red heart in a Tiffany window above the dossal. The heart was much larger in the dream, and beside it were two faces looking toward it. They were beneficent and smiling.

As a result of these dreams, the church leaders adopted a statement that this is a 'church with a heart', and the weekly bulletin begins with a statement that 'we welcome you as an honored guest or a treasured member'. The leaders decided that if they were to disband, it would be with a complete programme. They hired a member to develop a new approach to the Sunday school programme. The choir director instituted a music programme for children from ages three through high school. Educational activities for adults were strengthened, and there were renewed efforts to help the homeless and the poor.

As a further result, there has been an influx of members with young children. A number of these are former Roman Catholics, same-sex couples and several Jewish persons who, while they have not formally joined the church, worship regularly and participate in the activities of the congregation. At the same time, while the congregation is theologically liberal, there are conservative members who are active and whose contributions are respected. The congregation has become more racially diverse.

This growth in numbers led to a concern that was discovered in the Social Dreaming Matrix. The new members were not well grounded in the principles and polity of the Presbyterian tradition, and many of them were newcomers to the community. Some of the more established members were concerned that the influx of newcomers might bring about unwelcome changes in the spirit and fellowship of the congregation. There were those who did not want the church to grow too large (a remarkable idea given the usual desire of most American Protestants to equate success with bigness). There had been some disagreements about the direction of some programmes, and this was, rightly or wrongly, attributed to the differences between new and longstanding members. The pastor reported a dream *in which he was the captain of a ship. There were two elephants on the ship, and both decided to stand up and rock the boat. He told them that if they did not stop he would have to send them off. He asked himself how he could actually do that, and he worried about how to feed them.* Another dream was about people in heaven who have *to use a phone booth to call earth, but they were fighting each other to get in the booth.* Other dreams involved *reconstructing rooms in the church basement or the parish hall, but they were being done incorrectly.*

These dreams led us to engage in frank discussions about our feelings toward newer members. Our attitudes and concerns were made available for thought, and we have found ways to integrate these new members into the community much more readily. As I write this, I am struck by the similarity between our experience and that of the early church in its controversy between the Judaizers who supported Peter and James and the followers of Paul who wanted to open the church to Gentiles as well as Jews.

Without our being aware of it, we do seem to have taken up themes from the Biblical Matrix. We have realized important elements of the teachings of Jesus. It would be impossible to say that Social

Dreaming was the only cause of these developments. We can only offer the working hypothesis that Social Dreaming can be a resource for deepening understanding of the faith, and can make it possible to strengthen the community. As practiced in this congregation, it does appear to have helped change the culture. One participant in the dreaming Matrix recently suggested that 'We are dreaming the church.'

In recent months, the Matrix has met, but the dreams do not appear to clarify any themes. I have wondered if the Matrix has come to the end of its usefulness, if we could use that term. Recently, I asked if, under these circumstances, we should stop. Nobody in the Matrix wanted to do so. One participant spoke for all when he said, 'This gives us the opportunity to have the most meaningful conversations we have ever had.' We are available for thought.

CHAPTER SEVENTEEN

The creative frame of mind

Gordon Lawrence and Susan D. Long

The purpose of this essay is to explore the mental posture, or frame of mind—phrases with sufficient common-sense meaning for enquiry—by examining the mental phenomena evoked subjectively when in the process of creative thinking. For this purpose we take the original meaning of creativity, that is, the bringing forward of new ideas through the courage to go beyond the existing and institutionalized domains of knowledge. This meaning has been diluted and nowadays the term 'creative' is applied to anything novel. There are, however, human beings who perform daring, creative acts, often outside of the confines of current thinking and discourse: the discovery of a scientific law, the authorship of new writing, the making of a poem, the configuration and striking image of a painting, or any work of art, for instance. These acts have special value for society and civilization. Yet, despite the plethora of research, the essential nature of creativity still lies beyond the grasp of scientific investigation, not quite able to encompass the combination of uniqueness of process and daring of endeavour involved.

We believe that the crucible of creativity lies outside of conscious, goal-oriented thinking. Although conscious thinking has a place insofar as creative products are integrated into culture, it is from another place that the creative spark comes. How that place is reached, or better, how it reaches us, is our concern and also with what frame of mind we entertain it. To develop our enquiry, we adopt ideas from systems theory, especially ideas of complex, chaotic systems together with ideas from psychoanalysis, in particular, the psychoanalytic thinking of Wilfred Bion.

We start with the essential idea that everything is connected to everything else. Only as thinking observers are separations made in all that is. It is from within the domain of the observer that descriptions arise and order our connections to nature and each other (Maturana, 1980). Thinking is powerful in that it orders the universe, but can it do more than observe and order? The connectedness of our biological being with our psychological mind has always been a mystery. Mind arises from body as an emergent phenomenon, but does mind affect body?

Since the 1990s neurobiological research has been pursuing the idea that the mind can act on the brain to cause physical changes (Begley, 2007). This metamorphosis can be furthered by thinking about thinking. The capacity of the human nervous system to detect its own patterns and processes and to discern whether these originate as perturbations from sensory phenomena, or within the system itself, are the essence of self-consciousness and produce an observer (Maturana, 1980). It is this recursive process that enables new patterns to develop—indeed infinity of new patterns despite the closed organization of the nervous system itself.

> A living system capable of being an observer can interact with those of its own descriptive states which are linguistic descriptions of itself. By doing so it generates the domain of self-linguistic descriptions within which it is an observer of itself as an observer, a process which can be necessarily repeated in an endless manner. (Maturana and Varela, 1980: 121)

But descriptions, language, and conscious discourse are not the only form of thinking:

> The neurophysiologic process that consists in its interacting with some of its own states as if these were independent entities

corresponds to what we call thinking ... thinking is a mode of operation of the nervous system that reflects functionally its internal anatomical projection (possibly multiply) onto itself ... *and* is necessarily independent of *natural* language. (Maturana, 1980; emphasis added)

The biologists Maturana and Varela give us some ways of thinking about how we think (Maturana and Varela, 1980). All living things are limited by the set of interactions possible for them. This sounds tautological but it is definitive. This closed set of interactions is its cognitive domain and this set creates its ecological niche. The possible interactions within an ecological niche are a closed and finite system, given Maturana's definition of life as autopoetic. Autopoetic means that a living system is defined as a system that creates the components that in turn create the processes that create them (the components) in a self-sustaining and self-reproducing manner. The cognitive domain is subservient to this autopoetic process, that is, cognition serves life. What is outside the niche cannot, by definition, be known. Humans, however, although equally limited as other organisms in their cognitive domain by their possible interactions, enter into linguistic and reflective interaction domains. This takes them to into self-consciousness.

There are two points of interest to note here. First, humans have a nervous system able to give rise to an observer who can discern its patterns of activity and to discern whether or not the pattern of nervous system activity is internally or externally initiated. This allows for the distinction between fantasy and reality, thinking and perception. The human nervous system, in its complexity, gives rise to consciousness and a human observer who makes the distinctions. It is this emergent observer in her domain who distinguishes, not the nervous system itself. That system cannot know such differences. It just is. This is a first paradox. It is the paradox of emergence where the observer is both of the nervous system, and yet transcends it. The difficulty is that in transcending it, the observer—a psychological entity—no longer intimately and immediately knows that from which it arose. There is a gap.

The human observer makes descriptions of what is observed and then interacts with these descriptions in an infinite regress. In other words, the human observer can extend his or her descriptions infinitely. This makes their cognitive domain and their thinking capacity theoretically infinite. We are observers of observers.

Second, in the domain of the observer, humans communicate by orientating each other toward their own nervous system activity. That is, communication involves directing others towards apprehension of their own minds rather than transmitting information. We all know the difficulties of communication and how misunderstandings frequently occur. What you think you heard that I said is not the same as what I think I said. But, the infinite is in our minds, accessed unconsciously, and we can direct each other to look there. When we do this together we extend our cognitive niche. We can recognize what is common to us and act together within that.

These two ideas: that we are observers of observers and that we communicate through orientating each other to observe ourselves, will become important to our argument about the frame of mind for creativity.

The nervous system, the mind (which is emergent from it) and the whole cultural domain (the psycho/biological niche of the mind as it were) are interlinked and co-evolve. The infinite patterns possible in the nervous system/mind/culture are only described through the discursive domain of the conscious observer. Their operation is independent and closed, recursive to itself. There is always a gap between what we can explain in discourse and what exists *in itself*.[1] But, is it possible that the spark of creativity jumps this gap if we find a state of mind to attend to what exists in itself (Hayles, 2000: 129)?

---

[1] There are differences among theories in the area of complex systems with regard to whether or not transcendence in cognition is possible. While Maturana and Varela believe that the observer is locked into a cognitive domain which includes descriptions of an environment, but that cannot be in contact with anything outside of itself—hence, we cannot know of any outside 'reality', or if indeed there is one, thus to talk of the reality of things in themselves is dubious—some later theorists dispute this. For example, Katherine Hayles (2000) says, 'language has a logical structure and part of that logical structure is to provide for a space for the unknowable and the unspeakable, even though paradoxically that space has to be provided within the linguistic domain'. See Niklas Nuhmann, N. Katherine Hayles, William Rasch, Eva Knodt and Cary Wolfe 'Theory of a Different Order: A conversation with Katherine Hayles and Niklas Nuhmann' in William Rasch and Cary Wolfe (2000) *Observing Complexity: Systems Theory and Postmodernity*, Minneapolis, University of Minnesota Press, p. 129.

Phenomenology of creativity and the unconscious infinite

We wish to explore the phenomenology of creativity. What is its state of mind? The linking of creativity on, the one hand, to madness and irrationality, and, on the other, to religious ecstasy or inspiration, has a long history. Early ideas about creativity linked it to madness. Both Plato and Aristotle saw the poet as 'inspired and, as it were, mad' (Plato, 1949 cited in Hatterer, 1965: 17). In the middle ages, St. Augustine considered creativity as divine inspiration, although by the seventeenth century the idea that creativity was natural and came from the human mind was well accepted and Leibnitz introduced the idea of unconscious inclinations in the mind. 'The discovery of musical proportions, he called unconscious arithmetic' (Ibid.: 18).

With Freudian psychoanalysis came the linking of creativity to eros and sexuality. For Freud, madness is avoided through the process of sublimation. Libido and sexual tension is transformed in creative endeavour. Freud's theories brought back the link of creativity with madness, and the predominance of libido theory in early psychoanalysis emphasized a traumatized picture of the unconscious mind, with creativity as the only healthy way out and the creative artist as one caught between past traumas and highly sublimated artistic devotion. Some later psychoanalytic writers moved toward understanding the role of the ego; Ernst Kris argued for the creative process as a regression in the service of the ego—a kind of going mad with a more rational purpose. The total creative process then became seen as involving a variety of mental states and an ability to move or be moved between different levels of consciousness. For example, Ehrenzweig describes the creative process in terms of moving between conscious focus and unconscious scanning as the artist, through projecting part of him/herself into his work enables the work to take on a life of its own. As this occurs, the artist must surrender to the process and become, for a time, ego-less (Ehrenzweig, 1967). But, how can we prepare ourselves to move through different levels of consciousness and awareness, especially when this involves surrendering ourselves to the unknown?

The phenomenology of mental experience leading to creativity, Polkingthorne describes:

> ... that there is a dimension to our minds more profound than that of the conscious rational ego seems clear to me.

> It is a common scientific experience that a period of intense but unsuccessful engagement with a problem, when followed by a fallow period in which unconscious processes are presumably at work can yield the sudden appearance into consciousness of the solution, fully formed, as it were by subterranean process.
> (Polkingthorne, 1996: 54)

After months of struggle Henri Poincarre found the answer to a mathematical problem just as he was stepping on to a bus for an expedition. Others have had a similar experience in lesser ways.

Mark Rothko (2004: 1), in his philosophy of art writes of 'the irrational quality of inspiration, [the] finding between the innocence of childhood and the derangement of madness that true insight which is not accorded to normal man'. Creativity begins with the irrational, irrespective of the form in which it is realized, whether that is a scientific discovery, an innovative engineering achievement, an original building, or a work of art. The creative well-springs that, finally, bring any of these artifacts to realization are located in the unconscious mind as it engages with the existence of the unknown of infinity (used in a poetical sense, not scientific).

The irrational arises from the unconscious which is pure primary process. It is timeless and eternal and without place and is, therefore, infinity. Symbolism it produces through displacement and condensation. It contains the juxtaposition of opposites that are paradoxical. Fantasy and reality are equivalent, which can be seen as the unreal and the real (Grotstein, 2001).

The unconscious mind, which holds sway during sleep, operates on logic that is totally different from the rationality of conscious awareness. Where in waking life asymmetrical logic is deployed, always distinguishing between words and concepts, in sleep symmetrical logic is used. The unconscious occurs when the finite sets of the conscious mind are relaxed (Matte-Blanco, 1975) and the rules of logic are suspended because the sleeper is temporarily ego-less. The 3Rs (reading, writing, and arithmetic) are prime examples of finite sets, operating on rules of logic, and common to all human beings, enabling them to communicate. Alternatively, the unconscious operates on infinite sets characterized by pure imagery, metaphor, and logic that is non-sequential. Images are juxtaposed asymmetrically while dreaming in an associative manner that could not be thought of while awake and conscious. It is in these bizarre, surreal juxtapositions that new thinking is heralded.

Although it is difficult to accept the unconscious as the fundamental source of creativity because it is unknown, horrendous, dreadful, and awesome to contemplate, it can be regarded as a positive element in human life because it always surprises and is the portal to the infinite. This is supported by the empirical evidence that the 'bright idea' comes from dreaming (Meier, 1984: 18). The problem in accepting this insight is that the experience of dreaming, when it is recalled, is diffuse, unclear, incoherent, surreal, and does not provide a clear map for the everyday puzzles or existential problems facing people in their society. Furthermore, as Freud (1900: 11) identified, 'There is at least in one spot in every dream which is unplumbable—a navel, as it were, that is its point of contact with the unknown.' This is the point at which we as observers reach our limits of observation. Language and its concepts fail us.

The matching of the dream to reality is no simple parallel because the infinite possibilities of the meanings of the dream have to be made through the use of free association and amplification of the narrative. The problem of the 'navel' may still exist. That which is implicated in the dream thinking can be illuminated, but this just reveals more that is connected. The dream is a source of creativity, is idiographic and experienced as accidental and contingent. It becomes a tangible idea that conforms to abstract universal principles in consciousness. Freud, in his revision of his theory of dreams, acknowledged that in addition to being a repository for unsatisfied wishes, the dream also was 'a particular form of thinking' (Ibid.: 506). This form of thinking, coming as it does from the illogical sets of the unconscious, is cryptic.

> Visual images become the best possible choice for the unconscious to reveal itself during sleep ... are used by the unconscious, instead of words, in order to create messages, like ideograms or symbolisms, but lack the exactness of written or spoken lexis. (Lopez-Corvo, 2006: 127)

That human beings live in a double reality, the internal world of unconscious phantasy, and the external one, is evident through subjective experience. Dreaming is one way that unconscious phantasy is tested against reality. Does daydreaming perform the same function? Not quite, because of the element of control in daydreaming. Dreaming, arising from sleeping, is never controlled or managed, and this is its supreme value—it belongs to the unconscious mind—which is why 'lucid' dreaming has to be treated with suspicion.

> Day dreaming, fantasizing, experimenting with different versions of reality in one's mind is part of normal functioning; it has both a 'research' function and a defensive, escapist one. We need both to survive. Longing for a more ideal world, a wish for a more perfect union with one's love object, in fact a search for the paradise lost of infant love is, I think, an essential aspect of human nature. (Sodre, 1999: 62)

Pathological daydreaming takes over the mind, and replaces natural life with something which is purely self-constructed and managed. It becomes an activity that can have deadly consequences. Ignes Sodre, in her discussion of Flaubert's novel, *Madame Bovary*, shows convincingly 'how the misuse of imagination can lead not just to the impoverishment of mental life, but to an active corruption and perversion … [demonstrating] in a most powerful way how death can be caused by daydreaming' (Ibid.: 62).

Although the extraordinary creative idea may originate in a dream, there is reluctance to admit this for it is embarrassing to acknowledge the irrational. Einstein was honest enough to admit that the solution to the general theory of relativity, after years of fruitless calculations, came from a dream: 'like a giant die making an indelible impress, a huge map of the universe outlined itself in one clear vision' (Brian, 1996: 159).

We argue that the 'bright idea' paradoxically comes both from outside of the system and yet also from inside it. It is outside insofar as it has previously been un-thought or un-enacted. It is inside, insofar as it comes from the unconscious infinite of possibilities potentially within us. Even if the 'bright idea' from dreaming can be disavowed, rejected, there is still the issue of how extraordinary creative thinking is made possible. How to prepare consciously for creative thinking? How the individual perceives the environment is relevant.

Modes of apprehending reality

The working hypothesis here is that being available for the 'bright idea' of the dream depends on the mode used by the individual to apprehend and experience reality.[2] Ernest Schachtel (1959) elaborated three such modes: (1) the auto centric; (2) secondary auto centricity; and (3) the allocentric. The first is the subjectively based modality; the third is grounded in objectivity. The second lies between these two. A mature individual can alternate consciously between these. Not only do these modes determine how the world and its objects are apprehended and perceived but they also structure how the world is presented and communicated to the perceiver.

The first mode, the auto centric, is governed by the needs of the individual such as hunger, thirst, and touch. It intimately involves the senses and is bounded by the pleasure-pain principle. It is essentially egocentric and the objects of the environment—people, animals, plants, and all natural features—are construed and responded to in terms of individual needs and desires. This mode is associated with the early stages of development.

In time, the individual acquires a secondary auto centricity which is the beginning of the glimmerings of the object as existing in its own right. This is paralleled by the acquisition of language, embedding the individual in his or her culture. The richness of the culture is transmitted through naming and classification. The individual acquires logical sets that define the nature of that culture. As the individual acquires these he or she has to relinquish direct experience of the objects that surround him or her because the very language used to describe them is socially constructed. Useful memory begins to supplant autobiographical memory. The freshness of childhood perception is replaced by the socially agreed, useful culture and language of the society.

---

[2] It is recognised here that by reality we refer to that which is real beyond the limited bounds of everyday observation. W. Rasch and C. Wolfe (2000) Introduction op. cit. point to the difficulties faced in postmodernity where positivistic realism is no longer tenable, but relativism too readily becomes the destroyer of meaning and slips to solipsism. They argue for a reworked representationalist framework to be found in systems and complexity theory as a rigorous theory for describing all systems.

Secondary auto centricity regards the environment and its objects in terms of their usefulness, their added-value. An equatorial forest, for example, is perceived as wood for building and for flooring, and as the raw material for paper-making. Its larger ecological significance is not perceived. The human observer in this mode apprehends his or her world in instrumental terms.

The most mature mode of perception, the allocentric, is to perceive the world and its objects in their fullness, irrespective of the personal feelings of the observer. It is to explore the object by sublimating ego-centricity to examine its 'being'. It is to grasp the reality of the object by transcending the definitions of natural language and culture. It is to be 'at-one' with the object, or phenomena, by having no 'I-ness' (being in a state of ego-lessness) so that everything can be perceived as if it had never been experienced before. Allocentric perception of an object is to take a *global* perspective in which the object as a whole is perceived both in its uniqueness and in its connectedness to everything else. This is to reach toward the infinite where all is connected to all in connections beyond those made by our limitations as observers.

How this can occur is a central issue for understanding creativity. Humans cannot transcend a domain from within that domain—for example, we cannot know what is outside language by using language to describe it. Organizations and cultures are closed cognitive systems unable to take in new knowledge, only able to be perturbed or disturbed by what is outside so that this disturbance makes them rethink from within the terms that they have available;[3] in Bion's (1970) terms, from within the establishment. Transcendence means moving out of the domain within which we normally operate. We believe that, in dreaming, a new set of interactions is possible—hence the niche of human existence is expanded. The dream accesses the unconscious infinite.

But, even when the call of the new idea touches us from, for instance, the dream, the fear of transcending the shared perspective

---

[3] W. Rasch 'Immanent Systems, Transcendental Temptations and the Limits of Ethics' in W. Rasch and C. Wolfe (2000) op. cit. It should be noted that, like Maturana and Varela we recognize that organizations and cultures are open to the importation of elements which they use in their autopoetic processes. It is their system of understanding and cognition that is closed.

of culture and consequently being left alone is the most powerful factor in preventing the allocentric perception of an object. The unknown experience of phenomena and objects in the environment can always be avoided by *not* thinking, *not* looking, by remaining locked in the familiar. Human beings, when presented with the new, are afraid that without their accustomed attitudes, perspective, and labels they will stray from the safety of their culture and fall into the abyss of the unknown.

One way of achieving allocentric perception is by way of Zen Buddhism when the individual attains enlightenment. This enlightenment is reached after a crisis that causes the individual to let go of his or her 'ego' with its thoughts, concepts, prejudices, desires, and involvement. This is prevented in some cultures and times because the social pressure of conformity is to stay firmly in the ego. This works against transcending the culture in which the individual is embedded. For example, Western thought has intellectual and linguistic conventions that reduce and generalize experiences—the finite sets.[4]

By contrast, the traditional Indigenous culture of Australia was able to achieve this allocentric mode of perception, or something akin to it, because of the Dreamtime. Dreamtime is the absolute ground of being or the fundamental universal continuum from which all differentiation arises, which is reinforced by traditional stories. The directly perceivable, which is synonymous with truth and reality, is made meaningful in the context of the Dreamtime. They each reflect the other. 'To designate the ultimate transcendent state as the Dreaming signifies to the Aboriginal that this "other world" is an intimate indispensable aspect of the tangible world, just as sleep and dreams are to the waking state.'[5]

Dreamtime has no equivalence in the Western thinking apparatus, but there is an unused multi-verse of dreaming waiting to be

---

[4] This culturally contrived conceptualization results from the actions of the physiological filtering mechanism of the brain, called reticular formation, which is strengthened as information from our senses is selected and reduced to fit our generalizing capacities.

[5] A.G.E. Blake (2007). Personal communication of Robert Lawlor's. *Voices of the First Day: Awakening in the Aboriginal Dreamtime.*

tapped. While anxieties can impede the reception of information to the mind, both from reality and dream, so can intellectual and linguistic practices, both of which might be re-thought and modified. Transcendence requires that we move to a niche shared with the other, even the other of natural objects; that we find ways into a totality currently beyond us.

Apprehending an object as a totality involves a total act of interest and a total turning to it. This turning towards the object with total interest is with contemplative attention, or what Zen Buddhism called 'right presence of mind'.

The poet Rilke gave much thought to the conditions in which an object will reveal itself to the poet, or artist.

> In order to have an object speak to you, you must take it for a certain time for the only one that exists, the only phenomenon which through your devoted and exclusive love, finds itself in the centre of the universe. (Schachtel, 1959: 225)

Rilke's method more suits the Western mind than the way of Zen Buddhism. The allocentric mode of perception is how we intuit the infinitude of the object under study. This is an act of imagining the object in infinity by willing ourselves into the same infinity. This is to dissolve the boundaries set up through the perspectives of particular observers and to connect to a larger system. It invokes faith.

Act of faith

How does the individual internalize a thinking attitude for apprehending the infinite? The most telling description of how one addresses the essence of an object is given by Bion (1970: 32) as he describes the 'act of faith' which he saw as the 'scientific state of mind'.

> It refers to a sense of experiencing the existence of reality and truth. Even though truth is not wholly reachable, comprehensible or amenable to being uttered or owned, its existence can be intuited and used … It is not the mystical posture it may seem but an acknowledgement that trained intuition can be developed and put into practice. It expresses a faith that truth exists. (Sandler, 2005: 292)

Faith denies in a disciplined way, memory, understanding, and desire (both derived from primary and secondary auto centricity modes of perception) in order to be available for thinking from K (processes of knowledge) to O (ultimate truth). The origins of these thought processes are found in the infant who, equipped with a pre-conception of breast, searches for a real breast to match it. This matching is only possible when the baby can tolerate the 'no-breast' as part of experience. 'It must evolve before it can be apprehended … when it is thought just as the artist's O is apprehensible when it has been transformed into a work of art' (Bion, 1970: 31).

The ability to be at-one with O requires faith in an ultimate reality and truth (*noumena*), the unknown and the unknowable, the formless infinite.

> This must be believed of every object of which the personality can be aware: the evolution of ultimate reality (signified by O) has issued in objects of which the individual can be aware. The objects of awareness are aspects of the 'evolved' O and are such that the sensuously derived mental functions are adequate to apprehend them. For them faith is not required. For O it is.
> (Bion, 1970: 31)

Thought processes

Both the mode of perception and the act of faith are ways in which humans offer themselves as containers for experience as they make themselves available for the transformation of raw experience into contained thinking and thought. Bion (1970) offers a model of what takes place in the mind. Thoughts and feelings are transmitted to the human mind through the experiences both of sensory and non-sensory data or information. The non-sensory experiences are difficult for the Western mind to entertain because this culture is more suited and accustomed to processing sensory data, or at least to attending to and observing sensory data.

While the human mind can be defended against the anxiety of the meaning of sensory data, it is most surely defended against the meaning of non-sensory material, based on the terror of the uncertain and the unknown, which makes for an intolerance of doubt and uncertainty. Madness and psychosis beckon when the individual goes beyond the culture that makes sense of their being and existence.

Raw sense data can be understood to be Beta-elements (Bion, 1967: 100–120). Such elements are only suitable for projection on to other objects and phenomena in the environment, and never for thinking. Such elements are full of nameless dread and render inchoate the individual. They are bizarre objects and remain undigested. As raw material though, they can be apprehended sensuously and can be decoded into elements that are suitable for thinking and dreaming. When they are deciphered by the mind they become Alpha-elements.

The mind is essential for this transformation. The intricate link between thoughts and mind is seen in Bion's (1992) formulation.

> For Bion thoughts require a thinker, that is to say, a mind, a place where thinking can happen to thoughts. The experience of discovering, is linked to, or the other side of the coin, having a mind. Both arise together. (Hinshelwood, 2003: 184)

The vulnerability of the apparatus of the mind in this process of transformation is affirmed by Bion who writes:

> The existence of the real objects can be denied, but the sense impressions persist … The next stage, imposed by yet more powerful intolerance, is the destruction of the apparatus that is responsible for the transformation of the sense impressions into materials suitable for waking unconscious thought—a dream thought. This destruction contributes to the feeling that 'things', not words or ideas, are inside. (Bion, 1992: 134)

When Beta-elements become Alpha-elements through the alpha-function of the mind, they can be used, provided that the mind is not destroyed through the incapacity to tolerate reality. Thinking requires the experience of no-thinking. The act of thinking changes the thinker because it affects the patterns of neural activity in the brain.

Thinking takes different forms. It could be said that intuition is the capacity to observe, discern, and describe those neural processes stimulated from within the inner patterns of nervous system activity—Bion's (1970) non-sensuous thinking, while scientific logic, that is, deduction and induction, is the capacity to work with the thinking initiated through sensory experience. Although, in reality, intuition and logic actually co-evolve and work together in apprehending both the sensuous and non-sensuous. This is all possible except where such thinking capacities are attacked and links destroyed.

Negative capability

The mind can be prepared for thinking by what Keats called 'negative capability'. When the individual 'is capable of being in uncertainties, mysteries, doubts, without any irritable reaching after fact & reason', he or she is in a state of negative capability (Bion, 1970: 90). French and Simpson (1999: 216–230) argue that their best work in consultancy happens when they don't know what their doing, and provide examples to illustrate this from their work. Key elements are the acts of 'waiting', or 'listening'. They quote Eigen (1981: 326), 'an attitude of pure receptiveness … an alert readiness, an alive waiting'. The waiting is for the emergence of the new patterns that come from the alert study of the object or phenomena. This involves listening to the silence in the encounter with objects. But, it also involves alertness to the interior world and to the patterns of thought that emerge from contact with the object. This echoes allocentric perception.

Curiosity

Another condition of availability for extraordinary creative thought is curiosity. This is derived from the epistemophilic instinct, identified by Melanie Klein in her work with babies. The search for knowledge is associated with life-giving forces. It starts with curiosity about the sexual organs in infancy and is transformed into curiosity about the mind and proceeds to a curiosity about the external world. This can be either scientific or artistic. The individual who as a mature individual can hold on to his or her sense of curiosity is well placed to acquire an allocentric mode of perception, the ability to act in faith by having a developed sense of awareness for searching for truth. The curiosity of a child is critical for the development of new knowledge derived from the infinite (cf Rothko, 2004).

Imagination

Imagination is another mental phenomenon in creativity. Etymologically it derives from 'making images'. At one level it can be used for flights of fancy, but it is really about the application of common-sense to the experience of phenomena. The transcendence of events and objects, even their mystical qualities, has to be treated with scientific method. Bion (1992) eschewed the idea that imagination should exist independently of fact by re-affirming common-sense. Observation was to be used in conjunction with the scientific method to arrive at truth, to facilitate the transformation of thinking.

By attempting to imagine an event, or object, **in** infinity, provides us with a dilemma. To imagine is to envisage something not in our immediate presence. It has to be viewed in terms of common-sense by being reality tested in empirical terms to avoid the traps of solipsism and idealism. Yet, imagining the object in the wholeness of creation, beyond immediate experience and beyond what is *known* is to see it as it is. The use of the imagination implies being available for intuition—the faculty of knowing without the use of deductive and inductive rational processes. The twentieth-century philosopher David Pearce (1992) argues that intuition uses abductive logic—a different kind of thinking based on association rather than linear deduction or empirical induction. This associative thinking echoes the activity of the nervous system that is self-referential and self-stimulated rather than that derived from the perturbations of sensuous perception.

What impedes intuition, and imagination, is institutionalized and sterile memory and desire; programmed thinking repeating old patterns. These can be avoided through mental discipline.

Infinity matters

The unconscious and infinity have been used here synonymously, based on Bion's (1965: 181) formulation that the unconscious is 'won from the void and formless infinite'. Perhaps, it would be better to refer to the individual as having unconscious processes but when the individual is joined by others, the term 'infinite' might be more apt in that it is available to all humanity.

Thomas Henry Huxley (1887: 204) described a near century ago that intellectually we stand on an islet of the known in the midst of an ocean of inexplicability which is the unknown infinite. The task of every generation is to reclaim more from the infinite; even though there is a paradox in this, in that as this is done the infinite itself expands.

The term infinite comes in three flavours, according to John Barrow. First and second are mathematical infinity and that of the physical universe. The third flavour:

> ... is the most familiar, the most controversial, and the least amenable to investigation. To some it is a matter of faith, to others a state of mind, and to most others a harmless mystical feeling about the Universe that does not have any real impact on the here and now. This is what we might call transcendental, or ... absolute infinity. It is the cosmic encompassment of everything. (Barrow, 2005: 110)

This flavour of infinity (the poetic) most closely approximates Bion's 'O', the absolute, the *noumenon*, the thing-in-itself, the unknowable. To partake of this infinity does not mean to reach beyond ourselves. The transcendence required is to move beyond our usual ways of encountering what is already in us. Infinity is in the mind but it is in struggling with its existence there that finite knowledge is realized.

What distinguishes humans from the animal world is their ability to observe their own process (through both empirical observation and intuition) while having all of their senses open towards the infinite world with its numberless aspects. In this they have the capacity to constantly explore new terrain, new ways of relating to objects in their inexhaustible being, without auto centrically remaining embedded in the known culture and self for reassurance.

The question that leads us to infinity is, 'Who or what are you who are part of the same world of which I am a part?' This question concerns the *totality* of the object as part of the organic and systemic *whole* of life.

Grappling attentively with the infinite of natural objects has led scientists to new discoveries. The observable universe was once interpreted from a Newtonian perspective, but Einstein overthrew it with his special relativity theory. The discoveries of quantum physics gave us not only a new understanding of the nature of the universe, but also of our roles as observers in that universe. Observation of dissipative structures and spontaneous systemic self-organization challenges the idea of necessary entropy in systems. These discoveries expose hidden aspects of the infinite flux. They were brought into existence as scientists probed beyond the surface of immediately observable phenomena, drawing new distinctions.

> What the theory of observation holds, then, is that the world is not given—as in the traditional representationalist frame—tbut is rather brought forth in the dynamic interaction of observer observed ... Since that bringing forth takes place by means of paradoxical distinctions, it means, as Maturana and Varela put it, that, 'every world brought forth necessarily hides its origins. By existing we generate cognitive "blind spots" that can be cleared only by generating new "blind spots" in another domain.'[6]

It is the dynamic interplay that is creative. The blind spots are that which is unconscious whenever a new distinction is made. The infinite becomes apparent through actively imagining the object by the suspension of narcissism or auto-centric perception, whatever one knows, ridding oneself of memory and desire to be free to intuit what might be its truth.

Thinking alone, thinking together

But how is the extraordinary creative leap made possible? The idea of the genius working alone to produce a creative insight or artifact is questionable. Ideas do occur at the same time to different individuals. What happens is that the infinite, that which is implicate in the universe of what is, becomes available for thinking. The cognitive niche is extended to include that which was hitherto outside it—through access to the infinite. The field of possible interactions is amplified. How? It is through the contact with dream. Humans hold in common the ability to dream, whether acknowledged or not.

---

[6] Rasch, W. and Wolfe, C. (2000). Eds. Introduction. In: *Observing Complexity: Systems theory and post modernity*. Minneapolis: University of Minnesota Press. p. 13. They quote Maturana and Varela *The Tree of Knowledge, the Biological Roots of Human Understanding* Rev. ed. Boston Shambala, 1992.

We cannot *not* dream, even if, in waking life, we do not remember those dreams. Our hypothesis is that dream provides the link between the conscious observer (embedded in his or her systems of language and culture) and the unknown, spontaneously organizing system of thinking that is the human ecological niche.

Moreover, dream is a shared manner of creation waiting to be realized. Although dreaming tends to be construed in terms of the individual, Social Dreaming takes a different starting point in that it is done simultaneously with many people. It takes place in a Matrix, not a group, focusing on the allocentricity of the dream and **not** the dreamer).[7] What happens is that the infinite sets of the mind are agitated, or excited, by the dreaming, and in contemplating the dream in consciousness (the Matrix), by using free association and amplification, new thinking is made available. There is a point in a Social Dreaming Matrix when the unconscious minds of the participants begin to resonate. The dream of one perturbs the dreams of others, so that each is re-oriented toward the unconscious shared infinite where the possibility of new insight, understanding, and knowledge can be realized.

Conclusion

In this essay, an attempt to understand creativity has been made by focusing on the state of mind required in the process of creation. We argue that the 'bright idea' paradoxically comes both from outside of the system and yet, from inside. It is outside, insofar as it has previously been unthought or un-enacted. It is inside, insofar as it comes from the unconscious infinite of possibilities potentially within us. Thinking about thinking is part of the recursive domain of the human as observer. Yet as observers, we are limited by our language and culture. True creativity only occurs when we transcend these limitations. But how? The allocentric mode of perceiving provides stimulation that can be transformed into thinking and dream by means of

---

[7] Lawrence, W.G. (1998). *Social Dreaming @ Work*. London: Karnac Books; (2003) *Experiences in Social Dreaming*. London: Karnac Books; (2005) *Introduction to Social Dreaming: Transforming Thinking*. London: Karnac Books; (2007) *Infinite possibilities of Social Dreaming*. London: Karnac Books.

the Alpha function. These thought processes become conscious and accessible by means of the personal unconscious, dreaming, 'negative capability', imagination, curiosity, intuition, faith, and the infinite. One working hypothesis is that dreaming is the pivot of creativity (the bright idea), whether acknowledged or not.

BIBLIOGRAPHY

Altan, F. and Forni, E. (2005). *La prospettiva del ranocchio*. Torino: Bollati Boringhieri.
Ambrosiano, L. (2003). La scoperta del Social Dreaming. In: Lawrence, W.G. a cura di *Esperienze nel Social Dreaming*. Roma: Edizioni Borla s.r.l.
Armstrong, D. (1998a). Introduction. In: Lawrence, W.G. Ed. *Social Dreaming at Work*. London: Karnac Books.
Armstrong, D. (1998b). Thinking aloud: contributions to three dialogues. In: Lawrence, W.G. Ed. *Social Dreaming @ Work*. London: Karnac Books.
Armstrong, D. (2005). *Organization in the Mind*. London: Karnac Books.
Arnheim, R. (1997). *Visual Thinking*. London: University of California Press, Ltd.
Baglioni, L. (2002). Associazioni e riflessioni sul 'Social Dreaming'. *Funzione Gamma Magazine*, 10. Mito, sogno e Gruppo due. http://www.funzionegamma.edu
Baglioni, L. (2004). Disturbi della regolazione affettiva: fra sopravvivenza e sviluppo tollerabile nel gruppo omogeneo. In: Corbella S., Girelli, R. and Marinelli, S. (a cura di). *Gruppi Omogenei*. Roma: Edizioni Borla s.r.l.

Balamuth, R. (2003). Childreamatrix: dreaming with preschool children – or, bootlegging dreams into the school years. In: Lawrence, W.G. Ed. *Experiences in Social Dreaming*. London: Karnac.
Barrow, J.D. (2005). *The Infinite Book*. London: Jonathan Cape.
Bateson, G. (2000). *Steps to an Ecology of Mind*. Chicago and London: University of Chicago Press.
Begley, S. (2007). How Thinking can Change the Brain. *Wall Street Journal*. [http://online/wsj.com/article/SB116915058061980596.html]
Beradt, C. (1968). *The Third Reich of Dreams*. Chicago, IL: Quadrangle Books.
Bergner, M. et al. (1981). The Sickness Impact Profile: Development and final revision of a health status measure. *Medical Care*. 19. 787–805.
Bion, W.R. (1961). *Experiences in Groups*. London: Tavistock Publications.
Bion, W.R. (1965). *Transformations*. London: William Heinemann, Medical Books.
Bion, W.R. (1967). *Second Thoughts*. London: William Heinemann, Medical Books.
Bion, W.R. (1970). *Attention and Interpretation*. London: Tavistock Publications.
Bion, W.R. (1979). Making the best of a bad job. In: *Clinical Seminars and Other Papers*. London: Karnac Books.
Bion, W.R. (1987). *Clinical Seminars and Four Papers*. Abingdon: Fleetwood Press.
Bion, W.R. (1992). *Cogitations*. London: Karnac Books.
Bion, W.R. (1997). *Two Papers: The Grid and the Caesura*. London: Karnac Books.
Bion, W.R. (2000). Making the Best of a Bad Job. In: Bion, F. Ed. *Clinical Seminars and Other Works*. London: Karnac Books.
Biran, H. (2007). The Dreaming Soldier. In: Lawrence, W.G. Ed. *Infinite possibilities of Social Dreaming*. London: Karnac Books.
Blake, A.G.E. (2007). Personal communication of Robert Lawlor's.*Voices of the First Day: Awakening in the Aboriginal Dreamtime*.
Blake, W. (1979). In: Yeats, W.B. Ed. *The Poems of William Blake*. London and Henley: Routledge and Kegan Paul.
Bollas, C. (1987). *The Shadow of the Object*. London: Free Association Books.
Bonnerup, B. (2009). Personal Communication.
Borwick, I. (1997). *Group Study and Action Program*. New York: Borwick International.

Bosnak, R. (2007). *Embodiment: Creative imagination in Medicine, Art and Travel.* Hove, W. Sussex: Routledge.

Brian, D. (1996). *Einstein: A Life.* Chichester: John Wiley and Sons.

Briggs, J. and Peat, D. (2000). *Seven Lessons on Chaos.* New York: HarperCollins Publishers.

Brunning, H. (2006). *Executive Coaching-Systems Psychodynamic Perspective.* London: Karnac Books.

Cahill, T. (1999). *Desire of the Everlasting Hills: The World before and after Jesus.* New York: Anchor Books.

Claxton, G. (2006). *The Wayward Mind: An Intimate History of the Unconscious.* London: Abacus.

Correale, A. (1999). *Il campo istituzionale.* Roma: Borla s.r.l.

Darwin, C. (1887). Ed. The Life and Letters of Charles Darwin. Vol. 2. *On the Reception of the Origin of Species.* London: John Murray.

Di Donato, R. (2004). *Appunti di dotta ignoranza.* Pescara: ASSIR.

Ehrenzweig, A. (1967 reprinted 1993). *The Hidden Order of Art: A Study in the Psychology of Artistic Imagination.* London: Weidenfeld & Nicolson.

Eigen, M. (1981). Towards Bion's starting point: Between catastrophe and faith. *International Journal of Psycho-Analysis.* 66. 321–30.

Fernandez-Armesto, F. (1997). *Truth.* London: Bantam Press.

Francescato, D., Tomai, M. and Ghirelli, G. (2002). *Fondamenti di psicologia di comunità.* Carocci.

Frankl, G. (1979). *The Social History of the Unconscious.* London: Open Gate Press.

French, R. and Simpson, P. (1999). Our Best Work Happens When We Don't Know What We're Doing. *Socio-Analysis.* 1: 2. 216–230.

Freud, S. (1900). *The Interpretation of Dreams.* Translated by J. Strachey. Standard Edition Vol. IV. London: Hogarth Press.

Fubini, F. (2002). Sogni in cerca di un sognatore, *Funzione Gamma Magazine,* 10. *Mito, sogno e Gruppo due.* http://www.funzionegamma.edu

Gaburri, E. and Ambrosiano, L. (2003). *Howling with the wolves.* Turin: Bollati Borringhieri.

Gittings, R. (1970). Ed. *The Letters of John Keats: A Selection.* Oxford: Oxford University.

Gold, S. (1999). The sane madness of vital truth. *Psychoanalytic Studies.* 1:4. 435–446.

Goleman, D. and Kaufman, P. (1992 reviewed 2007). The Art of Creativity. In: *Psychology Today Magazine.*

Gordon, R. (1978 reprinted 2000). *Dying and Creating: A Search for Meaning*. London: Karnac.
Gray, J. (2002). *Straw Dogs*. London: Granta Books.
Grotstein, J.S. (2001). *The Unconscious, The Infinite, and God*. San Francisco: Paper presented to the Deep Springs Institute.
Grotstein, J.S. (2007). *A Beam of Intense Darkness*. London: Karnac Books.
Hahn, H. (1998). Dreaming to learn: pathways to rediscovery. In: Lawrence, W.G. Ed. *Social Dreaming @ Work*. London: Karnac Books.
Hartmann, E. (2000). The Psychology and Physiology of Dreaming. In: Gamwell, L. Ed. *Dreams 1900–2000*. Ithaca, NY: Cornell University Press.
Hatterer, L.J. (1965). *The Artist in Society*. New York: Grove Press.
Hayles, K. (2000). A conversation with Katherine Hayles and Niklas Nuhmann. In Rusch, W. and Wolfe, C. Eds. *Observing Complexity Systems: Theory and Postmodernity*. Minneapolis: University of Minnesota.
Heaney, S. (2001). Out of the bag. In: *Electric Light*. London: Faber and Faber.
Hinshelwood, R. (2003). Group Mentality and 'Having a Mind'. In: Lipgar, R. and Pines, M. Eds. *Building on Bion: Roots*. London and New York: Jessica Kingsley Publishers.
Holy Bible, New International Version. (1973, 1978, 1984). Grand Rapids, MI: Zondervan.
Howard-Jones, P.A. and Murray, S. (2003). Ideational Productivity, Focus of Attention and Context. In: *Creativity Research Journal*. 15: 2 & 3. 153–166.
Hunt, S., J. McEwan, and McKenna, S. (1989). *The Nottingham Health Profile: Users manual*. Revised edn. Dover, NH: Croom Helm.
Huxley, T.H. (1887). On the reception of the origin of species. In Darwin, C. Ed. *The Life and Letters of Charles Darwin*. Vol. 2. London: John Murray.
Irvin, P. (2003). *Directing for the Stage*. Switzerland: RotoVision SA.
Kapuscinski, R. (2001). *The Shadow of the Sun: My African Life*. Harmondsworth: Penguin.
Knight, R. (1980). *Edwin Muir: An Introduction to his Works*. London: Longman.
Laplanche, J. and Pontalis, J-B. (1988). *The Language of Psychoanalysis*. London: Karnac.

Lawrence, W.G. (1979). A Concept for Today: The Management of Self in Role. In: Lawrence, W.G. Ed. *Exploring Individual and Organizational Boundaries*. Chichester: John Wiley & Sons. Reprinted (1999) by Karnac Classics.

Lawrence, W.G. (1998a). *Social Dreaming @ Work*. London: Karnac Books.

Lawrence, W.G. (1998b). Prologue. In: Lawrence, W.G. Ed. *Social Dreaming @ Work*. London: Karnac Books.

Lawrence, W.G. (1998c). Social dreaming as a tool of consultancy and action research. In: Lawrence, W.G. Ed. *Social Dreaming @ Work*. London: Karnac Books.

Lawrence, W.G. (1998d). Won from the void and formless infinite: Experiences of social dreaming. In: Lawrence, W.G. Ed. *Social Dreaming @ Work*. London: Karnac Books.

Lawrence, W.G. (2000). The politics of salvation and revelation in the practice of consultancy. In: Lawrence, W.G. Ed. *Tongued with Fire: Groups in Experience*. London: Karnac Books.

Lawrence, W.G. a cura di. (2001). *Social Dreaming: funzione Sociale del Sogno*. Roma: Borla s.r.l.

Lawrence, W.G. (2001). Il sogno sociale come strumento di consulenza e ricerca-intervento. In: Lawrence W.G. a cura di. *Social Dreaming: la funzione sociale del sogno*. Roma: Edizioni Borla s.r.l.

Lawrence, W.G. (2002). Social Dreaming, *Funzione Gamma Magazine*, 10. Mito, sogno e Gruppo due. http://wwwfunzionegamma.edu

Lawrence, W.G. Ed. (2003a). *Experiences in Social Dreaming*. London: Karnac Books.

Lawrence, W.G. (2003b). Narcissism v. Social-ism Governing Thinking in Social Systems. In: Lipgar, R. and Pines, M. *Building on Bion: Branches*. London: Jessica Kingsley Publishers.

Lawrence, W.G. (2005). *Introduction to Social Dreaming*. London: Karnac Books.

Lawrence, W.G. (2006). Executive Coaching, Unconscious Thinking and Infinity. In: Brunning, H. Ed. *Executive Coaching Systems: Psychodynamic Perspective*. London: Karnac Books.

Lawrence, W.G. Ed. (2007). *Infinite possibilities of Social Dreaming*. London: Karnac Books.

Lawrence, W.G. (2007a). Creative Role Synthesis. Unpublished paper for the D10 Alumni Group.

Lawrence, W.G. (2007b). Dream Reflection Group. In: Lawrence, W.G. Ed. (2007). *Infinite Possibilities of Social dreaming*. London: Karnac Books.

Lawrence, W.G., Bain, A. and Gould, L. (1996). The fifth basic assumption. *Free Associations.* 6, 1:37, 28–55.
Lawrence, W.G., Maltz, M. and Walker, E.M. (1998). Il sogno sociale. In: Lawrence, W.G. a cura di. *Social Dreaming: la funzione sociale del sogno.* Roma: Borla s.r.l.
Lawrence, W.G. and Biran, H. (2002). The Complementarity of Social Dreaming and Therapeutic Dreaming. In: Neri, C., Pines, M. and Friedman, R. Eds. *Dreams in Group Psychotherapy.* London: Jessica Kingsley.
Lawrence, W.G., Baglioni, L. and Fubini, F. (2004). Il Seminario Internazione, Social Dreaming: funzione sociale del sogno e pensiero creativo, *Università di Roma 'La Sapienza',* Orto Botanico, 20-21-22 maggio.
Lawrence, W.G., Baglioni, L. and Fubini, F. (2006). Il Seminario Internazione, Social Dreaming: funzione sociale del sogno e pensiero creativo, *Università di Roma 'La Sapienza',* Orto Botanico, 8–9 giugno.
Lazar, R. and Lohmer, M. (2000). A Search for New Partners ... or an Invitation to a Harem? Paper presented to ISPSO Symposium in Paris. (Archives of the ISPSO.)
Lewis, C. Day (1969). *The Collected Poems of Wilfred Owen.* London: Chatto & Windus. p. 110. Draft of a fragment in BM.
Lopez-Corvo, R.E. (2006). *Wild Thoughts Searching for a Thinker.* London: Karnac Books.
Lopez-Rey, J. (1953). *Goya's Caprichos: Beauty, reason and caricature.* Vol. I. Princeton, NJ: Princeton University Press.
Martindale, C. (1995). Creativity and Connectionism. In: Smith, S.M., Ward, T.B. and Finke, R.A. Eds. *The Creative Cognition Approach.* Chapter 11. USA: Massachussetts Institute of Technology.
Martindale, C. and Hasenfus, N. (1978). EEG difference as a function of creativity, stage of creative process, and effort to be original. *Biological Psychology.* 6. 157–167.
Matte-Blanco, I. (1975). *The Unconscious as Infinite Sets.* London: Duckworth.
Maturana, H. (1980). The Biology of Cognition. In: Maturana, H. and Varela, F. Eds. *Autopoesis and Cognition: The Realization of the Living.* Holland: D. Reidel Publishing Co.
Maturana, H. and Varela, F. (1980). *Autopoesis and Cognition: The Realization of the Living.* Holland: D. Reidel Publishing Co.
McDuff, D. (1984). *Edith Södergran: The Complete Poems.* [trans., p. 63]. Newcastle upon Tyne: Bloodaxe.

Mednick, S.A. (1962). The associative basis of the creative basis. *Psychological Review*. 69. 220–232.
Meier, C.A. (1984). *The Unconscious in its Empirical Manifestations*. Boston: Saga Press.
Michael, T.A. (1998). Creating new cultures: the contribution of social dreaming. In: Lawrence, W.G. Ed. *Social Dreaming @ Work*. London: Karnac Books.
Michael, T.A. (2003). Deep calls unto deep: Can we experience the transcendent infinite? In: Lawrence, W.G. Ed. *Experiences in Social Dreaming*. London: Karnac Books.
Neri, C. (2002). Introduzione al Social Dreaming e resoconto di due workshop tenuti a Rissa e Clarice Town, *Rivista di Psicoanalisi*, anno XLVIII, 1.
Neri, C. (2003). Social Dreaming: Report on the workshops held in Mauriburg, Raissa and Clarice Town. In: Lawrence, W.G. Ed. *Experiences in Social Dreaming*. London: Karnac Books.
Oeser. F. (2005). *Bunyip Stories*. London: The Sicnarf Press.
Oeser, F. (2008). *Reflections: Aspects of the Unconscious*. London: The Sicnarf Press. pp. 73–74.
Oeser, F. (2010). *Changes*. London: Sicnarf Press.
Ortona, D., Planera, E. and Selvaggi, L. (2007).Vous êtes embarqué: Social Dreaming with a group of political Refugees. In: Lawrence, W.G. Ed. *Infinite possibilities in Social Dreaming*. London: Karnac Books.
Oxford Reference Dictionary (1987). London: Guild Publishing.
Pearce, D. and Wansing, H. (1992). *Nonclassical logic information processing*. Berlin: Springer-Verlag.
Perini, M. (2000). L'analisi delle organizzazioni secondo il modello Tavistock, *Il Nodo Group, Pubblicazioni psycomedia*. http://www.psycomedia.it
Pines, M. (1977). Prospect of group analysis. In: *Group Analysis*. 10:1. 49–55.
Polkingthorne, J. (1996). *Beyond Science*. Cambridge: University Press. Canto edn.
Rasch, W. and Wolfe, C. (2000). *Introduction, Observing Complexity: Systems Theory and Postmodernity*. Minnesota, MN: University of Minnesota Press.
Ravenna, A.R. and Todino, B. (1998). Verso una società interculturale: La Gestalt come modello di integrazione sociale interattiva. *Rivista Babele*. Numero 9.

Revised English Bible: With Apocrypha (1996). Cambridge: Cambridge University Press.
Ricci, P. (2003). Salute e qualità della vita: quali servizi per fornire risposte adeguate ai bisogni individuali, *Convegno 'Governare il sistema salute'* – 6 maggio. Roma: Istituto Italiano di Medicina Sociale.
Roberts, V.Z. and Brunning, H. (2007). Psychodynamic and Systems-Psychodynamic Coaching. In: Palmer, S. and Whybrow, A. Eds. *Handbook of Coaching Psychology: A Guide for Practitioners*. London: Routledge.
Rothko, M. (2004). *The Artist's Reality*. New Haven and London: Yale University Press.
Sasson, S. (1968). *Selected Poems of Siegfried Sassoon*. London: Faber & Faber, p. 28.
Sayers, J. (2007). *Freud's Art: Psychoanalysis Retold*. London: Routledge.
Scaparro, F. (2003). *La bella stagione*. Milano: Vita e Pensiero.
Schachtel, E. (1959). *Metamorphosis*. New York: Basic Books, Inc.
Slade, L. (2005). Social Dreaming for a Queer Culture. In: *Self & Society*. 33:3. 32–40.
Sodre, I. (1999). Death by Daydreaming: Madame Bovary. In: Bell, D. Ed. *Psychoanalysis and Culture*. London: Karnac.
Stapley, L. (2006). A Large-System Intervention. In: Gould, L., Stapley, L.F. and Stein, M. Eds. *The Systems Psychodynamics of Organizations*. London: Karnac Books.
Stevens, W. (1997). *Collected Poetry and Prose*. Ed. Kermode, F. California: Library of America.
Sutton, R.I. and Hardagon, A. (1996). Brainstorming Groups in Context: Effectiveness in a Product Design Firm. *Administrative Science Quarterly*. Vol. 41.
Tatham, P. and Morgan, H. (1998). The social dreaming matrix. In: Lawrence, W.G. Ed. *Social Dreaming @ Work*. London: Karnac Books. Translated in Italian, La Matrice del sogno sociale. In: Lawrence, W.G. a cura di. (2001). *Social Dreaming: La funzione sociale del sogno*. Roma: Borla s.r.l.
Thomas, D. (1971). *Dylan Thomas: The Poems*. London: J.M. Dent & Sons Ltd.
Thomas, D. (1975). In: Gardner, H. Ed. *The New Oxford Book of English Verse 1250–1950*. London: Oxford University Press.
Tisseron, S. (2004). *Manuel à l'usage des parents dont les enfants regardent trop la télévision*. Paris: Bayard Éditions.

Vallino Macció, D. (1992). Atmosfera emotiva e affetti. *Rivista di Psicoanalisi.* XXXVIII, 3.

Walker, M. (2003). The confusion of dreams between selves and the other: Non-linear continuities in the Social Dreaming experience. In Lawrence, W.G. Ed. *Experiences in Social Dreaming.* London: Karnac Books.

Wells, S. and Taylor, G. (1991). Eds. *William Shakespeare: The Complete Works.* Oxford: OUP.

Wilson de Armas, D. (1993). Quoted according to Murray, L.W. (1999). The angel of dreams: Toward an ethnology of dream interpreting. *Journal of the American Academy of Psychoanalysis.* 27:3. 417–430.

Winnicott, D.W. (1950). Thoughts on the meaning of the word democracy. *Human Relations.* 4. 171–85.

Winnicott, D.W. (1970). *The Child, The Family and The Outside World.* Harmondsworth: Penguin Books.

Winnicott, D.W. (1971). *Playing and Reality.* London: Tavistock Publications.

Winnicott, D.W. (1986). *Home is Where we Start From.* Harmondsworth: Penguin Books.

Winnicott, D.W. (1999). *Playing and Reality.* London and New York: Routledge.

Woolf, V. (1994). *The Second Common Reader.* Harmondsworth: Penguin.

Yeats, W.B. (1969). *The Poems of William Blake.* London and Henley: Routledge and Kegan Paul.

INDEX

A Midsummer Night's Dream 29
Abolition project 68
Act of faith 224–225
    Bion description 224
African-Americans and Whites
    in New York 170
Agresta, Domenico 41
Alpha function 232
Alpha-elements 226
American Protestants 210
Apprehending reality,
    modes 221–224
Armstrong, David 66
Artistic creativity 1
ATV (All Terrain Vehicle) 209
Autopoetic, life as 215

Babylonian captivity 202
Back-and-forth movement 152
Baglioni, Lilia 147
Bain, Alistair 6

Baptism 95
Beradt, Charlotte 143
Beta-elements 226
Bible matrix 205
Biblical matrix 203, 208, 210
Bion, Wilfred 6–7, 222, 224
    idea about imagination 228
    act of faith 224–225
    basic assumptions 136
    concept about learning
        from experience 51
    formulation of infinity
        matters 228–230
    formulation 226
    insight 52
    non-sensuous thinking 226
    paraphrasing 164
    psychoanalytic thinkers 8
    thought processes 225–227
Biran, Hanni 3
Blake, A.G.E. 223

Blake, William 73
Board of Social Dreaming, Ltd. 178
Bosnak, Robert 31
Brainstorming event 124
Brainstorming session 108–109,
    112, 115–116, 122, 125–126, 128
Breaking the Chains 66
Bridge of Dread, The 11
British Empire & Commonwealth
    Museum 66, 79
    British authority 66
Brown, Ford Madox 75–76
Brunning, Halina 187
Bubble up 27

Cadet pilots, selection of 95–104
    considerations 103–104
    creative role synthesis 99
    dialogue 103
    'group 1' 99–101
    'group 2' 102
    intervention description 97–98
    intervention methodology
        and its evolution 96–97
    purposes 96
    social dreaming matrix 98–99
Cabot, John 78
Castillo Theatre 169
Central Intelligence Agency
    and the Mafia 43
'Chief-Founder-Father'
    relationship 194
Chimney sweep 71–74
Christian movement 205
Clownish dreams 57
Creative consciousness 26, 39
Creative frame of mind 213–231
Creative power
    of dreams 188–189
Creative role synthesis (CRS) 97,
    99, 107–108, 137, 144, 149–150,
    158, 187–198
    applied to clinical cases 134–135

definition 190
    example as part of group
        relations training 195–196
    example of one-to-one
        coaching 194
    'group 1' 99–101, 192
    'group 2' 102
    in action 187, 191
    primary task 189
    psychoanalytic therapy 188
    psychoanalytical model 108
    run a session of 190
    use as part of teaching
        and training in systems-
        psychodynamic coaching
        196–197
    use of Brainstorming
        in place of 122
Creativity
    phenomenology
        of 217–220
    Polkingthorne description
        about mental experience
        217–218
    spark of 216
Crown Heights incident 169
Curiosity
    Klein, Melanie 227

Daydreaming,
    pathological 220
Deadness and rigidity 143
Differentiated thinking 26
Directing Programme 29
Dossal 209
Down's syndrome 126
Dreamers, Priesthood of 199–211
Dreaming
    acts of violence 46
    competitiveness 46
    in a primary school 53–63
    matrix 170
    network of 42–47

to emergence in general
    hospital 147–167
  vulnerable 46
Dream reflection dialogue 5, 149
Dream reflection group (DRG)
    42, 47, 51, 133
Dreams 55, 171
  children to 'cultivate' 63
  clowning around 56
  clownish 57
  cluster of 135
  creative power of 188
  death 58
  example of the use of 193
  falling 57–58
  false 58
  hyperbole 56–57
  migrant 83–93
  real 58–60
  reflection group 133–134
  sharing 63
Dreamtime 223

Eden, Angela 177
Ego-centricity 222
Egypt captivity 202
Egyptian Pharaoh 202
Ehrenzweig, Anton 2
  psychological theory 27
  The Hidden Order of Art 26
Elements of Emergency
    Psychology 148
Eli, Prophet 201
Ellwood, Colin 25
  intuitive sense 35
Emergency task force 150
Erasmus High School in Brooklyn 170
Eyes Wide Shut 45

Family Mediation training
    course 108–109
Family mediators, training
    of 105–118

Family therapist 192
Faraday cage 10
  mechanistic activity 11
  mental 3
Flying Dutchman, The 78
French psychoanalyst Serge
    Tisseron 62
Freud's theories 217
Freudian psychoanalysis 217
Fubini, Franca 131

Gladiator, The 59
Goal-oriented thinking 213
Gordon, Rosemary 27
Goya, Francisco 26

Hartmann, Ernest 2
Hayles, Katherine 216
Hebrew Scriptures 206
Heroes, mentors, and idols
    of identification 174–175
Hidden Order of Art, The 26
Huxley, Thomas Henry 228
Hyperbole 56

Imagination 227–228
  Bion idea 227–228
Infinity matters
  Bion's formulation 228–230
Inhibition and exhibition 65–81
Inspirational thinking 28
Israeli-Palestinian paintings
    project 169–170

Joseph 203
Judaism 206

Kafka's *Metamorphosis* 45
Karibù Cooperative, Rwandan
    director 83
Keats, negative capability 227
Klein, Melanie
  Curiosity 227

Korzybski, Alfred 79
Kris, Ernst 217
Lawlor, Robert 223
Lawrence, Gordon 1, 28, 177, 189, 199, 201, 213
Lazar, Ross A. 193
Liccardo, Tiziana 95
Lohmer, Mathias 193
Long, Susan D. 213
Low-shot on reality 53–63
Luther, Martin 199

Macabre dream 151
Madame Bovary 220
Madness and psychosis beckon 225
Manley, Julian 65
Martindale, Colin 27
Mathematical infinity 229
Matrix 109–110, 117, 120, 122
   after 186
   associations in 155
   bible 205
   biblical 203, 208, 210
   climate 111
   composition 121
   dream of last 166
   dreaming intelligence of 164
   dreamless colleague 158
   dreams 44, 114–115, 133
   dreams of first 164
   emotion of curiosity 155
   experience 119
   first dream 110
   first 151
   functioning 120
   King-Kong in the third 161
   last and synthesis 160
   making use of 139–141
   mirrors 131
   of undifferentiated unconscious 131
   organizational 165
   participants comments 166
   primary task of 151
   second and third 153–158
   second experience 163–166
   social dreaming in 206
   third, six dreams shared 156–157
   thirty-eight meetings of 207
   water and fire 153–158
Maturana's definition of life as autopoetic 215
Maxi emergency 147
Mental Faraday cage 3
Mental health service 131–146
Metamorphosis 214
Michael, Thomas A. 199
Migrant dreams 83–93
Military Academy Pilot 95
Mood-sharing and struggle 16
Modern-day Christians 200
Muir, Edwin 11
Mukamitsindo, Marie Therese 83
   conference re-launching 86

National Health Service 138, 143
National Theatre 29
Neapolitan professionals' association 122
Nebuchadnezzar of Babylon 202
Negative capability 227
Non-sensory experiences 225
Nunziatella 102
Nursing School of the Hospital 150

Oeser, Francis 9
Organizational dreaming 6
Ortona, Donatella 83
Oxford Reference Dictionary 188

Panic-stricken actors 44
Panopticòn project 43

Panopticòn's association 44, 51
Patel, Bipin 189
Paul, Apostle 200, 209
　death 206
Pearce, David 228
Persephone's Bridge 13, 19
Peter's dream 205
Pharisees 206
Physiological filtering mechanism of brain 223
Planera, Eleonora 41, 83
　cultural mediators 91
Playing and Reality 80
Poincarre, Henri 218
Political refugees and immigrants in local Italian community 83–93
Poseidon Adventure, The 78
Presbyterian tradition 210
Presentation of role puzzle 190
Presented dream 192
Presented puzzle 192
Presenter, associations of 192
Priesthood of dreamers 199–211
Psychiatric consultancy unit 148
Psychic deadness 163
Psychic pond 131
Psycho/biological niche 216
Psychological course 166
Psychology Service 148, 152
　Director of 152

Red fox dream 160
Resurrection of Jesus 206
RMS *Titanic* 78
Role puzzle 190–191
Role-system reflection 190–191
Roman Catholics 210
Roman cross 206
Romano, Sezze 83
Rose Bruford College 25
　directing programme 25

Rothko, Mark 218
Royal Shakespeare Company 31
Rumanian film, *4 months, 3 weeks, 2 days* (2007), 89
Rumanians, final matrix 90

Sailors and songs 76–77
Scaparro, Fulvio 63
Scare and frustration 162
Schachtel, Ernest 221
Screens and fences 77–78
Selvaggi, Laura 53
Service of psychology 147
Sexuality 46, 99
Sezze community 91
Shakur, Tupac 174
Ships and boats 78–79
Slade, Laurie 25
Slavery in the mind, inhibition and exhibition 65–81
　background 66–67
　children 74–76
　chimney sweep 71–74
　sailors and songs 76–77
　screens and fences 77–78
　ships and boats 78–79
　social dreaming matrices 67–71
Social deterioration 87
Social dreamers and poets 22
Social dreaming 28, 108, 133, 146, 183, 204, 211, 231
　adolescence according to adolescents 47–49
　at the UN Shelter Home 83
　auto-generative thoughts 50
　children's perception 53
　children's rights 53
　community 178
　emergent theory and culture of 179
　event 110

248 INDEX

experience 109–110, 119–120, 122–127
Faraday cage 10
for millennia 7
further thoughts 7–8
hosting 184
in Sezze 90
intimation of absolute reality 7
knowledge and thinking of the dream 3
Lepage, Robert (Director) 29
main hypothesis 61
master plan experience with 41–52
matrix 169, 177
of participants 3
physical contact 47
possibility of dialogue 28
prefigure creativity 10
principles of 179
program 131
psychoanalytical training 106
reality of 1
technique 109, 120, 128
third-generation of people 177
to creativity 9–23
training activities planning 106
transgressions 47
understanding the inexplicable 65
validity of 110
viewed as a system 2–7
with black rappers in New York 169–175
with children 53
with lawyers 119–129
with student theatre directors 25–40
working note on 1–8
workshop 1 (YG 2004): 7 March 2005 29–31
re-formulating the project 31

workshop 2 (YG 2005): 19 November 2005 32–34
developments 34–35
workshop 8 (YG 2006 and 2007): 27 October 2007 37–38
evaluating the project 38–40
workshops 67, 170
Social dreaming board 183
Social dreaming matrices (SDM) 1–2, 5–7, 10, 12–16, 30, 34, 38, 41, 67, 73, 80–81, 84, 86, 91, 97–99, 120, 132–133, 135, 137–138, 146, 149, 173, 175, 179–181, 183–184, 190–191, 199–200, 204, 209–210
abilities 44
at Castillo theatre, 42nd Street, Manhattan, New York 172–174
association 174
car 42
characteristic of 110
climate 111
death 42
emerges in 16
enquiry of 68
experience of 7
for African political refugees 84
goal-orientated configurations 6
images and thoughts 67–71
important aspects of 111
infinite qualities of 8
learning dialogue 180
learning to host 177–186
meaning of the dreams 4
methodology 149
mother, father and child 67–71
organization's unconscious dynamic 109
organizational dreaming 6
powerlessness 43

protection 10, 21
questions for hosting 182
reflection and learning 179
role of hosting 178
roles and abilities 41
socio-centric thrust 4
with dreams 137
with limited anxiety 4
working hypotheses 181
working technique 97
Social unconscious 70
Södergan, Edith 16
 The Stars 14
Sognando & Sognando 83
Sonenburg, Janet 31
Stars, The 14
Stevens, Wallace 10, 12, 21
Story of the Weeping Camel, The 159
Systems-psychodynamic coaching 196–197
System synthesis 190–191

Taylor, Tom
 Ticket-of-Leave Man, The 30
Therapeutic dreaming 3
Thinking alone, thinking
 together 230–231
Third Reich of Dreams, The 143
Thomas, Dylan 75
Thought processes 225–227
Ticket-of-Leave Man, The 30

Tiffany window 209
Tortono, Francesco 105
Tortono, Mattia 119
Totalitarian toddlers 131–146
Totalitarianism, growth 141
Totalitarian-state-of-mind 141–145
Tough honing 10
Transcendence 222
Turquet, Pierre 8
Twin Towers 152

Unconscious infinite,
 phenomenology 217–220
Unconscious sense-making
 processes 149
Undifferentiated thinking 26–28

Waitman, Alexis 194
Walker, Martin 200
Werdigier, Wolf 169
Western style fast-food
 meals 88
Williams, Andy 208
Winnicott, Donald 10, 144
Winter's Tale, The 14
Woolf, Virginia 19
Wright, Richard 174

Zechariah 203
Zen Buddhism 223–224
Zion 203